Scene Thinking

How is cultural activity shaped by the places where it unfolds? One answer has been found in the 'scenes perspective', a development within popular music studies that explains change and transformation within musical practices in terms of the social and institutional histories of scenes. *Scene Thinking: Cultural studies from the scenes perspective* takes up this framework – and the mode of analysis that goes with it – as an important contribution to cultural analysis and social research more generally.

In a series of focused case studies – ranging across practices like drag kinging, Bangladeshi underground music, urban arts interventions, and sites like single performance venues, urban neighbourhoods in various states of gentrification, and virtual networks of game consoles in countless living rooms – the authors demonstrate how 'scene thinking' can enrich cultural studies inquiry. As a humanistic, empirically oriented alternative to network-based social ontologies, thinking in terms of scenes sensitizes researchers to complex, fluid processes that are nonetheless anchored and made meaningful at the level of lived experience.

This book was originally published as a special issue of *Cultural Studies*.

Benjamin Woo is Assistant Professor in the School of Journalism and Communication at Carleton University, Ottawa, Canada. He studies the social worlds of contemporary 'geek culture', with a particular focus on the producers, intermediaries, and audiences oriented to comic books and graphic novels.

Stuart R. Poyntz is Associate Professor in the School of Communication at Simon Fraser University, Vancouver, Canada. His research addresses children's media cultures, theories of public life, and urban youth media production. He is President of the Association for Research in the Cultures of Young People.

Jamie Rennie is an instructor in the Communications Department at Douglas College, Vancouver, Canada. His research focuses on media literacy in Canadian schools and the various pedagogical approaches to teaching about and through contemporary media.

Scene Thinking

Cultural studies from the scenes perspective

Edited by
Benjamin Woo, Stuart R. Poyntz and Jamie Rennie

LONDON AND NEW YORK

First published 2017 by Routledge

2 Park Square, Milton Park, Abingdon, Oxfordshire OX14 4RN
711 Third Avenue, New York, NY 10017

Routledge is an imprint of the Taylor & Francis Group, an informa business

First issued in paperback 2018

British Library Cataloguing in Publication Data
A catalogue record for this book is available from the British Library

ISBN 13: 978-1-138-68418-8 (hbk)
ISBN 13: 978-0-367-02846-6 (pbk)

Typeset in Perpetua
by RefineCatch Limited, Bungay, Suffolk

Publisher's Note
The publisher accepts responsibility for any inconsistencies that may have
arisen during the conversion of this book from journal articles to book chapters,
namely the possible inclusion of journal terminology.

Disclaimer
Every effort has been made to contact copyright holders for their permission to
reprint material in this book. The publishers would be grateful to hear from any
copyright holder who is not here acknowledged and will undertake to rectify
any errors or omissions in future editions of this book.

Contents

Citation Information

The chapters in this book were originally published in *Cultural Studies*, volume 29, issue 3 (May 2015). When citing this material, please use the original page numbering for each article, as follows:

Introduction

Scene thinking: Introduction
Benjamin Woo, Jamie Rennie and Stuart R. Poyntz
Cultural Studies, volume 29, issue 3 (May 2015) pp. 285–297

Chapter 1

Border scenes: Detroit ± Windsor
Michael Darroch
Cultural Studies, volume 29, issue 3 (May 2015) pp. 298–325

Chapter 2

'We weren't hip, downtown people': The Kids in the Hall, the Rivoli and the nostalgia of the Queen West scene
Danielle J. Deveau
Cultural Studies, volume 29, issue 3 (May 2015) pp. 326–344

Chapter 3

When scenes fade: Methodological lessons from Sydney's drag king culture
Kerryn Drysdale
Cultural Studies, volume 29, issue 3 (May 2015) pp. 345–362

Chapter 4

Copy machines and downtown scenes: Deterritorializing urban culture in a pre-digital era
Kate Eichhorn
Cultural Studies, volume 29, issue 3 (May 2015) pp. 363–378

Chapter 5

Little big scene: Making and playing culture in Media Molecule's LittleBigPlanet
Sara M. Grimes
Cultural Studies, volume 29, issue 3 (May 2015) pp. 379–400

For any permission-related enquiries please visit:
http://www.tandfonline.com/page/help/permissions

Benjamin Woo, Jamie Rennie and Stuart R. Poyntz

SCENE THINKING

Introduction

In 'Postmodernism', Fredric Jameson famously posited a 'new (and hypothet ical) cultural form' he called 'cognitive mapping' (1991, p. 51). Like signs guiding us through 'total spaces', such as airports, university campuses and luxury hotels (p. 39), cognitive mapping would allow individual and collective subjects to feel their way through the increasingly opaque and complex 'spaces' of postmodern societies. It perhaps goes without saying that one only needs way finding aids when in unfamiliar territory, where the path is not self evident; one only needs a map, that is to say, when lost.

Theories and concepts are also a kind of map. They mark the contours of a domain, identifying its constituent parts and their relationships. They give us an idea of what to expect, and we use them to orient our way through the world of immediate social experience. They not only describe the paths we take but also help us figure out where it is we want to go. But it seems as though our maps have become less useful, less reliable, and less relevant today.

On the one hand, turn after turn within social and cultural theory has left many of us incredulous towards formal, grand theories. The postmodern critique was necessary, calling attention to the will to power lurking within theoretical paradigms that once seemed settled   and to the exclusions inherent in declaring something settled. But in its extreme forms postmodernism's standpoint epistemologies left us suspicious of truth claims attempting to transcend personal and idiosyncratic experiences of the world, threatening to delegitimize any conceptual maps whatsoever.

On the other hand, many of the assumptions about the social world undergirding our inherited concepts need to be re examined. Chief among these is the tidy identification of 'cultures' and 'societies' with nation states. Such assumptions are increasingly untenable in the era of robust globalization: the processes that constitute 'local' phenomena are almost always transnational, as communication systems and commodity chains entangle us with global others in countless ways. Meanwhile, boundaries between domains of inquiry are increasingly porous. As a consequence, it now seems obvious and unavoidable that the cultural *is* the social *is* the political *is* the economic, and so on.

Thus, the contemporary situation is not merely postmodern but also in important respects 'post society'. Nonetheless, most of us still have some ambition to say things about the conditions under which we live. As meaning making animals, we could hardly do otherwise. Indeed, risking performative contradiction, we rarely hesitate to do so in everyday life, reaching for familiar, ready to hand concepts to describe or explain some feature of our experience. But, while we are surrounded by the remains of premodern philosophy and modern social science, the contexts in which they were originally embedded, and from which they drew their logic, are no longer our context. Thus, the notions we intuitively deploy may not mean what we think they mean.

It is in this context that we see an ongoing need to interrogate our old concepts, refining them when possible and developing new ones when they are found lacking. The cultural studies tradition   theoretically and methodologically catholic, open to both imaginative theorizing and empirical testing   is particularly well positioned to generate new ways of characterizing our collective situation. It is in this spirit that we have assembled this special issue on scenes. It has three main objectives. The first is to collect empirical case studies of a variety of cultural scenes, showcasing the concept's utility across a range of domains of social life. Second, we want to advance an analytical stance we call 'scene thinking'. In each of the cases explored by our contributors, naming a group or cluster of activity a scene says something about how these concrete practices and spaces disclose the social's inherent relationality. Third and finally, we hope that this revisiting and interrogation of *scene* models a theoretical practice that can rise to the challenge of social inquiry and cultural analysis in these times.

The scene perspective

Although Blum (2003) has read the scene concept all the way back to antiquity, arguing that Socrates' circle of Athenian dilettantes was the 'original urban scene' (p. 176), a more manageable genealogy would arguably begin with the Chicago tradition of sociology. For Park (1925, p. 1), like the Socrates of *The Republic*, the city was a complex, structured and structuring apparatus: 'The city is not, in other words, merely a physical mechanism and an artificial construction. It is involved in the vital processes of the people who compose it; it is a product of nature, and particularly of human nature'. It is in this sense that we make the urban environment, and it in turn makes us. Perhaps more importantly, the Chicago urbanists worked to disaggregate the city through careful field studies that acknowledged the distinct social and cultural character of (classed and racialized) neighbourhoods and communities.

Later developments in American sociology were also influential. Goffman's (1959) dramaturgical theory points to scenes' theatrical or performative character. Scenes are not only places to do certain kinds of activity, but places to be seen doing them by significant others. Drawing inspiration from the youth slang of the 1960s to describe 'what one is "into"', Irwin (1977, p. 18) not only used the term explicitly but definitively pushed it into the sociology of leisure.

Without discounting the importance of these early developments, the concept as it is used most frequently today undoubtedly owes its currency to its adoption within the field of popular music studies. In particular, in a 1991 issue of this journal, Will Straw published the essay, 'Systems of Articulation, Logics of Change: Scenes and Communities in Popular Music', which advanced a Bourdieusian theory of musical scenes as a social space of circulation. Three years later, Barry Shank (1994) published his work on the history of the Austin, Texas, music scene as *Dissonant Identities*. Although they were not the first scholars to take up the ordinary language concept of *scene*, Shank and Straw popularized it as a way of talking about the roles of place, participation and circulation in the production of popular music. While not quite a paradigm or school, some have nonetheless identified this as a 'scenes perspective' (Bennett 2004), and Anahid Kassabian named *scene* one of popular music studies' distinctive theoretical concepts (cited Hesmondhalgh 2005).

Rather than focusing on aesthetic or cultural criticism of musical texts, the emergent scene perspective drew attention to the field of social relations in which music circulated. Thus, a bar or club was as important as a record label, and audience members were as important as musicians, for they all made the scene together. As Pepper Glass puts it, 'members, through their everyday interactions, collectively produce these settings'. 'Doing scene' is thus both extraordinarily creative and an ordinary, practical accomplishment (2012, p. 696).

From popular music studies, *scene* was quickly picked up by other scholars interested more generally in youth cultures. Through this work, *scene* became one of a number of concepts competing to replace the Birmingham School's subcultural theory within the 'post subcultures' debates of the late 1990s and early 2000s (see Muggleton and Weinzierl 2003, Bennett and Kahn Harris 2004, Bennett 2011). In a constellation with concepts like *subculture*, *club culture* (Thornton 1996, Redhead 1997), *Bund* (Hetherington 1998), and *(neo)tribe* (Maffesoli 1996, Bennett 1999), it became much easier to think of scenes as a kind of social group and not only the place where one hangs out. Around the same time, Straw (2001, 2004) returned to the concept, gradually expanding it to embrace a greater variety of cultural activities unfolding in urban environments. This expansion has enabled its transition from a simple, ready to hand descriptor for a kind of neighbourhood or clique to a complex theoretical object, referring equally to micro level interactions and global cultural flows. Interestingly, the term seems agnostic to the nature of its subjects, applying equally to collections of people, spaces, practices, and modes of participation, yet people are able to use it intuitively:

> In everyday life we speak regularly about scenes, and it is in such ways that the scene first appears to and for us. Then we ask, what are we talking about when we address the world in these ways, is there a persistence underlying this diversity? (Blum 2003, p. 165)

Not surprisingly, we contend that there is indeed a real persistence underlying diverse uses of *scene* in both everyday discourse and academic theorizing.

Summarizing and synthesizing some of their common features, we note that scenes are a basic part of the social imaginary of urban life. They are typically understood as loosely bounded social worlds oriented to forms of cultural expression. They provide systems of identification and connection, while simultaneously inviting acts of novelty, invention and innovation. Scenes are set within the fabric of everyday life but also function as an imagined alternative to the ordinary, work a day world. They can be utopian in moments, especially when scenes allow otherwise ignored or disappeared communities and subjects to find a home, but problems of institutionalization and coordination often push back against utopian aspirations. A scene may endure in one form or another for many years or it might quickly give way to the next big thing or hip neighbourhood. Sensitive to the particularity of immediate geographical and institutional settings, it nonetheless recognizes that locally enacted practices may be oriented to trans local or virtual collectivities (Bennett and Peterson 2004). The concept is thus supple enough to capture both the continuity and the constant transformation that characterize the social worlds formed around culture. It prioritizes neither production nor consumption, recognizing that both 'moments' are constituted relationally by participation and circulation. Finally, *scene* does not imply a restrictive model; the classification of a phenomenon as a scene is a starting point and not an ending point for investigation. For these reasons, we contend that *scene* can do important work for the cultural analyst.

Thinking through scenes

Scene's own ambiguities draw our attention to the dual nature of cultural life: It appears ephemeral, expansive, and elusive, yet it 'comes off' through routine even dull practices that are somehow greater than the sum of their parts. Ricoeur's (1967) aphorism that the symbol gives rise to thought is instructive here. For observers as much as participants, scenes have become part of the taken for granted social reality of life in the city. Thus, the *idea* of the scene the scene as symbol of a particular mode of effervescent sociability and as a mutually oriented to object of social action leads us to new ways of thinking about cultural activity. We argue that such 'scene thinking' can map (always incompletely, to be sure) how social and cultural life are lived in space, in time and in relation with others whose participation as consociates in the scene (Schutz 1967) makes them always already significant.

This is more than a question of terminology. Thinking in terms of scenes enables us to pick out objects of study from the on going flow of everyday life and to sense the larger structures of power, temporality and hope that gird our lives. Scenes 'emerge from the excesses of sociability that surround the pursuit of interests' (Straw 2004, p. 412). In this way, they are experiential and productive of what Ricoeur would call a 'surplus of meaning', an excess through which it becomes possible to chart the social imaginaries of a specific time and place.

Scene thinking seems to entail a view of the sociocultural domain as made up of agents in relationship around shared practices of meaning , place and community making. Our challenge is to see this domain as members do, beginning from the lived experience of a complex but coherent whole, and understanding how that whole comes into being. It is in this sense that this concept pushes us to take a 'scenic view': tracing the pathways and connections feeding into cultural activity in its myriad forms in order to develop a genealogy of the actors, spaces, material objects, discursive and tacit knowledges, and affects that give shape and character to our asymmetrical worlds.

Scene thinking and network talk

It is perhaps clear from the foregoing that what we have in mind is no longer simply a catch all label for vaguely defined clusters of cultural activity. We have greater designs on *scene*. In advancing it as a key concept for social research and cultural analysis, we are not asking that researchers and others abandon their research sites for a city's bohemian enclaves. Rather, we are advocating an analytical stance that takes the culturally constituted world of social experience as a scene.

It may be instructive to compare scene thinking with another concept that, on the surface, appears to do similar things. In recent years, another way of describing dispersed and yet apparently organized and structured chains of action has become ubiquitous and even commonsensical: We call it 'network talk'. This discursive formation comprises not only explicit network approaches among academic theorists such as the Actor Network Theory (ANT) of Latour, Callon, Law and others, Castells's network society thesis or the methodological innovations of social network analysis but also looser, more metaphorical uses of *network* among laypeople. Almost 20 years of Internet hype have rendered networks a commonsense way of thinking about social relationships. Indeed, networks have become a metonymy for the social itself.

But where network talk is certainly useful for describing the coordination of diverse actors and the production of intended and unintended consequences through complexly mediated political economic processes, it is freighted with cyberutopian ideologies of the 'transcendence' and 'substitution' of space

(Graham 1998). Indeed, in its cruder forms, network talk often reduces to technological determinism. These accounts, moreover, seem to flatter the scholastic habitus as much as the transhumanist imagination, promising that pure thought can conquer, abolish, or otherwise overcome the constraints of 'meatspace'. As a result, network talk has had little to say about the embodied, intentional and affective dimensions of human life. What we mean by this in short is that network talk lacks a robust conception of action:

> ANT is interested in the celebration of human agency in terms of its entanglement with technology, and not any other dimensions of human agency   all this, in spite of the fact that from other perspectives networks are at most the infrastructure of human action, not its dynamic content. (Couldry 2008, p. 101)

Pushing back against network talk's dominance is entirely in keeping with the humanist core that distinguishes cultural studies as a mode of analysis. Rather than stopping once we have described how actants are enrolled into a network, we would rather ask how individual and collective human agents invest these networks with meaning and use them to accomplish practically constituted goals.

Like networks, scenes enable, mediate and constrain action, emphasize the relationality of their members, and have an emergent, decentralized order. But the latter concept also avoids many of the limitations of network approaches. The language of networks reduces the meaningful and value laden world to a jumble of nodes and links in a featureless, mathematical space. Where network talk captures the linear processes of transmission through its architecture, scenes evokes the totality of circulation and exchange of cultural energies. Where networks are structured by more or less central nodes, scenes may also include passing memberships and ephemeral connections. Where networks promise to transcend space, scenes invest spaces with meaning, anchoring social and cultural practices in particular places.

The cultural phenomena we describe as scenes could also be diagrammed as networks, but in doing so, important features of those phenomena   the things that make them specifically *cultural*   drop out of view. We lose the subjective viewpoints of members and how they use a whole array of cultural practices actively to produce and maintain social structures. Conversely, attempts to add texture, context and substance back into networks will arguably make them more like places or communities   more like scenes. Blum (2003, p. 165) suggests that scenes are places 'that contribute to making the city itself a place', and people's investments of time and emotional labour in their networks provide a way of inhabiting the social. Studying the 'nodes' that produce a surplus of creative energy and the pathways that connect scenes to the environments we inhabit, we move away from the totalizing discourse of network talk, towards a generative sociology of action.

Scene *as a sensitizing concept*

This is asking a lot of a humble concept like *scene*. Is it up to the task? In a trenchant article reviewing several theorizations of youth cultures and popular music, Hesmondhalgh (2005, pp. 28 29) critiques *scene* as 'ambiguous' and 'downright confusing'. He acknowledges that ambiguity is typically numbered among the concept's strengths, but concludes that 'the term has been used for too long in too many different and imprecise ways [...] to be sure that it can register the ambivalences that Straw hopes it will' (p. 30).

If one suggested that it names a class of objects that are simply 'out there' in the world, then Hesmondhalgh has a point: it is impossible to operationalize something with such an underdetermined conceptual definition. We, however, are not making that suggestion. Indeed, we believe Hesmondhalgh's criticism is based on a category mistake, treating an epistemological category as if it had ontological substance in a straightforward, realist sense. But, as Blum (2003, p. 165) suggests, *scene* is given as an object of discourse, a way of describing and addressing ourselves to certain characteristics of the world of everyday social experience. That is to say, *scene* has always been better understood as a 'sensitizing concept', one that enables researchers (and others) to be responsive to the world, to pick out 'the proliferating co presence of varied textual/cultural forms in all their mobility and mutability' (Straw 2010, p. 26), without falling prey to the belief that our concepts are ontologically equivalent to things in themselves.

We make the distinction between definitive and sensitizing concepts with reference to the work of Blumer (1954). Blumer noted a fundamental problem in social theory: its concepts. Mainstream sociologists of his day mostly believed that their concepts represented social facts. However, these supposed facts failed to reliably and validly denote the things of the empirical world:

> [Social scientific concepts] do not discriminate cleanly their empirical instances. At best they allow only rough identification, and in what is so roughly identified they do not permit a determination of what is covered by the concept and what is not. Definitions which are provided to such terms are usually no clearer than the concepts which they seek to define. (p. 5)

Of course, this was not a new criticism, recapitulating as it did earlier debates over the nature of the cultural sciences and, especially, between 'positivist' and 'interpretive' traditions within them. But Blumer argued that his colleagues' impulse to correct this by refining *particular* concepts and measuring them better was wrong headed, because they were overlooking the epistemology of social scientific concepts in general namely that, they are *sensitizing* concepts.

Whereas definitive concepts, like those of the natural sciences or pure logic, '[refer] precisely to what is common to a class of objects, by the aid of a clear definition in terms of attributes or fixed benchmark', sensitizing concepts only give 'the user a general sense of reference and guidance in approaching empirical instances' (Blumer 1954, p. 7). For example, it is very difficult to set out a clear, universally valid definition of social rules, but that does not mean that we do not know a rule when we see it and cannot, with practice, get better at identifying them and saying something about how they work. Sensitizing concepts are less like rubrics or definitions, in other words, and more like models or exemplars. Keeping them in mind teaches us to think in particular ways, sensitizing us to certain problems.

All this is to say that scene does not name a thing, or even a class of things, but an orientation to things. The 'scene perspective' is literally a point of view, a way of seeing the world, and 'scene thinking' represents a decision to treat a set of individuals, institutions and practices *as if* they constitute a scene. Arguably, this is what members themselves do, sweeping discrete people, places, events and artefacts up into what comes to be called a scene. Focusing on the scene switches figure and ground, bringing taken for granted conditions of possibility to the fore. In the hands of different analysts, these might include spaces, organizations and infrastructures; affects, emotions and structures of feeling; or routes, networks and practices that make a particular scene part of the texture of a place. But to identify any or all of these as constitutive features of a scene sensitizes us to the ways they provide the setting for action.

Approaching *scene* in this way does more than simply add yet another concept to our theoretical toolbox. Rather, scene thinking ought to animate every stage of research: alerting researchers to possible sites of inquiry; helping us pose questions that bring into focus the unseen or overlooked in everyday life; and suggesting categories based on the meaning of circulation and flow, rather than what presents itself as permanent and thus somehow more significant. This is what Swedberg (2012), drawing on C.S. Peirce, refers to as 'theorizing in the context of discovery', where theorizing is an active practice that generates questions, suggests methods and analytical approaches, and drives further theory building. Fully metabolizing the concept, we would produce not studies of scenes or studies that use scene but scene based analyses, analyses sensitized to the on going, relational constitution of culture. This bias towards research practice means that the best way to understand what we mean by scene thinking and scene based analysis is to look at some examples of the concept at work.

How to read this issue

This is the part of an introduction, where we describe the issue's organization, explaining how each article will build on the one that came before to provide a conceptual trajectory through the issue. We have elected to order the contributions alphabetically by author and to provide a series of different pathways through them. Each of these 'tours', through the issue, is organized around a different set of comparisons and contrasts and a different set of key theoretical concerns.

There and back again

A first way to read these essays illustrates the expansion of *scene* as a concept, tracing its application across a growing range of research sites, starting with accounts of the cultural spaces most commonly recognized as scenes: Deveau on alternative comedy in Toronto's Queen West neighbourhood, Eichhorn on New York's downtown arts scene, or Darroch on artistic interventions in Detroit and Windsor. Participants in these scenes are or were likely to see the scene itself much as the researcher might, identifying the central role played by particular places and people.

These essays also exemplify the most common methodological approaches in the scenes literature, focusing on published accounts by journalists and participants. Contributions from Quader and Redden on the underground music scene in Dhaka, Bangladesh, and Drysdale on Sydney's vanishing drag king scene also describe familiar sorts of subcultural scenes. However, they are written in a more explicitly social scientific voice and add new data sources drawn from interviews, participant observation and focus groups.

Moving further afield, Silver and Clark challenge the exceptional nature of scenes by taking a scenic view of the amenities in literally every neighbourhood in the United States and Canada, Grimes's essay on the Playstation game franchise LittleBigPlanet interrogates the idea of space in relation to a 'virtual' scene, and Yoshimizu attempts to locate constitutive absences in a former red light district. These articles not only move us away from the more conventional scenes but also explore different ways of approaching them, from 'big data' to auto ethnography.

Scene thinking has encouraged all these authors to trace connections that may be unseen to the people involved. This is true whether we are talking about artists using photocopiers in their local bodegas, video gamers creating their own custom levels in *LittleBigPlanet*, or the traces of the global sex trade left behind in a neighbourhood.

Across the macro micro divide

A second route through this collection of essays is the question of scale. In the theoretical literature, it is noted that scene may equally refer to both 'our favourite bar and the sum total of all global phenomena surrounding a subgenre of Heavy Metal music' (Straw 2001, p. 248). Indeed, the 'same' scene may extend across several dimensions simultaneously. Describing it at any particular level invites a certain degree of structural comparison with the other levels at which the scene may operate. When one considers a popular music scene, such as the Bangladeshi rockers studied by Quader and Redden, for example, it is apparent that the local scene is often connected to regional, national and global scenes, whether through relationships of affiliation or distinction.

Like the larger scenes literature, the authors in this collection are operating at a range of levels. Despite this diversity of scope, scenes always remain their unit of analysis. Deveau and Drysdale examine single performance venues (Toronto, Ontario's Rivoli and the Sly Fox Hotel in the Newtown area of Sydney, Australia, respectively) and their relationships to a set of cultural practices (sketch comedy and drag kinging). Silver and Clark and Yoshimizu both look to neighbourhoods as the site of scenes, whereas Darroch and Quader and Redden describe whole cities as their hosts. Eichhorn concentrates on a tight cluster of neighbourhoods in New York City, but also looks at the ways that photocopiers enabled artistic and activist organizations to circulate beyond them. Finally, as Grimes shows, LittleBig Planet uses a global, virtualized network of game consoles to connect private bedrooms and living rooms. Reading these articles, whether from the micro to the macro or vice versa, we can appreciate how cultural activity organized through scenes occupy both the smallest, most intimate spaces and the broadest, most public ones.

Maps in motion

Another significant feature of scene based analyses is how scenes offer a means to study spaces and places that refuse more traditional 'mapping' techniques. Researching cultural life is often made far more difficult by the fact that the people and groups producing it are frustratingly nomadic. However, people and things 'do not just move through (or around) the city'; sometimes, the people and places producing scenes 'coalesce into momentary and temporary collectives' (Boutros and Straw 2010, p. 11). These temporary collectives can be studied in and of themselves, or they can be understood as the residuum of culture's restless energies. How, then, does one map a social space that is continually re inventing itself and re drawing its own boundaries?

Contributors have each, perforce, addressed this challenge, using *scene* to explore the emergence of cultural activity in space and time. This may involve studying scenes which have moved from one neighbourhood to another, as in Deveau, or which have dissipated, as in Drysdale or Yoshimizu.

Brief snapshots   such as Silver and Clark's index of neighbourhood amenities, Eichhorn's archival research, or the qualitative fieldwork of Quader and Redden or Drysdale   can help us characterize scenes in a particular moment. Yet, scene based analysis reminds us of the impermanence of the things we study: by the time we can identify a scene, it may have moved on, mutated into something else, or become far too mainstream for the tastes of its founding members.

Policing the culture

As Straw (2001, p. 248) notes, *scene* often connotes a sense of 'cozy intimacy', yet anyone who has participated in a scene knows they have their hierarchies and politics. Beyond personal grudges and feuds, there is the Bourdieusian struggle to impose one's own definitions of the field and its boundaries. Thus, a fourth thematic strand running through this issue is the question of power in scenes.

This is most obvious in Yoshimizu's treatment of Koganecho in Yokohama, Japan, where this brothel district was quite literally policed out of existence in a major raid and its subsequent Floridian re invention as a creative hub. Despite efforts to erase the memory of Koganecho's migrant sex workers, traces remain in nearby shops and restaurants and in the memories of area residents. The question of who gets to define public space is important for Darroch as well. Competing scenes seek to claim the city of Detroit on the one hand, as a crumbling wasteland for the urban explorers or, on the other hand, as a radical workshop for cultural entrepreneurs and artists.

Drysdale's informants seem quite attuned to the transformations that were dismantling the Sydney drag kinging scene. This involved them recognizing that spaces were being redefined around them. Conversely, Deveau explores how a moment in a scene's history uniting a certain set of actors (the Kids in the Hall) in a certain place (the Rivoli) can continue to function as a rhetorical source of legitimacy many years afterwards.

Grimes shows a more governmental side of these processes; the LittleBigPlanet network is privately controlled, and player conduct is regulated by its terms and conditions. But, just as importantly, the games' publisher, Media Molecule, shapes player participation by provisioning virtual objects all of which share their aesthetic and some of which are branded with media tie ins for players to construct their own environments.

These analyses powerfully remind us that, however familiar a scene is and no matter how stably 'coalesced' it seems, it is a social object defined by the discourses and practices of its members.

***

In putting together this collection of essays, we were not simply looking for intriguing social activities that are generally recognizable as scenes. We were looking for case studies where scene thinking could add something new. Our contributors have used this sensitizing concept to orient themselves to their research objects in new ways, and we hope the results will push readers towards a similar revisiting of other concepts: to what do they sensitize us and where might they lead us?

Notes on Contributors

Benjamin Woo is Assistant Professor of communication studies in the School of Journalism and Communication at Carleton University in Ottawa, Canada. He was recently a SSHRC Postdoctoral Fellow at the University of Calgary. His current research project examines creative labour and working conditions in the comic book industry. Previous research examined the practical grounds of 'nerd culture' in an urban scene.

Jamie Rennie is a Doctoral candidate in Social Justice Education at OISE, University of Toronto. His research explores media and technology in Canadian education, including both formal and informal sites of teaching and learning. Jamie teaches Communication Studies in Canada, and writes about pop culture online. He is currently completing his dissertation, and watching some very good television shows.

Stuart R. Poyntz is an Associate Professor in the School of Communication at Simon Fraser University. He is the lead editor of *Phenomenology of Youth Cultures and Globalization* (Routledge), co author of *Media Literacies: A Critical Introduction* (Wiley Blackwell), and has published widely in various journals, including, the *Journal of Youth Studies*, and the *Review of Education, Pedagogy and Cultural Studies*, as well as numerous edited collections.

References

Bennett, A. (1999) 'Subcultures or neo tribes? Rethinking the relationship between youth, style and musical taste', *Sociology*, vol. 33, pp. 599 617.

Bennett, A. (2004) 'Consolidating the music scenes perspective', *Poetics*, vol. 32, nos. 3 4, pp. 223 234.

Bennett, A. (2011) 'The post subcultural turn: some reflections 10 years on', *Journal of Youth Studies*, vol. 14, no. 5, pp. 493 506.

Bennett, A. & Kahn Harris, K. eds. (2004) *After Subculture: Critical Studies in Contemporary Youth Culture*, New York, Palgrave Macmillan.

Bennett, A. & Peterson, R. A. eds. (2004) *Music Scenes: Local, Translocal*.

Blum, A. (2003) *The Imaginative Structure of the City*, Kingston & Montreal, McGill Queen's University Press.

Blumer, H. (1954) 'What is wrong with social theory?', *American Sociological Review*, vol. 19, no. 1, pp. 3 10.

Boutros, A. & Straw, W. eds. (2010) *Circulation and the City: Essays on Urban Culture*, Kingston & Montreal, McGill Queen's University Press.

Couldry, N. (2008) 'Actor network theory and media: do they connect and on what terms?', in *Connectivity, Networks and Flows: Conceptualizing Contemporary*

Communications, eds. A. Hepp *et al.*, Cresskill, NJ, Hampton Press, pp. 93 109.

Glass, P. G. (2012) 'Doing scene: identity, space, and the interactional accom plishment of youth culture', *Journal of Contemporary Ethnography*, vol. 41, no. 6, pp. 695 716.

Goffman, E. (1959) *The Presentation of Self in Everyday Life*, Garden City, NY, Doubleday Anchor Books.

Graham, S. (1998) 'The end of geography or the explosion of place? Conceptu alizing space, place and information technology', *Progress in Human Geography*, vol. 22, no. 2, pp. 165 185.

Hesmondhalgh, D. (2005) 'Subcultures, scenes or tribes? None of the above', *Journal of Youth Studies*, vol. 8, no. 1, pp. 21 40.

Hetherington, K. (1998) *Expressions of Identity: Space, Performance, Politics*, London, Sage.

Irwin, J. (1977) *Scenes*, Beverly Hills, CA, Sage.

Jameson, F. (1991) *Postmodernism, or: the Cultural Logic of Late Capitalism*, Durham, NC, Duke University Press.

Maffesoli, M. (1996) *The Time of the Tribes: the Decline of Individualism in Mass Society*, London, Sage.

Muggleton, D. & Weinzierl, R. eds. (2003) *The Post subcultures Reader*, Oxford, Berg.

Park, R. E. (1925) 'The city: suggestions for the investigation of human behaviour in the urban environment', In *The City*, eds. R. E. Park, E. W. Burgess & R. D. McKenzie, Chicago, IL, University of Chicago Press, pp. 1 46.

Redhead, S. (1997) *Subculture to Clubcultures: an Introduction to Popular Cultural Studies*, Oxford, UK, Blackwell Publishers.

Ricoeur, P. (1967) *The Symbolism of Evil*, Boston, MA, Beacon Press.

Schutz, A. (1967) *The Phenomenology of the Social World*, Evanston, IL, Northwestern University Press. First published in German 1932.

Shank, B. (1994) *Dissonant Identities: The Rock 'n' Roll Scene in Austin, Texas*, Hanover, NH, Wesleyan University Press.

Straw, W. (1991) 'Systems of articulation, logics of change: communities and scenes in popular music', *Cultural Studies*, vol. 5, no. 3, pp. 368 388.

Straw, W. (2001) 'Scenes and sensibilities', *Public*, vol. 22/23, pp. 245 257.

Straw, W. (2004) 'Cultural scenes', *Loisir et société* [Society and Leisure], vol. 27, no. 2, pp. 411 422.

Straw, W. (2010) 'The circulatory turn', in *The Wireless Spectrum: The Politics, Practices and Poetics of Mobile Media*, eds. B. Crow, M. Longford & K. Sawchuk, Toronto, ON, University of Toronto Press, pp. 17 28.

Swedberg, R. (2012) 'Theorizing in sociology and social science: turning to the context of discovery', *Theory and Society*, vol. 41, no. 1, pp. 1 40.

Thornton, S. (1996) *Club Cultures: Music, Media, and Subcultural Capital*, Middle town, CT, Wesleyan University Press.

Michael Darroch

BORDER SCENES

Detroit ± Windsor

A multi layered artistic scene of site specific urban interventions crosses the border cities of Detroit, Michigan, and Windsor, Ontario. Consumption oriented approaches to scenes as clusters of urban amenities would disqualify these cities as loci of scenes: Detroit's scattered hip enclaves have had little influence upon neighbouring acres of abandoned buildings and vacant lots, whereas Windsor has promoted a new downtown cultural district and university campus but remains dotted with empty storefronts and boarded up structures. Yet, scenes are deeply engrained in their imaginaries   famously in Detroit's many musical scenes, but also historically in cross border mobilities of peoples and goods. Simultaneously integrated and divided, Detroit/Windsor is riddled with tensions between cross border circulation and the border's increasing impermeability, and between images of stasis and transformation. An experimental scene of creative collectives and site specific projects has responded to these tensions, disordering the material character of urban spaces and the built environment, the people, things, and media that pass through them, and their legal and institutional frameworks. Empty spaces, low rents, the circulation of discarded objects, the shifting economic conditions of skilled labour and 'making' cultures, and the availability of academic institutions have all contributed to these creative initiatives. Projects to stabilize neighbour hoods within Detroit are complemented by projects in Windsor that address forms of urban crisis deeply linked to Detroit's future. Windsor art collectives enter into an asymmetrical dialogue with site specific projects in Detroit as both insiders and onlookers, not in the sense of idle urban spectators but as an audience expressing its intimate knowledge of Detroit's history and current conditions. In opposition to each city's hurry to demarcate cultural districts and creative economies, the projects I describe are oriented to cautious and considered transformation grounded in dialogue, workshops, research and planning.

> Detroit is attracting artists in numbers large enough to earn it a designation as another Berlin: a city with a struggling economy where creative types can live and work cheaply and where, like [Matthew] Barney, they can realize projects that would be impossible most anywhere else. In Berlin, though, artists pursue international careers; in Detroit, they speak only to Detroit because, they say, anywhere else they would just be making art. In Detroit, they can make a difference. (Linda Yablonsky, 'Art Motors On', *W Magazine*, November 2011)

In the wake of the 2008 2009 financial recession, the many symbolic roles that Detroit occupies heart of industrial innovation, arsenal of democracy, Mecca for techno enthusiasts, icon of urban decline were eulogized in dozens of newspaper headlines, weekly features, urban arts blogs and glossy new histories of the Motor City. Detroit is metonymic for the auto industry and its ineluctable decline as well as for 'vital' or 'authentic' urban cultural scenes; its image hovers between that of a city in perpetual ruin and a petri dish of cultural experimentation, which has largely operated outside prevailing market forces since the financial downturn. As Detroit edged ever closer to municipal bankruptcy, which was finally declared in July 2013 following the state appointment of an Emergency Financial Manager, it captured the attention of international media as a city whose enigmatic past and current state of destitution rivalled only pre and post wall Berlin. (This comparison culminated recently in the Detroit Berlin Connection 'Congress for Subcultural Exchange for Urban Development', bringing together 'creative individuals and commu nities in the two cities with the goal of driving cultural and economic growth in Detroit' [*Detroit Berlin Connection*, 2014].) If this romantic comparison over looks serious distinctions between these cities, notably the history of racial tension in Detroit and other northern American industrial cities, it has contributed nonetheless to a steady stream of writings seeking to map the cultural terrain of the American metropolis in ruins. *Time* magazine launched a 1 year 'Assignment Detroit' project in September 2009, after editors bought a house for their embedded reporters. Articles in the *New York Times* and other major publications consistently described the ruined city as a fecund field of cultural production: 'Attracted by cheap space and driven by a sense of civic responsibility, young artists are turning crumbling homes into art centers, converting factories into studio and exhibition spaces, and planting community gardens as artworks' (Yablonsky 2010). While art scenes have long been associated with the aesthetic of a bohemian lifestyle, deriving in particular from the material conditions of cities with depressed economies (Forkert 2013), Detroit's contemporary art scene is extolled as largely detached from the international circuit of art commodities and global markets. Detroit is different, as the above comments suggest, because a wide range of art makers and cultural creators live and work outside conventional notions of private or public property and, moreover, are civically engaged in ways specific to Detroit, which resist easy exportation. In a series of blogs, Vince Carducci has theorized the conditions of Detroit's contemporary creative cultures, suggesting that the cartography of artistic initiatives is best understood as deriving from the 'art of the commons' and, following Jacques Rancière, consisting of an 'aesthetic community'. Art of the commons results from the breakdown in distinctions between private and public property, while the 'conception of [aesthetic] community isn't defined by the network of producers so much as it is by the conscious collective of ideas they are making tangible' (Carducci 2012). These different accounts portray Detroit's art scene as intensely localized, contained essentially within the city's physical boundaries, and oriented to shared understandings of civic engagement that exist outside the logic of the market economy which has so dramatically failed the city.

This pervasive emphasis on Detroit's internal dynamics, however, also serves to overshadow its location directly on the Canadian international border and North American Free Trade Agreement (NAFTA) trade corridor. Few cultural commentators are curious about this geography, past or present. A generation of auto industry decline in Detroit seems to have eradicated any historical sense of the origins of the city as *le détroit*, the narrows of the Detroit River. Across the Canada US border, Windsor, Ontario, a city of some 200,000 residents, and its neighbouring suburbs, have developed and declined alongside Detroit's colonial and industrial history. In many ways, Detroit Windsor is a simultaneously integrated and divided urban environment in which patterns of cross border circulation and impermeability are integral to each city's character conditions neglected or merely footnoted especially in the many histories of Detroit's racial, economic and infrastructural struggles. Cross border connections mark these cities in ways that distinguish them from the globalized flows of people, materials and information that regularly pass through them. While artists have long drawn upon cross border affinities, a multi layered Detroit Windsor creative scene has become evident in an array of creators and collectives that all strive to counter the cheap aestheticization of empty industrial spaces and structures through site specific initiatives, incre mental urban transformation and neighbourhood stabilization.

Prior to 9/11, the international border between Canada and the USA was relatively open; today, it appears to be ever thickening for people, even as cross border trade is ever more urgently promoted. While Detroit has witnessed revitalization and gentrification in parts of its centre, few benefits have trickled down from these hip urban enclaves to neighbouring acres of abandoned factories, buildings and storefronts, rundown residences, and vacant lots (Sugrue 2005, p. xxv). Windsor, long classified as Canada's Detroit (albeit less dramatically 'ruined'), also began promoting a new downtown Cultural District and university arts campus in 2011. It too is nonetheless dotted with empty storefronts and boarded up structures. Images of dense urban sociability are reduced in Detroit to a few blocks of tourist destinations in Corktown, Greektown, Midtown and the Sugar Hill Historic District, or the Saturday morning Eastern Market (Herron 1993, p. 18), and in Windsor to a number of downtown streets that for decades have been oriented to hospitality industries bars and clubs as a draw for young Americans. If urban scenic life only takes shape as part of the trend towards 'creative cities', alongside urban density and the availability of amenities (see Silver *et al.* 2010, 2011), then Detroit and Windsor would be largely devoid of cultural scenes. Yet scenes are deeply engrained in their imaginaries certainly in Detroit with musical scenes including Motown, metal, techno and hip hop, but also historically in cross border patterns of mobility of people, labour and goods [consider, e.g. the cases of the Underground Railroad, prohibition smuggling, or early twentieth century cross border labour movements (see Klug 1998)].

The narrative of Detroit as a city of ruins provides a peculiar backdrop to creative initiatives: ruined Detroit produces an aura of stasis through which the city is characterized either as 'dramatic' or 'an open canvas'. This stage like atmosphere is often interpreted as a space for nostalgia, recalling and replaying Detroit's 'golden era of Fordist prosperity' (Steinmetz 2008, p. 211), but it also generates discussion about cultural initiatives that place Detroit on the path to urban renewal and sustainability. Site specific urban experiments in Detroit have taken shape within this distinct ruined landscape of the city. These projects are scenic when they collectively circulate understandings of Detroit's conditions and broadcast an expanding narrative of Detroit as a model city in which creative endeavours prefigure ambitious forms of urban transformation.

For Windsorites, Detroit forever looms. The panorama of the Detroit skyline beckons to Windsor, and in turn, Windsor bears witness to Detroit from the position of an observation post, a lookout connected to yet separated from the economic forces and racial tensions that engulf its larger neighbour; an observation post closely linked to the vast Detroit 'canvas'. Through the integration of Detroit's imaginary into Windsor's sense of self, the border operates less as boundary and more as an interval of resonance, in McLuhan's sense of borderline (McLuhan 1977, p. 226). When it comes to Detroit, Windsorites are a particular brand of urban spectator. They are not idle, but rather intimate onlookers. The border's many spaces and forms of circulation yield creative energies that work against the overwhelming sense of stasis associated with abandoned landscapes and ruins. Within Windsor, I argue, a creative community strives to work as intermediary between Windsor and Detroit. Numerous Windsor based artists embraced Detroit's famed Cass Corridor scene of the 1960s and 1970s, a period of artistic fomentation that took place in the district south of Wayne State University. Windsor's ArtCite, one of Canada's first artist run collectives and an early Windsor Detroit institution to pay an artist fee, has often reflected the depth of involvement of Windsor's creative community's within Detroit, represented, for example, in its 1986 retrospective *Borderlands: Art from the Edge*. Artists such as Susan Gold and Chris McNamara have long studied, practiced and taught in both cities. Acutely aware of the constant cultural trajectories of movement across the border, this community negotiates the ambiguity of the border as both porous and impermeable. In this sense, a smaller Windsor scene of site specific projects and collectives has taken root, adapting the specificity of Detroit's internal creative scene by commenting on Windsor's asymmetrical relationship to Detroit and the international border. In Detroit, projects such as the well established *Heidelberg Project* and more recently *Power House Projections*, the *Unreal Estate Agency*, *ArtsCorps Detroit*, among others, all work through incremental, contem plative urban interventions to counter states of dereliction and to urge neighbourhood stabilization (Rodney 2014, pp. 261 262). And in Windsor the *Green Corridor Project*, the *Broken City Lab* (*BCL*) and the *Border Bookmobile* have reacted to Detroit's experimental cultural activity by reconceptualizing various border spaces as places equally open to transformation. These projects underscore specificities of Detroit Windsor that resist simple identification with other experimental urban arts scenes, perhaps most prominently because they also resist a bohemian attitude about 'artists' exemption from social responsibility' (Deutsche and Ryan 1984, p. 105). Attentive to the minutiae of everyday life in one or both cities, this cross border scene does not operate as a coordinated network of creators, but collectively works to circulate ideas for intervening in the underlying social, economic and political processes engulfing the region.

Will Straw has noted how the term 'cultural scenes' is frequently used either 'to circumscribe highly local clusters of activity' or 'to give unity to practices dispersed throughout the world' (2001, p. 248). If a Detroit scene appears distinctly local, circumscribed by the city's specific political and economic conditions, the asymmetrical relationship between Detroit's scene of site specific experimentation and a Windsor scene rooted in the cities' border culture affords us a unique opportunity to observe the elastic, yet overlapping, boundaries of such highly localized scenic activities and energies. Detroit Windsor provides a case study for interrogating the ways in which asymmetrical relationships between border cities, within the context of global cultural flows, are also distinctly manifested in local forms of cultural expression.

Creativity for or against the city

> Fuelled by artisanal coffee, grassroots ethics, and a whole lot of elbow grease, Detroit's Arts and Crafts scene is revving up again. (Alexandra Redgrave, *En Route* magazine, 2013)

According to the April 2013 edition of Air Canada's in flight magazine *En Route*, 'Detroit's *Arts and Crafts* scene is revving up again' (Redgrave 2013, p. 45). This image of creative life in Detroit stands in stark contrast to media reports of municipal bankruptcy and countless coffee table books of Detroit 'ruin porn'. According to the article, a Detroit creative scene is now identifiable by its concurrent traits of pseudo bohemian middle class values (artisanal coffee), bottom up culture (grassroots ethics) and creative labour (elbow grease). In highlighting the few blocks of Corktown and other enclaves flirting with gentrification, Redgrave suggests that this arts and crafts scene extends to all of Detroit   and conceals the city's hardest realities. As the white owner of a renovated Corktown inn and artisanal showroom explains: 'Detroit attracts a resourceful type of person who thinks, I'll just build it […] There's not a vague notion of local here'. In Detroit, 'the artist is your neighbour, and you know how that person helps the community' (2013, p. 46). The narrative of a blossoming creative scene in Detroit seems closely connected to a combination of close knit communities, making cultures and do it yourself (DIY) resource fulness, yet it neglects the diffusiveness of Detroit's cultural character and the many ways it is stratified by economics and race. Nevertheless, even if this story disguises Detroit's internal racial divisions and economic struggles   facts that re emerged when the city filed for bankruptcy only a few months later   it also acknowledges a DIY culture deeply connected to forms of creative expression that are intensely local, pulled between nostalgia and possible futures, as captured in the popular slogan 'made in Detroit'.

As with many cities, Detroit and Windsor have listened intently to the discussion in urban scholarship and popular news media about the virtues of investing in creative industries and fostering a creative class (i.e. Florida 2002, 2005). This is the image portrayed by the author of the *En Route* article, who describes her emotional response to walking through Detroit's Russell Industrial Centre, a post industrial hub of artisanal and creative activity:

> Walking around the cavernous space, aptly described by one artist as 'a whole neighbourhood in a building', gives me the sense that the RIC stands in for Detroit itself: a work in progress propelled by elbow grease and creative clout. (Redgrave 2013, p. 48)

Creative labour, in this account, is metonymic for the city. It is a familiar story: renovated buildings and young artists will yield Detroit's salvation. The RIC's website previously claimed that 'the historic façade of each building, combined with the repopulation of new, young artists is a great start to bring Detroit back'. In the *En Route* article, a studio operator at the hip Signal Return Letterpress in Detroit's Eastern Market district explains to a customer: 'You work with wood and metal … It's just like building a city' (2013, p. 51).

Like larger Canadian cities such as Toronto and Montréal, Windsor has turned to cultural planning as a means to urban revitalization, adopting its Municipal Cultural Master Plan in 2010 and promoting a Cultural District through a series of development projects announced in 2011: a new Aquatics Centre; collaborations between the Art Gallery of Windsor and a new City

Museum; and redevelopment of the Windsor/Detroit Tunnel Plaza. The University of Windsor has invested in this process with plans to open a downtown campus in 2016 by relocating its creative arts programming to the original Windsor Armouries and former Greyhound bus terminal. These investments acknowledge the presence of culturally expressive energies and are driven by the notion that related creative economies could be mobilized politically towards the resuscitation of struggling small city downtowns. At the same time, both the creative city model and attendant definitions of creative labour present a selective and limited definition of what constitutes a cultural scene.

The grammar of scenes: theatricality, seeing, project

From 2001 to 2006, I participated in a study of the culture of four cities (Montréal, Toronto, Dublin and Berlin) that sought to develop comparative frameworks for examining the specificity of urban cultures. How do cities retain their distinctiveness in an age of global and transnational cultural flows? One area of cross disciplinary interest that emerged from this Culture of Cities Project was the notion of the 'urban cultural scene', one of the foci among the contributions to this special issue of *Cultural Studies*. At the time the project's director, Alan Blum, suggested that 'scenes' are:

> recurrences envisioned as master categories that organize the very description of the city   the gay scene, the music scene, the drug scene, the art scene, the tango scene, the rave scene. Here, it sounds as if scenes, like commodities, circulate in ways that might bring them to some cities rather than others or to all cities in varying degrees. (2003, p. 166)

Yet scenes are also integral to the sense of specificity that we associate with particular urban enclaves, or as Blum argues:

> if the scene points to a recurring feature of all cities, or of any city worth its name (imagine a city that could not claim any scenes), then this universal function is distributed differently. Scene resonates with some concerted activity, an activity to a degree specialized, at least differentiated, but not necessarily covert. (2003, pp. 166 167)

For Blum, the ambiguity of the urban scene is marked by a series of tensions that he unpacks as the grammar of scenes. What we think of as a 'scene' is characterized by a tension between its regularity and its ephemerality   the commitment of its practitioners, on the one hand, versus the casual engagement of visiting, yet idle, onlookers on the other; a tension between its level of integration in, or removal from, the city (when are scenes only part of a city and when do they become indistinguishable from what we know of a city?); and finally a tension between the scene's coming to be and its perishing: the scene always contemplates its own mortality. Will Straw, a project co investigator, later noted that:

> scenes may be distinguished according to their location … the genre of cultural production which gives them coherence (a musical style, for example, as in references to the electroclash scene) or the loosely defined social activity around which they take shape (as with urban outdoor chess playing scenes). *Scene* invites us to map the territory of the city in new ways while, at the same time, designating certain kinds of activity whose relationship to territory is not easily asserted. (2004, p. 412)

In both of these accounts, the theatricality of city life is a central feature of the scene. Every scene is marked by the act of seeing: subjects who participate in a scene as onlookers are also:

> in the struggle to do seeing and to being seen   to be seen seeing, and so, to be absorbed in the action rather than an idle onlooker   [which] marks its subject as exhibitionistic rather than voyeuristic, that is, as one who is actively seen seeing and so, as engaged by the reciprocity of seeing as an act of mutual recognition. (Blum 2003, p. 172)

To be visible as an onlooker, in other words, is part of one's engagement in the scene, by the 'reciprocity of seeing'. On the other hand, to remain visible as an idle onlooker leaves the spectator of the scene, literally, out of place:

> A scene, as it gathers strength, makes those who are idle and detached, appear out of place. This reminds us that a scene is always a project, and as such, makes the encounter with place a test for all those who fall under its spell. (Blum 2003, p. 188)

These notions   the visibility of being seen and doing seeing, and the scene as a project   are fundamental to what I wish to describe as cross border scenic life in Detroit Windsor, for they allow us to identify the emplacement, on one the hand, of onlookers within Detroit and, on the other hand, of Windsorites as intimate onlookers between the two cities.

Detroit ruinscapes

> The vast population decline in [Detroit] has created a scene that looks as if it has never left the year 1968, kept in an eternal freeze frame, while nature grows over it. (Mitch Cope 2004, p. 11)

George Steinmetz (2008) has described the ruins of Detroit as eliciting a particular form of 'Fordist nostalgia' that constantly invites spectacular and dramatic representation, conjuring up hollow comparisons with ancient ruins. For instance, ruin photographer Camilo José Vergara (1995) famously suggested that Detroit 'place a moratorium on the razing of skyscrapers' (p. 36) in order to establish a segment of downtown as an 'American Acropolis' (p. 33), and *New York Times* travel writer Brian Park equated Detroit's ruins with those in Greece or Italy: Detroit's 'once mighty structures can exude a dilapidated wonder … Most dramatic is the former Michigan Central Depot … its 18 blown out floors … looming against the sky, its railroad station interior looking like an abandoned Roman settlement' (Park, B. 2005). More recently, French photographers Yves Marchand and Romain Meffre attempted to document the city of ruins as 'a contemporary Pompeii, with all the archetypal buildings of an American city in a state of mummification' (2010, n.p.). Ruined Detroit is conjured up as a vast stage on which primarily white suburbanites trace the storied histories of the 'Fordist metropolis in its golden age' physically by automobile or through a variety of websites and books, which offer guided tours and ruin maps. The digital tagging of Detroit's abandoned spaces in website tourism and blogging is what Marcel O'Gorman has called apocalypse tourism, as championed by urban explorers or 'urbexers'. As O'Gorman writes, 'for visitors, Detroit is a sort of mysterious archaeological site' (2007). Here, ruingazing almost evokes the sense of transgression that Blum describes as essential to any scene (2003, pp. 173 175); yet the suburbanite's act of transgression is not the same kind of performance that Blum feels opens up the scene to exhibitionism or the reciprocity of seeing. Rather, ruingazing is contained within acts of voyeurism, and thus while we might be tempted to consider these urbexers as forming a 'ruingazing scene', O'Gor man's account reminds us that there is no 'project' (in Blum's terms) involved with this collective action   despite claims that digitizing Detroit might save the city [see Rice (2005) and O'Gorman's (2007) critique of Rice]. In O'Gorman's words, referring to dozens of 'bad urbex blogs' that 'portray Detroit as the set of *Blade Runner*':

> What could potentially be a community of individuals working collabora tively to give a city a voice and restore its vitality, is overrun by a network of isolated, narcissistic individuals shouting, 'Look at me! Look at this dangerous place I visited! Make me your hero!' (2007)

For Steinmetz, suburban ex Detroiters' fascination with the ruined city is nostalgic rather than, as with other communities grappling with ruined environments, melancholic. Detroit's Fordist past is an 'object for historical contemplation', and the 'texts, films, and tours that resurrect Fordist Detroit are unambiguous about the fact that this prosperous city is located firmly in the past'. Nostalgia for Fordism is 'a desire to relive the past, to re experience the bustling metropolis as it is remembered or has been described' (Steinmetz 2008, p. 218).

As Lee Rodney (whose *Border Bookmobile* project I discuss below) writes, 'ruin porn simultaneously offends and appeals as we see something of ourselves in the theatricalized, extreme scenarios pictured in the glossy, large format photographs' (2014, p. 263). But an alternative sense of the city's creative scene is emerging against the backdrop provided by such theatricalized accounts of Detroit as a scene of ruins. In contrast to the image of Detroit as a stagnant stage for 'ruin exploration', urban interventions by artists with both local and international roots   some supported, others contested by local communities   attempt to engage with the city as a site of change, where empty spaces are characterized by constant movement: the circulation of waste and abandoned artefacts, and the gradual transformation of the built environment's material character, either by the process of decay or by intervention. By highlighting the *transformational* character of ruins (Edensor 2005) and inviting spectators to be visible as engaged participants, these projects dislocate the commonplace narrative of Detroit's cultural implosion, shifting our attention to the ways in which we might re construct disconnected stories and individual lived experiences whose traces are discernible only in fragments.

Scenes of Detroit

> The rumors are true: Detroit's contemporary art scene thrives. (Colin Darke 2011)

In *The Unreal Estate Guide to Detroit* (2012), architectural theorist Andrew Herscher has compiled a directory of creative projects emerging from Detroit's property of crisis in the guise of a tourist guidebook. 'Unreal restate' is 'urban territory that has fallen out of the literal economy, the economy of the market, and thereby become available to different systems of value, whether cultural, social, political or otherwise' (2012, p. 8). According to Herscher, Detroit's unreal estate urbanism has 'inspired many of its inhabitants to re think their relationship to the city and to each other' (p. 7)   inhabitants whose socio economic status, in many instances, falls outside the purview of an imagined 'creative class' associated with clusters of urban amenities (see also Rosler 2011). As a compendium of local initiatives, some undertaken by choice and others by necessity, Herscher's *Unreal Estate Guide* itself supposes a scene of 'unreal estate development' that includes 'creative survival as well as cultural critique, and it includes the ephemeral aesthetic servicing of those supposedly in need as well as material responses to objective needs through long term self organization' (2012, p. 13). Herscher's guide is not alone in positing Detroit as a scene of dispersed collective behaviour, ideas and values: individual acts of creativity caught up in the project of re thinking the city. Consider this 2005 description of Detroit's creative scene by Stephen Vogel, former Dean of Architecture at the University of Detroit Mercy and a co founder, with Kyong Park and Andrew Zago, of the *International Centre for Urban Ecology* in Detroit:

> My love for Detroit began with the hearty souls who occupy the city because they are reminiscent of the rural farming families among whom I spent my childhood. Their inventiveness, individualism, persistence, and ability to deal with enormous daily frustrations are a constant wonderment. The 'frontier' mentality that dominates large areas of Detroit is illustrative of great opportunity. It is also a mentality that is less concerned with race than with individual fortitude. There are a host of creative urban experiments taking place throughout the city that illustrate this individu alism. These include large scale urban farming enterprises, guerrilla gardening, ad hoc public transportation systems, green building experi ments, 'found object' constructions, food cooperatives, co housing enclaves, and vigorous art and music installations and performances. The city is ripe with opportunities for cultural experimentation with or without the approbation of government. (Vogel 2005, p. 19)

Here, creative urban experiments seem to combine individuality the 'individual fortitude' of creators whose skill sets may derive from manufac turing and making cultures with a kind of collective mentality of resistance and persistence. This situation resembles the scene described by Peter Lang in his introduction to Kyong Park's *Urban Ecology: Detroit and Beyond* (2005):

peeling back of Detroit's scarred past to reveal its bucolic but tragic destiny is an exercise inspired not from mainstream academia but from a subversive counter tendency involving artists, artist collectives, curators, cross disciplinary researchers, writers, film directors, and disillusioned professionals all hot wired together into an expansive global network. (Lang 2005, p. 11)

The heterogeneity of these creative urban experiments is itself one of the central characteristics of such a scene. Their proponents may have little contact with one another, but they share a commitment to Detroit as a place for experimentation.

Herscher's *Unreal Estate Guide* itself started as a project, the *Unreal Estate Agency*: an 'open access platform for research on urban crisis, using Detroit as a focal point' (2012, p. 2). Launched in 2008 as a collaboration between Herscher, fellow University of Michigan architectural scholar Mireille Roddier, Dutch curator Femke Lutgerink, as well as Christian Ernsten and Joost Janmaat of the Amsterdam based collective *Partizan Publik*, the *Agency*'s founding principle was to regard 'Detroit as a site where new ways of imagining, inhabiting and constructing the contemporary city are being invented, tested and advanced' (p. 2). Working with *Power House Projections* founders Gina Reichert and Mitch Cope (discussed below), the *Agency* hosted a residency for the Dutch artists. As Lee Rodney reports, the collaboration at first:

proved an awkward clash of worlds and ideals. [...] Many of the visiting artists expressed their discomfort and ambivalence about responding aesthetically to Detroit as outsiders. However, in spite of the uneasy situation they produced a makeshift outdoor chandelier that ran from electrical wires of a vacant lot without street lights. (2009, p. 11)

Here, we might recall Blum's (2003, p. 178) concern that scenes bring 'to view the affiliations which bind people as a collective of co speakers, as if they are dwelling in nearness to one another'. The deliberate encounter between insiders and outsiders, as with the *Agency*'s collaborations, perhaps troubled the sense that the local scene is one that demonstrates the vitality of shared intimacy as itself a form of creativity (2003, p. 179). The local and international character of the *Agency*, notes Rodney, is 'at once their strength and, arguably, their weakness' (2009, p. 11). In opposition to a longstanding trend to disavow one's affiliation with Detroit [as with Jerry Herron's (2005, p. 156) claim that 'we are   all of us   not from Detroit'], the city's shrinking population has tended to foreground moments of cultural vitality and outbursts of city pride. Celebrations of Detroit techno, for example, suggest natural affinities with the Berlin music scene, drawing many a European techno enthusiast to Detroit and vice versa. In this context '*Ich bin ein Detroiter*' has become a popular slogan representing 'made in Detroit' self respect (Rodney 2009, p. 11), a narrative of sociocultural resilience expressed through the mythical character of the city's enduring vitality in spite of its popular representation as a fallen and ruined city. Numerous site specific projects that challenge superficial acts of urban exploration absorb and propagate these forms of city pride.

Detroit's primary site specific venture that seeks vitality in ruins is the *Heidelberg Project*, initiated by artist Tyree Guyton in 1986. Over nearly three decades, Guyton has adapted and appropriated abandoned properties along a block of Heidelberg Street in his childhood neighbourhood on Detroit's Eastside. *Heidelberg* is a curious amalgam of artefacts both made and found that Guyton has assembled out of the detritus that circulates through the neighbourhood. Houses, cars, trees and streetscapes are decorated with coloured polka dots. By imposing patterns of regularity to the display of decaying stuffed animals, rotary telephones, shoes, vacuum cleaners, tires and other objects of everyday urban life, Guyton's project is a 'defamiliarization of what was conventionally perceived to be mere garbage' (Herscher 2012, p. 286). The *Heidelberg Project* has appropriated both objects and adjacent properties, opening a debate with the city about its status as art or a form of squatting. Partly in response to community anger over the project's transformation of the site, the City of Detroit has twice endeavoured to demolish the project in 1991 and 1999. In 2013 and 2014, a number of the project's main houses burned down in apparent acts of arson   but if the *Heidelberg Project* is representative of Detroit's site specific cultural scene, we glimpse the scene's capacities not only to reflect upon its own mortality but also to extend itself into the narrative of the city as a whole. As an article in the *Detroit Free Press* declared 'the art, like Detroit, will survive' (Stryker 2013).

Heidelberg's focus on neighbourhood stabilization is often compared with *Power House Projections*, a collective on the edge of the city of Hamtramck (a stand alone municipality within Detroit) that has also won international acclaim. Initiated by artists Gina Reichert and Mitch Cope, who together had previously established the collective *Design 99*, the project is centred on the renovation of one particular property, the Power House, but has expanded to a number of neighbouring houses and spaces. Hamtramck, a more densely populated, diverse (including a substantial Bangladeshi population), and comparatively more affluent district than *Heidelberg*'s Eastside, has nonetheless experienced its share of abandonment, criminality and vandalism. Cope, an artist by training, and Reichert, an architect and designer, bought the Power House 'a former foreclosed drug house' for $1,900 in 2008, and soon purchased adjacent lots valued even less (*Power House Productions* 2013). Renovated with solar and wind power, the Power House represents a self sustainable urban enclave, aiming to power adjacent properties, as well as a process of neighbourhood empowerment through participatory action. While Cope and Reichert do not hail from this area, unlike Guyton who grew up on Heidelberg Street, they nonetheless envisage the project as equally invested in the neighbourhood. As the Power House has transformed into *Power House Productions*, an artist run, neighbourhood based non profit organization funded through grants from local and national foundations, nearby houses have been purchased and transformed into, or proposed as, such concepts as the Sound House, the Skate House, the Play House, the Squash House, the Jar House Office & Guest Home, and the Ride It Sculpture Park, a skate park where you ride the art. All these 'concepts' aim to increase neighbourhood participation through meeting and performance spaces for community members and youth. In each of these instantiations of the project, slow and considered architectural processes, focused on sustainable activity and resourced through local and found materials, are themselves primary performative acts (Herscher 2012, p. 246). The Power House unfolds as living architecture, in which contemplative process resists and counters the demand for efficiency and haste in a housing market that so badly failed at the height of the 2008 financial crisis.

If the *Heidelberg Project* and *Power House Productions* each instantiate a project (in the theory of scenes) of living and surviving in Detroit, they diverge from another initiative that received widespread media attention: the *Ice House*, a proposal to encase an abandoned Detroit house in ice. Undertaken in 2010 as a commentary on the housing crisis, the *Ice House* appeared to some to be another venture by artists who appear in Detroit ready to take advantage of the 'open canvas'. Instead, the project recalled rather than criticized the aestheticizing tendencies of 'ruin porn', which, as John P. Leary has lamented, 'dramatizes spaces but never seeks out the people that inhabit and transform them' (2011). As one Detroiter remarks in Mark Binellli's book, *Detroit City is the Place to Be:*

> People don't understand how offensive 'urban exploration' is to us. Just the arrogance of it. What do you think would happen if four black kids went into one of those buildings? They'd be arrested. White kids? All right, go home son. *Freezing houses.* Detroit isn't some kind of abstract art project. It's real for people. These are real memories. Every one of these houses has a story (Binelli 2012, p. 285)

Ultimately, the *Ice House* was little oriented to participation in the sense of being seen or doing seeing. In contrast, *Power House Productions*, which draws a considerable international audience and hosts a regular visiting artist programme, is committed to neighbourhood participation and espouses the desire to be seen seeing. The *Heidelberg Project* and *Power House Productions* thus embrace the idea of a scenic *project* as an assemblage of devalued local spaces, found materials, a DIY mentality and continual neighbourhood participation. The *Ice House* is indicative of interventionist projects that use Detroit as a backdrop for critiquing the failure of the free market system, but stands outside of the city's aesthetic community because it overlooks the possibility of neighbourhood stabilization.

Close ties between creative initiatives and cultural institutions in art education and exhibition are also a notable feature of the experimental art scene of Detroit. According to Straw, 'scenes take shape, much of the time, on the edges of cultural institutions which can only partially absorb and channel the clusters of expressive energy which form within urban life' (2004, p. 416). All of the artists discussed either studied at local art colleges or are affiliated as instructors and curators with local institutions. Guyton studied at the private College for Creative Studies, one of the central incubators for design culture in Detroit's manufacturing history. Reichert and Cope each undertook art degrees at Detroit's Cranbrook Academy of Art, through which Cope participated in the Detroit-leg of the international Shrinking Cities Project that investigated conditions of population decline and restructuring facing urban regions in Berlin, Detroit and other cities. Reichert has taught university and college students at local universities, and Cope also served as one of the first curators at the up-and-coming Museum of Contemporary Art Detroit, located in a former auto dealership, which is now emerging as a hub of creative experimentation in urban settings. Marion Jackson, former Chair of Art and Art History at Wayne State University, served on the Board of the *Heidelberg Project* for 12 years and is one of the key organizers of *Arts Corps Detroit*, a Wayne State-affiliated 'service-learning' course and art project that has partnered with local community groups, including *Heidelberg*. Working with neighbourhood groups, *Arts Corps'* 'LOTS of Art!' project invites Wayne State affiliates to repurpose selected underutilized parcels of land as interactive, community art spaces. Closely affiliated with local institutions, *Heidelberg* and *Power House* offer their own youth internships and training programmes, and thus serve as hubs for the dissemination of creative energies outward from the internal dynamics of their neighbourhood projects.

If these dispersed site-specific creative initiatives give shape to a Detroit experimental art scene, it is nonetheless a scene that contemplates the particularities of Detroit without overtly extending itself to other cities. Detroit's scene appears unusual and unique, as with Detroit itself, paralleled only by select shrinking cities such as Berlin in the 1990s with their own specific economic and political histories (Forkert 2013). Nevertheless, a related experimental scene has emerged in Windsor through its bordering relationship with Detroit (as both local suburb and transnational neighbour), a scene that invites us to consider Windsor as a site of both spectating and participating. The asymmetrical relationship between Detroit and Windsor is mirrored in the flow of cultural energies between their scenes as spaces of integrated cross-border cultural activity, and simultaneously throws into relief the constant transnational movement of capital, goods and people that characterizes the border culture of the greater Detroit metropolitan area.

Onlooking Detroit: cross-border circulation

The border with Detroit yields a magnetism that is central to Windsor's imaginary. My first impression of Windsor was of a thin strip of land opposite an entrancing skyline, a city built as a lookout. Travelling at dusk from the train station along Riverside Drive, I realized that I had never fully grasped the proximity of Windsor to Detroit. Only in subsequent visits did I begin to take in how Windsor was organized, stretching away from the river along numerous arteries oriented to industrial infrastructure. Detroit's skyline is embedded in Windsor's visual identity (a student once commented that Windsor 'owns' the Detroit skyline). Similarly, tour guide images of Detroit frequently portray the city from the vantage point of Windsor, as if Detroit's best view is from outside the city (Rodney 2014, p. 268). When Detroit Emergency Financial Manager Kevin Orr held a press conference regarding the city's filing for bankruptcy (19 July 2013), he stood in front of an image entitled 'Reinventing Detroit' depicting a view of the Detroit skyline taken from Windsor.

Faced with Detroit's epic history, and witnessing parallel economic and infrastructural downturns, Windsor is in many ways its little cousin. At other times, Windsor operates as an additional suburb of Detroit alongside established suburban centres such as Grosse Pointe and Royal Oak. Yet as a city on the other side of the border, Windsor retains an individuality that also sets it apart from the greater Detroit area. While Windsor's population has declined by 2.6 percent since the economic downturn of 2008, Detroit City has lost some 20 percent of its population since 2000. In real numbers, Windsor's last census population count of 210,891 (in 2011) is not wildly smaller than Detroit City's last count of 684,799 (in 2012; City of Detroit, Office of the Emergency Manager 2013, p. 1), acknowledging of course that the ethnic composition of these cities remains very different. However, these numbers do not capture the population of the greater metropolitan area surrounding both cities: including Detroit's many suburbs, the population of greater Detroit–Windsor is close to 6 million. To consider this greater urban region requires attending to cross-border patterns of circulation and impermeability that are constitutive of the simultaneously integrated and divided environment of the Detroit–Windsor borderlands.

Cross-border mobilities – of populations and media forms, of invasive species and industrial materials – have long underscored the ambiguity of this border as a physical boundary, its status as both a permeable waterway and a political obstacle. This point was driven home by international media attention in 2013 on a three-story pile of petroleum coke, covering one city block, that built up unannounced on underused railway spurs on the Detroit side of the river, reviving fears of environmental cross-border contamination and galvanizing local community groups on each side to coordinate resistance efforts (Austen 2013). Standing opposite the greened landscape of Windsor's Odette Sculpture Park, the petcoke piles brought into relief marked distinctions between values associated with urban space: while Windsor's parkland is built on former industrial sites, similar spaces in Detroit to be zoned for industrial use merely hundreds of metres away.

Cross-border trade and traffic has of course always been integral to the borderland economies, regardless of the US Department of Homeland Security's attempts to redefine North American border control and security. When Ford established assembly plants in Windsor, he quickly had access to the tariff-free zones of the British Commonwealth and thereby established one of the earliest international trade corridors. Thomas Klug has documented the complexity of the Detroit Labour Movement throughout the late nineteenth and early twentieth centuries, where daily commuters and strikebreakers from Canada were perceived as a threat to Detroit labour-market security (Klug 1998, 2008). Prohibition era and post-war economies deriving from illicit industries flourished through cross-border relationships and shifting discrepancies between USA and Canadian currencies, while fomenting moralistic debates about legal and illegal forms of vice. In both cities, these debates extended into the late twentieth century with regard to the legalization of gambling (see Karibo 2012).

Just as thousands of Windorites today cross the border daily to work in manufacturing, health and other NAFTA-regulated industries, agricultural goods and industrial materials – especially within the automotive sector – circulate regularly across the border. Bill Anderson describes a 'distinctive pattern of US–Canada automotive trade whereby Canada exports a larger share of vehicles to the US and the US exports a larger share of parts to Canada', but as many smaller automotive parts are required for major components, 'it is possible for the same part to cross the border several times' before arriving at an assembly plant (2012, p. 493). At the same time, the rise of free trade in the 1990s and the increasing implementation of more stringent border security in the 2000s have contributed to the transformation of Windsor and Detroit's border spaces from local points of contact to corridors of global trade, favouring flows of products over people (Rodney 2014, pp. 267–269). Stricter identification requirements – passports or enhanced ID cards – introduced through the Western Hemisphere Travel Initiative in 2009 have not only slowed cross-border tourism but also blocked the passage of undocumented people who might well contribute to local labour markets on both sides of the border. And while economic linkages through the automotive sector have long defined the cities and neighbouring regions, political cooperation between local authorities has curiously remained distant (Nelles 2011). Thus, a peculiar condition of economic interpenetration and political separation contribute to the cultural landscape of the Windsor–Detroit borderlands.

Arguably, one generative cross-border literary and artistic scene evolved in the early years of the renowned *Christian Culture Series*, initiated in 1934 by Father J. Stanley Murphy at Windsor's then Assumption College (now Assumption University, an institution federated with the University of Windsor), which brought dozens of writers, artists, philosophers and Catholic labour activists to the border cities. In the late 1960s and 1970s, notably throughout Detroit's tumultuous uprisings during the Civil Rights Movement, Windsor-based radio station CKLW's *The Big 8* Top 40 show claimed the number one spot in Detroit ratings, introducing numerous Motown and other performers to cross-border audiences. Describing the 1990s Detroit techno scene, Marcel O'Gorman (himself a Windsorite who has worked in both cities) captures the intimacy of the border cities in the clandestine movements of Richie Hawtin, or Plastikman:

> For a long stretch of Saturday nights in the mid-1990s, young suburbanites crossed 8-mile road and headed into Detroit's East side, packing themselves like lemmings into the long-abandoned Packard automotive plant. They went there to get high on inner-city danger, ecstasy washed down with Evian, and the thumping sensorium of Detroit's king of darkno, Richie Hawtin, a.k.a. Plastikman. When all the feel-good was rubbed off on the dance floor, and the sun began to rise, they returned to the safety of their homes in So-and-So Woods and Something Hills. Plastikman was the pied piper of apocalypse tourism. Even in 1995, after being banned from the US for 18 months for working without a permit, Hawtin bootlegged himself into Detroit to mix and spin at underground raves. As always, beckoned by word of mouth, deftly designed flyers, and electronic airwaves, the suburban crowds swarmed the abandoned Packard Plant.

There is a certain poetry in the scene of a techno DJ working the crowd at an automotive assembly plant. Plastikman, 'mashing together' (an expression I have come to despise) deep strings, subsonic base, and an outer-space plink-plonk backbeat, is at home on the assembly line. (O'Gorman 2007)

Perhaps as a response to the political disjuncture between the municipalities and regions, it is not surprising that such instances of cross-border cultural activity have sprung up throughout their histories. The three Windsor projects I discuss next – *Green Corridor*, the *BCL* and the *Border Bookmobile* – work to bridge the border by fostering cross-border recognition of the ways in which Windsor's own urban predicament complements Detroit. Detroit appears again a stage, but one for which Windsorites form a particularly engaged audience – an audience of intimate onlookers.

Windsor: border scenes

While Detroit's contemporary experimental art scene engages with abandoned, demolished or ruined spaces in specific neighbourhoods, creative communities in Windsor are challenging states of dereliction by reminding us that the border city is part of a greater urban environment that has constantly experienced spatial transformations. Windsor-based projects on their own may not constitute a scene, in Barry Shank's sense of an 'overproductive signifying community' (1994, p. 122). Yet in the context of Windsor's onlooker relationship with Detroit, these projects mobilize local energies in multiple directions. On one hand, they constitute a form of cross-border circulation, a local instantiation of what Gaonkar and Povinelli (2003) have called the movement of the 'edges of forms' (p. 391). On the other hand, within Windsor, creative collectives draw on their position as intimate onlookers to propose new forms of connection between Windsor and Detroit, negotiating the ambiguity of the border as simultaneously porous and impermeable.

As with the Detroit-based projects discussed in this paper, creative communities in Windsor are directly and indirectly connected to educational institutions and respond, in Lee and LiPuma's (2002, p. 192) sense, to 'the interactions between specific types of circulating forms and the interpretive communities built around them'. Straw notes that 'universities everywhere generate forms of learning and expressive practices that are in excess of their intended function as places for the imparting of formal, disciplinary knowledge. Predictably, universities are important sites for the accumulation of social and cultural capital' (2004, p. 414). The University of Windsor's School of Creative Arts (merged in 2013 out of the schools of visual arts and music, and programming in cinema) is the locus of creative initiatives that engage border spaces in critical art education and of collectives that have emerged from this school and extended themselves into the scenic life of the city. Border spaces in part generate the school's cultural capital, and allow the school to connect to concentrations of subcultural capital (e.g. through cross-border teaching faculty and local sessional instructors). The overall proximity of the university to the border – the Ambassador Bridge's infrastructure and the university's central campus are integrated within the same geographical space – has fostered on-going student interest in understanding these weird spaces.

Border spaces in Windsor are thus an arena for experimentation in which artists and students work with and against the urban environment. The *Green Corridor* project, initiated in 2004 by artists Noel Harding and Rod Strickland, a University of Windsor visual arts professor, has sought to reclaim 2 km of the Windsor–Detroit gateway along Huron Church Road approaching the Ambassador Bridge. In its various manifestations as both an undergraduate course and an urban research forum, *Green Corridor* has challenged the fragmentation of the border environment into seemingly disconnected spaces: the Ambassador Bridge's vast customs and security zone focused on cycles of trade and travel, industrial zones, surrounding communities with a high proportion of low-income residents, and the campus of the University of Windsor itself. This area includes the adjacent blocks of Indian Road, a street of boarded-up houses owned by the American Ambassador Bridge Company as a part of its bid to twin the bridge's span but which Windsor's City Council listed as a designated heritage area in 2007 due in part to a First Nations settlement that once stood nearby. In contrast to these disconnected spaces, *Green Corridor* treats the entire border region as a total and harmonious environment facing related manifestations of urban crisis.

As Kim Nelson and I have argued (2010), *Green Corridor* challenges us to rethink the urban spaces of the border in terms of circulation rather than the linear metaphors of corridors or crossings. The project engages the border environment as a fluid space open to innovations in urban design and in so doing shifts the spatial bias of the border from an edge to an environment or field. The complexity of Detroit and its material conditions are not external to this field, but rather are necessarily part of an expanded understanding of borderline spaces as points of resonance. In 2009, for example, *Green Corridor* staged its *Open Corridor* intervention: an interactive and site-specific festival of arts, science, performance and community. Designed as a drive-through, open-air gallery along Huron Church Road running south of the Ambassador Bridge, *Open Corridor* staged public art projects and performances to engage both local and international travellers in seeing and listening. In keeping with Windsor's bid to be seen seeing, this border space was thus momentarily redefined and re-coded as an experience of the local rather than a transnational passageway. A 'Drive-Thru Symphony' relied on the participation of car and truck drivers in an interactive performance, a call-and-response exchange activating the corridor through visual projections, text and time-delayed images. Music ensembles performed sound works 'created in response to the themes of environment, traffic, and shifting time (the time it takes for sound to travel long distances, mobile audiences, and the streaming delay to the FM signal)' (Green Corridor Project 2009). The two-day performance proposed 'a "sensorial" approach to urbanism that explores how we use sight, sound, and even smell as a means of navigating and understanding the city' (Green Corridor Project 2009).

Much like Detroit's *Heidelberg* and *Power House Projections*, *Green Corridor* is motivated by the same logic of gradual and contemplative transformation, drawing our attention to the integrated material conditions of Detroit–Windsor and the 'challenges posed by living and working in places that are in critical condition' (Rodney 2014, p. 262). This practice of urban self-reflection is furthered by the *BCL*, an artist-led creative research collective working to promote civic change by acknowledging and disrupting Windsor's state of crisis. Initiated by local artist Justin Langlois as a research-creation project for his MFA in Visual Arts, the *BCL* includes a number of student artists with backgrounds in various fields.[1] Since its inception, the *BCL* has undertaken a range of urban interventions: environmental awareness and 'self-help' slogans for Windsorites (e.g. biodegradable, seed-filled balloons emblazoned with 'You Are Worth It' for the *Open Corridor Festival*); the *Text-in-Transit* project in partnership with Transit Windsor, featuring 100 statements and stories posted as bus advertisements ('The automobile can only take us so far' and 'There is a future here'); and *Scavenge the City*, 'algorithmic walks' based on randomly generated sets of instructions for navigating Windsor. As with *Green Corridor*, the *BCL* calls for new ways of mapping Windsor in relation to its own past, articulating a need 'to create the foundation upon which new border relations can be imagined and enacted in both Windsor and Detroit' (*BCL* 2011, p. 7). Having obtained an Ontario Trillium Foundation grant in 2012, the group established the Civic Space, a storefront meeting, research and gallery space in an under-populated stretch of Pelissier Street. As with Detroit's *Design 99* (which previously established a storefront workshop gallery in Hamtramck) and subsequent *Power House Projections*, the *BCL*'s success in obtaining a variety of arts funding grants has allowed it to pursue activities ranging from pop-up urban interventions, local workshops, international conferences such as *Homework: Infrastructures and Collaboration in Social Practices* (2011), and artist residencies such as *Storefront Residencies for Social Innovation* (2010) and *Neighbourhood Spaces: Windsor & Region Artist-in-Residence Program* (2013–2014). These residencies have invited multi-disciplinary artists and designers to occupy spaces in Windsor as interventions into the everyday realities of high rates of vacancy and underused properties. The movement of motivated young artists through the university and into the city indicates the intimacy of the local arts community (e.g. Langlois also served as the Director of the municipal Arts Council). The *BCL*'s activities have thus crossed the boundaries between student project, social collective, professional organization and academic think tank. As Straw contends:

> the knowledges required for a career in artistic fields are acquired in the movement into and through a scene, as individuals gather around themselves the sets of relationships and behaviours that are the preconditions of acceptance. Here, as in scenes more generally, the lines between professional and social activities are blurred, as each kind of activity becomes the alibi for the other. The 'vertical' relationship of master to student is transformed, in scenes, into the spatial relationship of outside to inside; the neophyte advances 'horizontally', moving from the margins of a scene towards its centre. A variety of urban media (from alternative weekly newspapers to Internet-based friendship circles) now act as way-finding aids in this process. (2004, p. 413)

In their 2011 online and self-published compendium *How to Forget the Border Completely* (2011), the *BCL* extended an earlier *Cross-Border Communication* project as a series of interventions 'based on the desperate need to communicate with Detroit, Michigan, from Windsor, Ontario' (Figure 1). This endeavour captured Windsorites' desire to be seen looking at Detroit. In its first manifestation, *Cross-Border Communication* (2009) projected messages such as 'We're In This Together' onto buildings facing Detroit at the riverside intersection of Windsor's main street, Ouellette Avenue (Figure 2). *How to*

FIGURE 1 Broken telephone by *BCL*. Image credit: Karlyn Koeser.

FIGURE 2 Cross-border communication by *BCL*. Image credit: Cristina Naccarato.

Forget the Border Completely documents a series of imagined interpenetrations between Windsor and Detroit, such as the disappearance of the river as Windsor and Detroit streets merge, or cross-border subways and portals. Actively forgetting the border is an attempt to imagine the impossible, a projection of an unattainable future vantage point from which we may nonetheless contemplate the present moment. Forgetting is thus a tactic to counter nostalgic ruingazing in the region as a whole, and the passivity of observing these cities as merely objects of historical contemplation. Lee Rodney's *Border Bookmobile* takes up questions of instituted versus tactical forgetting of the region's historical configurations through an archive of artefacts and stories that highlight changing attitudes towards the border cities.

The *Bookmobile* is an art-research project organized and curated by Rodney, a scholar of urban and visual cultures at the University of Windsor who also leads a senior undergraduate seminar on 'Border Culture'. Since 2009, the *Bookmobile* has been housed in a 1993 Plymouth minivan, an emblem of Detroit design made in Windsor's Chrysler Minivan Assembly Plant (Figure 3). Drawing on Detroit's neglect of its border city status as a starting point, Rodney describes the project as a 'mobile exhibition of books, photographs, maps, and ephemera on this border region' as well as USA–Mexico border relations, a 'memory project' that seeks to 'chart the changing relationship between Detroit and Windsor as border cities' by inviting 'viewers and participants to produce new narratives about the region that speak to the interrelationship between Windsor and Detroit' (Lee Rodney 2014, p. 255; Figure 4).

FIGURE 3 *Border Bookmobile* at Windsor's Ambassador Park on the Detroit River. Image credit: Lee Rodney.

In its most recent manifestation as the *Border Bookmobile Public Archive and Reading Room* (2013), an exhibition at the Art Gallery of Windsor alongside contemporary art curator Srimoyee Mitra's program *Border Cultures: Part 1 (Homes, Land)*, the mobile library was turned inside-out allowing visitors to browse the plethora of materials and border memorabilia (from pencils and badges to stamps and playing cards), read and view the many narratives of border crossings that the project has collected, and finally make copies of materials. As with *Green Corridor* and the *BCL*, the *Bookmobile* highlights the border's capacity to facilitate flows of products while often hindering flows of people.

By reifying the otherwise abstract border into specific visual spaces on which to project acts of resistance to the borderland's fragmented character, the *Green Corridor*, the *BCL* and the *Border Bookmobile* all draw attention to strategies for reimagining abandoned structures and underused spaces bound together by the Detroit–Windsor gateway. If each initiative appears staunchly local in orientation, their joint commitment to imagining a different cross-border urban experience is part of the scene's *project*. As Rodney puts it, 'if Detroit and Windsor prove to be resistant to gentrification, it is not merely because of the blue-collar legacy; it is because the critical issue facing neighbourhoods is stabilization' (Rodney 2014, p. 262). These initiatives are simultaneously

FIGURE 4 *Border Bookmobile*, Windsor downtown market. Image credit: Riaz Memhood

connected to and separate from Detroit's aesthetic community, a community which thus exceeds its own perceived local boundaries.

Conclusion: Detroit ± Windsor

Detroit and Windsor have emerged as sites of a multi-layered experimental art scene deeply embedded in each city's cultural landscape and educational institutions, where 'collaborative projects aim at neighbourhood stabilization against the tide of foreclosures, abandonment, and arson' (Rodney 2014, p. 262). Inhabiting the space between images of stasis and change, and between patterns of cross-border circulation and impermeability, the activities transpiring within the many projects discussed in this paper work to disorder the material character of urban spaces and the built environment, the people, things and media that pass through them, and even their legal and institutional frameworks. Yet to identify these many projects as a scene also invites us to consider what Straw identifies as the notion's 'elusive slipperiness' (2001, p. 252). The diversity of strategies and approaches they employ exceed more tightly circumscribed activities suggested by terms such as art world or movement. Moreover, the very slipperiness of scenes affords us the opportunity to consider cross-border affinities in cultural expression which cannot easily be identified in terms of class, community, or subculture, nor in terms of national strategies for fostering cultural citizenship. Blum's assertion that since 'the city breeds the celebration of intimacy [...] the culture of the city is located as much in its topography of scenes as in its formal institutions of "high art" such as the ballet, opera, theatre district, museums, and galleries' (2003, p. 183) is applicable to Detroit–Windsor: as cross-border cooperation between political, cultural and even educational institutions is severely limited, scene arguably describes the intimate relationship between site-specific projects afforded by Windsor's onlooker status with Detroit more efficiently.

Yet if a multi-layered art scene connects Detroit and Windsor, it also serves to highlight the distinctiveness of these cities. While Windsor's border-oriented collectives make forays into central Detroit with some frequency, neither city's projects have attempted to maintain a longer-term presence in the other city. And although the projects described on either side of the border are all overtly oriented to civic change or community transformation, their dispersal across multiple sites of encounter and their connections to educational and professional institutions may, arguably, also slow the pace of the systemic change they desire. Against each city's hurry to embed scenic life within officially demarcated cultural districts and economies, the projects I have described are oriented to cautious and considered transformation grounded in dialogue, workshops, research and planning. The sense of intimacy fostered within efforts to stabilize Detroit neighbourhoods is complemented by forms of intimacy between Windsor and Detroit generated through Windsor-based projects that address forms of urban crisis all deeply linked to Detroit's future. Windsor art collectives thus enter into a dialogue with site-specific projects in Detroit as both insiders and onlookers – not in the sense of idle onlookers, as with most ruin tourists, but rather as an audience expressing its deep knowledge and appreciation of Detroit's history and current conditions. In the gradual nature of transformation that these projects espouse, as they contemplate a perhaps unattainable future, the scene is afforded time to contemplate its coming-to-be and its potential perishing.

Note

1   The *BCL* includes Justin Langlois, Danielle Sabelli, Michelle Soulliere, Josh Babcock, Rosina Riccardo, Cristina Naccarato, Hiba Abdallah, Kevin Echlin and Sara Howie.

Notes on Contributor

Michael Darroch is an Associate Professor of Media Art Histories and Visual Culture at the University of Windsor and Director of the IN/TERMINUS Creative Research Collective. He has published essays on art, media, language, and urban culture and is co-editor of the anthology *Cartographies of Place: Navigating the Urban* (McGill-Queens, 2014). He is completing a book manuscript on transatlantic and interdisciplinary influences on Canadian media studies and the journal *Explorations* (1953–1959).

References

Anderson, W. P. (2012) 'Public policy in a cross-border economic region', *International Journal of Public Sector Management*, vol. 25, no. (6/7), pp. 492–499.

Austen, I. (2013) 'From Canadian oil, a black pile rises in Detroit', *New York Times*, 18 May, p. A1.

Binelli, M. (2012) *Detroit City is the Place to Be*, New York, Metropolitan Books.

Blum, A. (2003) *The Imaginative Structure of the City*, Montréal and Kingston, McGill-Queen's University Press.

Broken City Lab (2011) *How to Forget the Border Completely*, Windsor, Broken City Lab.

Carducci, V. (2012) *Envisioning Real Utopias in Detroit* [online] Available at: http://motownreviewofart.blogspot.ca/2012/02/envisioning-real-utopias-in-detroit.html (accessed 28 April 2014).

City of Detroit, Office of the Emergency Manager (2013) *Proposal for Creditors* [online] Available at: http://www.detroitmi.gov/Portals/0/docs/EM/Reports/City%20of%20Detroit%20Proposal%20for%20Creditors1.pdf (accessed 28 December 2013).

Cope, M. (2004) 'In Detroit time', in *Shrinking Cities Working Papers, Volume III: Detroit*, ed. P. Oswald, Halle an der Saale, Kulturstiftung des Bundes, pp. 11–12.

Darke, C. (2011) *An Insider's Guide to Detroit's Contemporary Art Scene. Hyperallergic: Sensitive to Art & Its Discontents* [online] Available at: http://hyperallergic.com/39737/detroit-contemporary-art-scene/ (accessed 28 December 2013).

Darroch, M. & Nelson, K. (2010) 'Windsoria: border/screen/environment', *Public*, vol. 40, pp. 56–64.

Detroit–Berlin Connection [online] (2014) Available at: http://detroitberlin.de (accessed 23 May 2014).

Deutsche, R. & Ryan, C. (1984) 'The fine art of gentrification', vol. 31, October, pp. 91–111.

Edensor, T. (2005) 'Waste matter – the Debris of industrial ruins and the disordering of the material world', *Journal of Material Culture*, vol. 10, no. 3, pp. 311–332.

Florida, R. (2002) *The Rise of the Creative Class: And How It's Transforming Work, Leisure and Everyday Life*, New York, Basic Books

Florida, R. (2005) *Cities and the Creative Class*, London, Routledge.

Forkert, K. (2013) 'The persistence of bohemia', *City: Analysis of Urban Trends, Culture, Theory, Policy, Action*, vol. 17, no. 2, pp. 149–163.

Gaonkar, D. P. & Povinelli, E. A. (2003) 'Technologies of public forms: circulation, transfiguration, recognition', *Public Culture*, vol. 15, no. 3, pp. 385–397.

Green Corridor Project. (2009) *Open City Festival*, Windsor, ON, Green Corridor Project.

Herron, J. (1993) *After Culture: Detroit and the Humiliation of History*, Detroit, Wayne State University Press.

Herron, J. (2005) 'Not from Detroit', in *Urban ecology: Detroit and beyond*, ed. K. Park, Hong Kong, MAP Book Publishers, pp. 155–156.

Herscher, A. (2012) *The Unreal Estate Guide to Detroit*, Ann Arbor, University of Michigan Press.

Karibo, H. M. (2012) *Ambassadors of Pleasure: Illicit Economies in the Detroit–Windsor Borderland, 1945–1960*. Unpublished doctoral diss., Toronto, University of Toronto.

Klug, T. A. (1998) 'The Detroit labor movement and the United States–Canada border, 1885–1930', *Mid-America*, vol. 80, pp. 209–234.

Klug, T. A. (2008) 'Residents by day, visitors by night: the origins of the alien commuter on the US–Canadian border during the 1920s', *Michigan Historical Review*, vol. 34, no. 2, pp. 75–98.

Lang, P. (2005) 'Over my dead city', in *Urban Ecology: Detroit and beyond*, ed. K. Park, Hong Kong, MAP Book Publishers, pp. 10–16.

Leary, J. P. (2011) *Detroitism. Guernica: A Magazine of Art and Politics* [online] Available at: http://www.guernicamag.com/features/leary_1_15_11/ (accessed 28 December 2013).

Lee, B. & LiPuma, E. (2002) 'Cultures of circulation: the imaginations of modernity', *Public Culture*, vol. 14, no. 1, pp. 191–213.

Marchand, Y. & Meffre, R. (2010) *The Ruins of Detroit*, Göttingen, Steidl.

McLuhan, M. (1977) 'Canada: the borderline case', in *The Canadian Imagination: Dimensions of a Literary Culture*, ed. D. Staines, Cambridge, MA, Harvard University Press, pp. 226–248.

Nelles, J. (2011) 'Cooperation in crisis? An analysis of cross-border intermunicipal relations in the Detroit–Windsor region', *Articulo: Journal of Urban Research*, vol. 6 [online] Available at: http://articulo.revues.org/2097 (accessed 28 December 2013).

O'Gorman, M. (2007) 'Digital Detroit: tourists in the apocalypse', *CTheory* [online] Available at: http://ctheory.net/articles.aspx?id=586 (accessed 28 December 2013).

Park, B. (2005) 'Going to Detroit', *New York Times*, 28 August, travel section, pp. D13.

Park, K., ed. (2005) *Urban Ecology: Detroit and Beyond*, Hong Kong, MAP Book Publishers.

Power House Productions [online] (2013) Available at: http://www.powerhouseproductions.org (accessed 28 December 2013).

Redgrave, A. (2013) 'Motor skills/Les moteurs du changement', *enRoute*, April, pp. 45–52.

Rice, J. (2005) 'Detroit taggin', *CTheory* [online] Available at: http://ctheory.net/articles.aspx?id=484 (accessed 28 December 2013).

Rodney, L. (2009) 'Detroit is our future', *Fuse Magazine*, vol. 36, no. 4, pp. 6–12.

Rodney, L. (2014) 'Art and the post-urban condition', in *Cartographies of Place: Navigating the Urban*, eds. M. Darroch & J. Marchessault, Montréal and Kingston, McGill-Queen's University Press, pp. 253–269.

Rosler, M. (2011) 'Culture class: art, creativity, urbanism, part III', *E-flux Journal*, vol. 25 [online] Available at: http://www.e-flux.com/journal/culture-class-art-creativity-urbanism-part-iii/ (accessed 28 December 2013).

Shank, B. (1994) *Dissonant Identities: The Rock'n'roll Scene in Austin, Texas*, Hanover, NH, Wesleyan University Press.

Silver, D., Clark, T. N. & Graziul, C. (2011) 'Scenes, innovation, and urban development', in *Handbook of Creative Cities*, eds. D. E. Andersson, Å. E. Andersson, & C. Mellander, Cheltenham, Edward Elgar, pp. 229–258.

Silver, D., Clark, T. N., & Yanez, C. J. N. (2010) 'Scenes: social context in an age of contingency', *Social Forces*, vol. 88, no. 5, pp. 2293–2324.

Steinmetz, G. (2008) 'Harrowed landscapes: white ruingazers in Namibia and Detroit and the cultivation of memory', *Visual Studies*, vol. 23, no. 3, pp. 211–237.

Straw, W. (2001) 'Scenes and sensibilities', *Public*, vol. 22/23, pp. 245–257.

Straw, W. (2004) 'Cultural scenes', *Loisir et société* [Society and Leisure], vol. 27, no. 2, pp. 411–422.

Stryker, M. (2013) 'Fire claims part of Heidelberg Project, but the art, like Detroit, will survive', *Detroit Free Press*, [online] Available at: http://www.freep.com/article/20130503/COL17/305030120/heidelberg-project-guyton-fire-detroit (accessed 4 May 2013).

Sugrue, T. (2005) *The Origins of the Urban Crisis: Race and Inequality in Postwar Detroit*, Princeton, NJ, Princeton University Press.

Vergara, C. J. (1995) 'Downtown Detroit: American Acropolis or vacant land?' *Metropolis*, April, 33–38.

Vogel, S. (2005) 'Surviving to create', in *Urban Ecology: Detroit and Beyond*, ed. K. Park, Hong Kong, MAP Book Publishers, pp. 16–19.

Yablonsky, L. (2010) 'Artists in residence', *New York Times*, 22 September [online] Available at: http://www.nytimes.com/2010/09/26/t-magazine/26remix-detroit-t.html?_r=2&adxnnl=1&adxnnlx=1285758007-VD4winfKUrKGnXhLd dn9+w (accessed 28 April 2013).

Yablonsky, L. (2011). 'Art motors on', *W magazine*, November [online]. Available at: http://www.wmagazine.com/culture/art-and-design/2011/11/detroit-art-scene (accessed 28 April 2014).

Danielle J. Deveau

'WE WEREN'T HIP, DOWNTOWN PEOPLE'

The Kids in the Hall, the Rivoli and the nostalgia of the Queen West scene

This paper examines how discourses about obscurity, ambivalence and nostalgia serve to perpetuate cultural scenes. I consider Toronto bar and performance venue the Rivoli and Canadian comedy troupe the Kids in the Hall (KITH) as part of a cultural scene that existed on Queen Street West in the early 1980s. I analyse this case study through media discourses found in reviews and interviews about the scene and argue that representations of KITH's participation in the early days of the scene continue to legitimize the troupe as a groundbreaking and counter-cultural comedy team. That is, even now that they have ostensibly left 'the scene' they are still defined by it. In contemporary interviews with the group, their origins on the Queen West circuit, particularly at the Rivoli, are consistently used to frame them as innovators in Canadian comedy. These discourses also work to obscure the extent to which scenes are constructed and at times part of profoundly predictable taste cultures.

Described by one cultural critic as a 'fashionable new wave watering hole', the Rivoli opened in Toronto, Canada, at 334 Queen Street West in February 1982 and quickly established itself as a prominent venue on the Queen West circuit, which was then part of a burgeoning punk music scene in Canada (Brunt 1982, Dale 1982, Lacey 1983). Hosting a range of hip, creative activities – from alternative theatre to esoteric, high-cultural activities such as literary readings and contemporary art symposia (Dale 1982, Mays 1983) – it was not simply a bar and performance venue but also clearly positioned as a critical hub in the Queen West arts scene around which symbolic capital circulated. The café, theatre and edgy music and art venue became the home club for the Kids in the Hall (KITH; comedians Dave Foley, Kevin McDonald, Bruce McCulloch, Mark McKinney and Scott Thompson), an alternative sketch troupe which formed in

1984 and rose from relative obscurity in the Rivoli's dark backroom to popular heights in mainstream comic media.

This comedy team has had a lasting impact on the Canadian comedy scene, as well as traditions of sketch comedy in both the USA and the UK. Almost 30 years later, they continue to work together, reuniting every few years for live performances and television specials. Their sketches have often engaged with banal aspects of everyday life such as suburban families and corporate workplaces, subverting these scenarios with absurd characters. Their portrayal of women, not as drag characters, but as 'real' women with appropriately styled hair, make-up and wardrobe became a signature element of their comedy. They were also particularly hard on Toronto's 'Bay Street' crowd, and regularly caricatured businessmen and corporate culture. For example, in a sketch from season one of their television series, they satirize business networking as a series of handshakes and meetings in which participants agreed to meet again. By the end of the sketch, this networking pays off for McCulloch's character as the buzz around his 'newness' gets him a business card from an enthusiastic Foley. The two exchange clichéd statements about unspecified local sports teams before parting ways to shake hands with other businessmen with whom they will network. The sketch includes observations about trying too hard (with one participant jumping on the back of another) and the success of a merger (depicted by two men ballroom dancing together). In another sketch, Dave Foley's character climbs the corporate ladder only to be mocked by his boss (McDonald) when he discovers Foley does not drink. He pressures Foley into having a 'girl drink' which results in Foley becoming a 'girl drink drunk'. We see his character binge drinking on brightly coloured beverages accented with paper umbrellas. His alcoholism eventually results in his losing his job. Many of their sketches are framed around absurd and/or incompetent characters featured in otherwise every day or banal scenarios. Arguably, this kind of comic style was at home in the Queen West scene where young people participated in what they perceived to be an alternative, anti-corporate lifestyle.

The historical conjuncture of the KITH, the Rivoli and the Queen West scene remains a significant component of contemporary discourses about the comedy troupe, the venue, and the city of Toronto. Consider, for example, the following introduction provided by Jian Ghomeshi (2008), host of the CBC Radio 1's popular programme, *Q*:

> You likely know the story, dear listeners. In the mid-80s a sketch comedy troupe featuring Dave Foley, Bruce McCulloch, Kevin McDonald, Mark McKinney, and Scott Thompson took up residency in the backroom of Toronto's Rivoli Restaurant. There they began honing a comedy revue as the Kids in the Hall, the twisted and scathing humour of their stage show soon became the talk of the town and caught the attention of *Saturday Night Live* producer Lorne Michaels. Michaels and the Kids developed a television

series for CBC. Canada tuned in. Thursday nights at 9:30 belonged to Kids in the Hall.

Ghomeshi's assumption that his listeners already know the story and his framing of this narrative as a formative moment in the troupe's comic style reinforce this 'original' moment in the cultural scene. The Rivoli here is described as a space to 'hone' a comedy style – indicating that it has a workshop or low-stakes element to it. At the same time, it is also framed as a site of good comedy, leading to the discovery of the troupe by one of the most significant cultural intermediaries in the industry. This narrative of obscurity, quality, discovery and continued legitimacy works its way through many media discourses about KITH, and they themselves regularly reinforce it in both past and present interviews.

As a hub for the comedy industry, Toronto boasts a range of opportunities for comedy performers; this comedy scene was still emerging in the early 1980s when KITH took up residency at the Rivoli. Even in these early days, however, important gatekeepers were circulating in the industry. Mark Breslin's empire of Yuk Yuk's comedy clubs was expanding, and many of the most popular sketch comics of the day (such as the cast of *SCTV* and many performers on *Saturday Night Live*) had spent formative years working in Toronto. Today, the Rivoli is not a peripheral performance space, but a respected and popular venue that is integrated into the mainstream field of comedy production. The Queen West art and culture scene that emerged in the 1970s as well as the punk and alternative culture scene that established itself there in the early 1980s are well known to scholars, participants – and even to outside observers who were never a part of this cultural space. As such, the scene lives on in urban lore, living memory, and the histories of spaces and venues that still operate in this now gentrified part of the city.

In this article, I argue that KITH and the Rivoli venue offer a useful example of the significance of legitimizing discourses in cultural scenes. I illustrate how particular spaces and moments are consecrated as 'scenes' in and through media discourses, often becoming part of the popular memory of a time and place. In order to trace how this is evident in the history of KITH and the Rivoli, I consider three narratives related to the comedy troupe, the space and their cultural legitimacy. The first is the privileging of obscurity and exclusivity. These define the scene as 'hip'[1] and unique, and enable people to make distinctions between insiders and outsiders, original participants and newcomers. Second, participants exhibit a selective ambivalence about success and 'selling out'. That is, the original scene is privileged as being authentic through its obscurity, but performers also seek better opportunities for exposure, frequently at the expense of their performative identities as hip and countercultural. Third, discourses exhibit a retrospective narrative based in the creative legitimacy of the space and nostalgia for the original scene.

These elements of the scene – obscurity, ambivalence and nostalgia – can be traced through media discourses.

Theorizing scenes

Cultural scenes are 'overproductive signifying communities' situated in relation to clusters of cultural amenities such as commercial activities or performance spaces (Shank cited Straw 2004, p. 412). In these spaces, consumption is closely linked to the expression of social ties and a common identity (Silver *et al.* 2004). Linked as it is with consumption as a meaningful activity, the use of the concept of 'scenes' has largely focused on spaces and activities that occur within the urban spaces of the 'bohemian metropolis' (Hesmondalgh 2005, p. 29). A generalized anti-establishment perspective is typical of such bohemian, avant-garde creative communities (Lloyd 2010), and has been so since the nineteenth century:

> What emerges in bohemia is a milieu that provides aspirants with both material and symbolic supports for the plying of such an uncertain trade, from inexpensive dwellings and tolerant cafes to a local status system unhinged at least partially, from the vagaries of the market. (Lloyd 2010, p. 56)

The symbolic capital imbued in such bohemian spaces continues to impact where artists choose to live and work and how the resulting artistic enclaves are ranked, even as the term 'bohemian' has taken an unpopular, even stigmatized, turn. This stigma is part of an increased cynicism about the performative claims to 'authenticity' that participants in bohemia have been thought to embody.

Like the concept of scene, Pierre Bourdieu's (1993) concept of 'fields' offers a spatial sociology of cultural production that engages with complex social spaces that often lack clearly defined boundaries. The extent to which these theories overlap can be seen in the positioning of KITH and the Rivoli as spaces of obscure culture which build symbolic capital in opposition to prevailing performance types and venues. Additionally, scenes are taste communities – a designation for which Bourdieu's theories of culture also provide some useful tools. As Will Straw (1991, p. 374) defines the logic of the field of cultural practices, 'those procedures through which principles of validation and means of accommodating change operate within particular cultural spaces so as to perpetuate their boundaries'. Here, we are offered a theory of cultural complexity which takes into account both the structural logics of the field and their reproduction, as well as the agency of actors within this field who, through their choices and cultural preferences, also alter the field in relatively predictable ways.

In scenes, what would ordinarily be inconsequential aesthetic choices become imbued with a politics of lifestyle. This aesthetic politics can reinforce the experience of a scene as important and exclusive, even if it is not, in the end, particularly innovative or transformative. Personal politics of style offer cues to other participants as to who belongs; obscure cultural knowledge, specific to the scene, allows for recognition between/amongst insiders (Gelder 2007). Knowledge of these unspoken codes is an element of cultural capital which participants must assimilate. A general definition of cultural capital, a term fundamental to Bourdieu's theories of cultural production and taste formation, is 'a form of knowledge, an internalized code or a cognitive acquisition which equips the social agent with empathy towards, appreciation for or competence in deciphering cultural relations and cultural artefacts' (Johnson 1993, p. 7). Cultural capital is not only at work in consumption but also within the system of production. The 'rules' that govern movement within the field are masked by appeals to cultural authority and the notion that cultural preferences are justified (Bourdieu 1984).

In contemporary culture, commercial activity is taken up as a meaningful and significant social process. The type of food that I buy, the cultural artefacts that I choose and display, and the activities in which I participate are not only elements of commerce but also make up a more profound experience of life in the city. Through scenes, moreover, these choices organize experiences of belonging in the cityscape, dividing urban space into a series of territories. In her comprehensive study of club cultures in the UK, Sarah Thornton argues that 'club cultures are *taste cultures*' (1996, p. 3). These subcultures reinforce shared cultural interests and 'crucially [...] embrace their own hierarchies of what is authentic and legitimate in popular culture – embodied understandings of which can make one "hip"' (1996, p. 3). This 'hipness' is an element of the participants' subcultural capital (1996, p. 11). While not a club like those considered by Thornton, the Rivoli in Queen West was also a space rooted in a particular type of subcultural capital which drew upon notions of 'hipness' for its emergent countercultural legitimacy within the scene.

The Queen West scene

The Queen West scene took root in the 1970s, following the rapid gentrification of the formerly bohemian Yorkville into one of Toronto's most expensive downtown neighbourhoods (Caulfield 1994, Henderson 2011):

> The bohemian community shifted south to Queen Street [...] and a cluster of small clubs, clothing shops, bookstores, and other uses dependent on the bohemian and arts communities took root here in the 1970s. An almost immediate consequence was that the Queen Street West strip became fashionable. [... Here], and in a number of other locales across downtown,

streetscapes are dotted by stores, coffee shops, bars, and other uses created or patronized by the bohemian and arts communities. (Caulfield 1994, pp. 90–91)

By the 1970s, Queen West had been largely abandoned by industrial and commercial interests, leaving space and, importantly, cheap rents for other types of production. As is fairly typical in underutilized, downtown spaces, an arts and culture scene emerged, drawing legitimacy from the grit and poverty of the area (for a discussion of this process in New York see also Eichhorn, this issue). As part of the development of taste cultures, artists and creative professionals act as 'creative scene makers' engaged in the pursuit of the 'cutting edge' (Lloyd 2010). According to Will Straw (2004), scenes are part of an urban infrastructure which allows for the exchange of cultural goods and encourages interactions within cultural spaces. Participants in bohemian cultural scenes such as those that develop in hip artists' neighbourhoods appeal to 'new culture hawks' who derive social capital from knowledge of, and participation in, obscure culture (particularly that which is destined to break out of obscurity) (Lloyd 2010). In the case of Queen Street West, the combination of artists and an emerging punk music scene created a vibrant cultural space where alternative performance venues such as the Rivoli could flourish (O'Connor 2002).

In his detailed ethnography of Chicago's Wicker Park neighbourhood in the early 1990s, for instance, Richard Lloyd offers an account of gentrification that closely mirrors that of Toronto's Queen West. Like Queen West, Wicker Park was 'discovered' by artists who moved into run-down industrial spaces, taking the rough elements of the neighbourhood as a sign of their creative authenticity. The cheap rents and ever-present risk of crime and violence became prerequisites for cultural consecration. As Lloyd argues, neighbourhoods like Wicker Park (and Queen Street West) become 'not only a target of gentrification, but also a bohemian-themed entertainment district where patrons are not starving artists but rather affluent professionals' (2010, p. 71). Yet the trope of the starving artist imbues such spaces with authenticity, with these supposedly authentic inhabitants (themselves often relative new-comers) positioning themselves against subsequent waves of ever more affluent residents. This process has played itself out across Toronto, with hipsters and artists moving ever westward in pursuit of cheaper rent and edgy lifestyles.

So, while urban scenes such as Queen Street West can accurately be defined as innovative spaces of cultural production, we might also acknowledge that there is nothing new about a generation of hipsters pursuing what they perceive to be 'authentic' cultural experiences in what they deem to be undiscovered, creative spaces; this process results in a frequently repeated cycle of urban gentrification and redevelopment. The gentrification of Queen Street has continued to move westward, culminating in the current hotbed of artistic talent and creative enterprises – Parkdale (Van Eyk 2010). The conditions in the Queen West of the Rivoli theatre at the time of the KITH were, however, similar to those experienced today in Parkdale. Notably, the term Queen West is synonymous with this creative scene, which has not always inhabited the same portion of Queen West, but rather moved along as the higher property values of gentrification have moved ever westward. For Michelle Van Eyk, writing her Master's thesis in Architecture in the late 2000s, Queen West is an area near Dufferin, rather than Spadina. Queen West acts as a moniker for an area of Queen Street that holds immense symbolic capital due to a thriving arts and culture scene. As Van Eyk notes of the Queen West area around Dufferin, 'In the early 2000s a handful of art galleries clustered along the Queen Street West strip likely migrating from the Queen–Spadina corridor where a vibrant bohemian arts scene existed in the 1970s after being priced out of Yorkville' (Van Eyk 2010, p. 65). The Queen–Spadina corridor which Van Eyk juxtaposes to the current Queen Street West scene is, for the purposes of this paper, 'Queen Street West'. While gentrification has displaced these 'alternative' arts scenes from their locales over the decades, it is important to note that this progression from Yorkville, to Queen West, to Parkdale lives on in popular narratives – often in tension with the commercial activities that come to define these spaces.

The Rivoli as countercultural space

Even as the 'scene' has drifted westward with its stretch of Queen Street West gentrifying into a trendy and expensive neighbourhood, the Rivoli, at Queen and Spadina, has managed to maintain its 'coolness'. As one critic notes:

> the chains have moved in and Queen Street has lost much of its funkiness. It has become more corporate and, therefore, more predictable. Still, the forces of gentrification have not succeeded in killing the eclectic vitality of the street, which survives in cafes, bars, and restaurants such as The Rex, Queen Mother, Rivoli, Horseshoe Tavern, and Peter Pan, all Toronto institutions. (Hume 2012, p. 4)

These so-called 'Toronto institutions' continue to represent the vibrant youth culture that gave Queen West its edge in the 1980s. The Rivoli remains an important venue in the comedy industry and on Monday nights is now home to the AltDot Comedy Lounge, a stand-up showcase that distinguishes itself from the 'mainstream' comedy of other clubs. Billed as 'Canada's most popular alternative comedy showcase', it features some of Toronto's most recognizable, yet still 'alternative' comedians. The contradiction between 'popular' and 'alternative' reinforces the extent to which the rhetoric of the scene reinforces its supposed obscurity while also depending upon being known – and even 'popular' – as a function of its legitimacy.

This tension between 'popular' and 'alternative' has long played out in media discourses about the venue. For example, in 1996, comedy critic Andrew Clark suggested that:

> The Rivoli is still one of the more 'out there' comedy joints but it is considered by those in the business as a marquee show. It's a place you play once you've perfected your work. Troupes that might once have cut their teeth at the Rivoli must now work their way up to booking the place. (1996, p. H8)

This balance between being 'out there' and being a prestigious venue drives the Rivoli's 'hip' reputation. In the same year, *Toronto Star* reporter Jamie Kastner called the Rivoli, 'arguably the hippest performance space on Queen West' (1996, p. C3). In part, this 'hipness' relates to the continued resonance of the venue as an important breeding ground for alternative culture, such as 'hit comics Kids in the Hall [... and] twang-and-crooners, Cowboy Junkies' (Kastner 1996, p. C3). In a 1996 interview, the booking agent for the Rivoli's backroom, Greg Bottrell, noted that demand for the room by established performers meant it was no longer a space to develop new, cutting-edge acts. Nonetheless, the venue still boasted countercultural credibility. Indeed, Bottrell was a high school dropout, turned heavy machinery mechanic, turned record store clerk, turned Charles Taylor – quoting philosophy major. Bottrell's exact blend of street credibility (dropout, tradesman) and intellectualism (philosophy student) was a perfect expression of the kind of bohemian eclecticism required by countercultural spaces such as the Rivoli.

Unlike the artistic field considered by Bourdieu, live music and comedy performers do not aspire to autonomy from the economy. Rather, live music, comedy and other 'commerical' arts can be consecrated through financial success as much as any other kind of consecration (e.g. respect from peers, positive media coverage and professional awards). The strategies of authors 'owe their form and content to the interests associated with the positions which they occupy in the structure of a very specific game' (Bourdieu 1993, p. 190). In the case of urban cultural scenes, where consumption practices are taken up as symbolic of identity, there is no necessary relation between legitimacy and profitability. Commercial culture may be legitimate and lucrative, legitimate and unprofitable, or lucrative but illegitimate; the producers' relationship to the cultural scene can confer or deny legitimacy to commercially successful products. Even within this commercial system, discourses of disinterestedness, a disdain for commercialism and rhetorical affiliations with non-market performance forms continue to circulate. In such popular cultures, oppositions to the privileging of economic gain are often rhetorical (rather than the consequence of an objective relation), and are generally aimed at securing a position of enhanced cultural capital.

In the case of Queen Street West, for instance, venues such as the Rivoli relate to avant-garde arts scenes, experimental music genres such as punk and jazz, and alternative theatre such as sketch comedy. In a review of the Rivoli's restaurant, one critic noted, 'Whatever their particular theme[...,] a restaurant hires staff that look and act the part. [...] New Wave, as in The Rivoli on Queen Street, wants artsy types who think that black is the sweetest color in the rainbow' (Kates 1984, p. CL2). However, it bears noting that the 'obviousness' of the scene also relates to your positioning within it. For example, 5 years later, another critic argues in the Toronto Star that the Rivoli is 'one of the most unpretentious cafes on Toronto's trendy Queen Street West' (Hume 1989). Over time, a venue that was initially 'a preferred artists' hang out' gradually became a perceptively accessible space for individuals who did not necessarily relate to the more obscure elements of the Queen West arts scene.

I note this transition because it is in this context that discourses about KITH comedy and their location in Queen West would be linked to 'counterculture' practices. While in popular uses of the term, counterculture is associated with falling outside of the mainstream; in this context, it should be read instead as a part of the social process of shifting cultural tastes and attitudes. According to Stuart Henderson:

> counterculture is best defined not as an alternate system of social interaction and ideologies existing *outside* the expected, dominant culture but rather as the shifting sets of responses, refusals, and acceptances performed by actors in the cultural process. (2011, p. 5)

Henderson frames this cultural process as being part of the 'call-and-response' between dominant and subaltern cultures. This is the process of cultural production and reproduction that Bourdieu outlines in his field theory. In art, for example, the artists, works and practices that are considered to be the 'avant-garde' are, by their very status as avant-garde, already in the process of being usurped by other, newer, more 'countercultural' artists and practices working at the margins of the artistic field. Participants, in other words, are never completely outside of this system of renewal. They are constantly implicated in its reproduction, as taste cultures shift and early career artists gain legitimacy and consecration.

'Cool' KITH, nostalgia and ambivalence about the mainstream

Featuring comedians Dave Foley, Kevin McDonald, Bruce McCulloch, Mark McKinney and Scott Thompson, KITH's comedy reflected the kind of countercultural attitude that was characteristic of the 'bohemian' strip of Queen West inhabited by venues like the Rivoli in the 1980s. Although the troupe would eventually break into television comedy, their time at the Rivoli was also spent honing their style with improvisational work which was not always intended to play well with a mass audience. This image of their comedy as falling outside of the mainstream is a major component of the troupe's narrative about itself. Indeed, in discussing their eventual popularity at the Rivoli, KITH member Dave Foley distances the group from the trendy, arts scene elements of Queen West, arguing that they were initially outsiders to the 'hip' culture that was developing there. In discussing the audience for their early shows at the Rivoli, Foley notes:

> at first we were loathed by the Queen Street crowd because they thought comedy was silly, uncool, this is back in a time when it was all very serious […] but eventually we got the art scene crowd and the punk rock crowd coming down. (Foley 2007)

Here, Foley distances the group from other types of 'cool' culture such as the art scene that was already established on Queen West. In interviews for the CBC documentary *Comedy Gold: The Hilarious Story of Canadian Comedy* (2005), both Kevin MacDonald and Dave Foley frame themselves as outside of such hip, urban scenes: 'We came from the suburbs' (MacDonald); 'We weren't hip, downtown people' (Foley). In distancing themselves from the 'established' scene and its habitués, they paradoxically engage in a discursive claim to 'coolness' through its rejection.

We see such a disengagement from cool in KITH sketches which lampoon businessmen, such as the head crusher, in which a character played by Mark McKinney stalks businessmen and 'crushes' their heads by holding his hand in front of the camera and playing with false perspective. The crux of the joke is that the character's anti-establishment rage is largely impotent as his 'victims' are not really harmed, and in many cases are completely unaware of, or indifferent to, his actions. Such anti-establishment sketches offered, in many respects, a quintessentially 'bohemian' outlook that rejected corporate consumer culture (albeit in favour of a different kind of stylized consumption). Indeed, the 'networking' sketch described earlier in this paper, with its emphasis on new, hip, participants can be read not only as satirizing business culture, but any 'scene' which makes a claim to coolness, even their own. As humorous utterances, these sketches send up the very countercultural attitudes that they espouse. They both critique ('the man') and turn the critique back in on themselves, in many ways acknowledging that critiquing 'the man' is not, in the end, a particularly innovative or original perspective on the corporate world. This is precisely the type of complex disinterestedness that sociologist Pierre Bourdieu associates with avant-garde art cultures, characterized by a rhetorical disdain for commercialism, while also taking up increasingly privileged positions within the field. In a related manner, KITH can be seen to perform a kind of counterculture which critically engages with the prevailing culture as its primary referent, negotiating in the spaces between mainstream and alternative. Such tensions are often made manifest in youth cultural scenes where hierarchies are set between 'the authentic' and 'the phony'; 'the hip' and 'the mainstream' (Thornton 1996, pp. 3–4). Importantly for Thornton, these kinds of discourses are not 'innocent accounts of the way things really are', but rather play into the ideologies and cultural agendas of the scene's participants (p. 10).

Consuming and producing obscure culture is an important aspect of 'hip' cultural capital. The various countercultural art and cultural scenes that have travelled across Toronto since the 1960s have all been associated with 'obscurity' by insiders. Only those 'in the know' have access to the scene. It cannot be explained, you must simply 'get it'. Somewhat contradictorily, this obscurity is also highly self-conscious and obvious in the artifice of its performance. As Liam Lacey writes in a review for *The Globe and Mail*:

> The spirit of self-conscious bohemia haunts the backroom of the Rivoli restaurant on Queen West: abstract geometric art decorates the right-hand wall, mirrors on the left. Not only are you surrounded by art, you can see yourself surrounded by art. Cool, or what? (1984, p. 20)

It is a rhetoric more than anything else, intended to delimit clear lines between insiders and outsiders. That the scene associated with the Rivoli in the 1980s might exclude some uses of the space is not an unspoken secret, but explicit. Indeed, Lacey notes that Dave McIntosh, organizer of Sounds from the Streets Festival, expressed reservations about using the Rivoli as a venue for his event which aimed to expand exposure of Toronto's underground music scene. McIntosh reportedly expressed concern that perceptions about the exclusivity of the Rivoli would deter kids from the suburbs from attending the festival, and that the audience would remain composed of the Queen Street regulars. According to John Irwin, exclusivity is a regular feature of urban bar scenes. He argues that:

> the heterogeneous city is crammed with different types of people, of whom many are antagonistic, incomprehensible, repulsive, or threatening to each other. [...] There are 'home territory' bars, which attract a particular crowd or persons who share some characteristic or characteristics [...]; in these cases, the clients and management discourage outsiders from using 'their bar'. (Irwin 1977, pp. 32–33)

This is the kind of exclusivity that McIntosh expressed concern about. What if the regular clientele of the Rivoli interfered with the larger aims of the music festival? As it turned out, the event did succeed in attracting a range of attendees, including kids from the suburbs, but the organizers' expression of concern draws attention to the extent to which spaces such as the Rivoli can become strongly defined by particular scenes, to the exclusion of other types of participants. The concern over the scene deterring 'kids from the suburbs' is an interesting one, as many of the scene's participants had also, likely, come from the suburbs, as had the scene-makers in Yorkville in the 1960s (Henderson 2011). Similarly, KITH themselves identified as being 'kids from the suburbs'. The issue was not being from the suburbs, then, but the extent to which the participants had (or had not) internalized the taste dispositions of hip, downtown culture.

In their discussion of hipsters and 'cool' culture, Cronin *et al*. (2014) argue that an opposition to 'mainstream' cultures defines these subcultural 'communities of consumption'. They claim that these communities 'often reinforce their joint emotional attachment through a united and sometimes ritualized opposition to dominant lifestyle norms and mainstream consumer sensibilities' (p. 2). The KITH brand of anti-cool cool was aggressively cynical about the mainstream, and was often deeply sarcastic. Forming in the 1980s during a recession, the troupe often mocked the traditional family and the nine-to-five grind. As Foley notes, they brought a punk mentality to the comedy stage, 'We sort of stumbled on stage half drunk and blasted punk rock music and did, you know, aggressively offensive material' (*Comedy Gold: The Hilarious Story of Canadian Comedy* 2005). All these served to reinforce their image as part of obscure culture, being offensive, inaccessible and resolutely anti-mainstream.

This cultural agenda continues to frame contemporary discourses about the comedy troupe, often resituating them within this original creative moment where they came to be representative of the Queen West scene. This has been, in part, reinforced by a consistent discourse of ambivalence about success and mainstream consecration. In discussing the troupe's transition into larger, more mainstream New York clubs, for instance, Thompson notes, 'I suppose your rebel status is lost. It looks as though you've been seduced by the mainstream' (Atherton 1990, p. E1). The television moment of KITH coincided with the growth of cable and the shattering of the mass network audience. Their comedy could be edgy and 'weird' with a cult following and still exist on HBO. In 1990, Foley remarked:

> Inevitably we're going to be the establishment. It happened as soon as we got the TV show. You're no longer on the outside … You just go on doing what you're doing. It's better than pathetically trying to cling to out [sic] street status. (Atherton 1990, p. E1)

In these instances, Foley and Thompson illustrate their awareness that their 'rebel status' is under threat with greater mainstream success. Nonetheless, this status is consistently rooted in an origin story which frames their early days in the backroom of the Rivoli as an artistically innovative and commercially unencumbered moment. As is the case in Thornton's study of club cultures, I do not take up these discourses as 'innocent accounts', but as ideologically grounded; they are part of a cultural agenda, both consciously and unconsciously generated by the scene's participants (1996, p. 10).

Media discourses, including interviews, often nostalgically refer to the troupe's early life as an alternative comedy act in a culturally relevant scene. No matter how much subsequent success they experience, they still have a discursive footing in the countercultural scene. This is precisely the nostalgic linking that we saw in Jian Ghomeshi's introduction which re-tells the familiar story of an innovative new comedy troupe at the Rivoli which suddenly obtains mainstream success. As another example, a review from 1990 also retold the discovery of KITH at the Rivoli, both reinforcing the importance of this venue as a vital performance space in the Queen West scene and establishing the inevitability that this talented group would rise from the backroom to primetime:

> A couple of years ago, Dave Thomas's [from popular television comedy *SCTV*] wife Pam caught their act at the Rivoli and tipped off CBC programming head Ivan Fecan, who tipped off *Saturday Night Live* producer Lorne Michaels and the Kids were off. (Atherton 1990, p. E1)

The Rivoli-based lore of KITH remains a defining element of the group's narrative. It absolves the group of moving from the 'underground' into the 'mainstream' – they were, after all, plucked from obscurity in the backroom of a dingy, artsy, club. The perceived artistic authenticity of this space remains a point of nostalgia for the group members. Even in the early history of the troupe, such as in 1986 when the popularity of KITH obliged them to play larger venues, Mark McKinney says of the Rivoli, 'I'd love for us to lead a double life in Toronto. We'd present our best work at places like the Factory and then go back to the Rivoli to go wild and experiment and be loose and be choppy for our old fans'. Foley similarly frames the Rivoli as a creatively satisfying venue, 'It's the best place in the world to try new material. If we didn't keep developing with Rivoli-type shows, we'd be dead in the water' (Mietkiewicz 1986, p. D13).

Through media discourses about their countercultural positionings as well as anti-mainstream themes of the comedic material, the group present themselves in direct opposition to the less confrontational sketch comedy that dominated the larger comedy scene in the city at the time. In an interview for the documentary *Comedy Gold*, Mark McKinney is critical of the apparent conservatism of the Toronto comedy scene in the early 1980s:

> Toronto seemed very conservative comedically. We were really surprised. Everyone seemed to just wanna get into the Second City touring company

or musical theatre or something, you know, squaresville. (*Comedy Gold: The Hilarious Story of Canadian Comedy* 2005)

This origin narrative is also rooted in an opposition to the established comedy field against which the performers claimed to be rebelling. Early in their careers, largely through word of mouth, the comedy troupe gained a reputation for edginess and irreverence. Not only did they succeed in attracting a dedicated fan base, but also 'industry insiders' such as Lorne Michaels who recruited two of their members to write for *Saturday Night Live* before eventually giving KITH their own television show which aired on CBC in Canada (1988–1994) and HBO in the USA (1989–1995). In spite of their general criticism of mainstream comedy, the group did eventually move from the economically peripheral space of the Rivoli into a much more mainstream position on the CBC and beyond.[2]

Notably, even prior to their 'big break', members of the group were engaged in more mainstream creative work. McCullough and McKinney worked briefly in New York on the writing staff for *Saturday Night Live*. Meanwhile, during this time, Thompson, Foley and McDonald performed with the Second City's touring company (Mietkiewicz 1986, Lacey 1988). So, while Mckinney describes the Toronto comedy scene, and in particular Second City, as 'squaresville' in contrast to their own work, KITH members were not separate from this field of comedy production, but selectively integrated themselves into it when experience or work were required. Even less credibly 'countercultural' is the fact that both Dave Foley and Bruce McCullough had small parts in Kevin Sullivan's *Anne of Green Gables: The Sequel* (1987). KITH lore overlooks the extent to which the process of 'making it' was an extended one. As McKinney notes in an interview, after the group had established itself as a saleable commodity, 'we played there [the Rivoli] a long time to nobody' (Bacchus 1989, p. 58). They were not taken up overnight as members of a thriving cultural scene, then, but gradually developed a following. Their discovery was based, in part, on luck and on the more mainstream comedy field that already existed in the city. At various times in their early development, members of KITH took work that could be considered less creatively free, in order to support their creative work together. They did not, then, emerge suddenly and perfectly from the cultural scene of which they were a part, but negotiated for space within it and at times needed to work outside of its framework.

This experience is telling. How scenes emerge in practice is always more nuanced and complicated than what is said about them. Nonetheless, legitimating discourses remain constitutive in how scenic practices take shape. Scenes are haunted by the idea that the places, people, and creative work housed within them were at their most creative and authentic in the original moment of the scene. This memory, however, only exists because the performers or works have left the scene and succeeded outside of it according to the terms set within the larger creative field. If KITH had never left the backroom of the Rivoli, would their symbolic capital as representatives of an alternative youth subculture have endured? Would an unsuccessful KITH still be a respected part of the former scene, or would they be a forgotten comedy show, the sad 'has beens' who never made it out? Succeeding outside of the scene is an essential consecration conferred retrospectively – on both the scene itself and the agents who leave it. Its existence in the present is in many ways dependent upon a future realization of the creative energy and success that derives from, but exists outside of it. Just as the current careers of the participants are linked to a past scene, the scene in its time is linked to a hypothetical future where it will become a source of cultural nostalgia.

While discourses of obscurity, ambivalence and nostalgia work to frame the scene as countercultural, distinct and innovative, then, they also overshadow some of the more pragmatic complexities of life in Queen West in the 1980s. The discourses that reinforce scenes work to obscure the extent to which they are constructed, ever-changing, and at times profoundly predictable in their taste cultures and social posturing, while at the same time being acknowledged spaces of innovation and cultural change. Obscurity, ambivalence and nostalgia as articulated in discourses about KITH and the Rivioli link to a countercultural past, consequently legitimizing their place in the comedy industry today.

Conclusion

Through a consideration of reviews of the venue and the troupe published during the area's countercultural heyday of the 1980s, as well as more recent media coverage, I find that both the Rivoli venue and the KITH comedy group are continually linked with this original scene. Indeed, even in interviews and features today, the story of KITH originating from the edgy, backroom of the Rivoli acts as a significant framing device which offers a legitimizing discourse that links the now successful group with an 'authentic' (non-commercial) past rooted in a localized, alternative arts scene. This venue offers a useful example of a performance space as it initially existed on the peripheries of commercial comedy production, eventually becoming a respected and privileged venue, mirroring in many ways the history of gentrification that has characterized the area of Queen West in which it is situated. In considering the Queen West scene, the Rivoli and the emergence of the KITH as a part of a countercultural, artistic scene, it becomes clear that perceptions of 'authenticity' of the time, space and artists within the scene are significant, perhaps even more so than the relation of these spaces and individuals to economic capital.

This does not however discount the fact that there is still an inextricable relationship to the economic sphere. The cultural scenes in these 'bohemian' spaces experience a narrative arc from edgy and exclusive, to increased legitimacy resulting in increased popularity, and thus, at a certain point, diminished 'exclusivity'. Scenes can be haunted by the constant sense that it *isn't what it used to be*. This nostalgia for a prior scene occurs consistently. There are seemingly endless *original* scenes for which the *authentic* participants lament. In relation to such lamenting of the former cultural scene in Toronto's Yorkville, historian Stuart Henderson asks, 'what if our memory of this place has become obscured, corrupted, transfigured by years of nostalgia?' (2011, p. 6). In relation to the Rivoli, the KITH, and the Queen West scene, I find this cultural scene to be, in part, constructed through similar tendencies towards insider discourses and nostalgia.

That a particular cultural scene developed on Queen Street West during the 1970s is well established in the history of Toronto's urban development. Such artist-driven scenes are neither naturally occurring nor contrived, but are a complex social space. Scenes, on the one hand, seem relatively predictable. Queen West was not the first bohemian infused art community, nor will it be the last. On the other hand, however, an element of perceived authenticity is required for participants to 'buy-in' to the scene and donate their symbolic energies to its reproduction. This complex interchange between structure and agency within scenes is a feature of fields of cultural production more generally.

Notably, in discussing the media discourses which frame KITH and the Rivoli as part of the Queen Street West scene, I do not offer a commentary on the motivations of the speakers. That is, I am not suggesting that KITH members were being consciously strategic in their framing of their comic work as part of an alternative cultural scene – this is an element of their performative identities. As social agents, we all make constant micro-decisions which are founded on structural elements of which we are not conscious, and balanced with conscious choices guided by self-perceptions and social goals. The type of comic 'taste' that KITH developed and promoted at the Rivoli in the mid-1980s was derived from a mix of conscious and subconscious social attitudes and fit in well with the larger, alternative art scene that was thriving on Queen Street West at that time. The construction of the KITH identity in relation to the Queen West scene is at times ambivalent, with members sometimes distancing themselves from its artsy coolness, while also maintaining countercultural capital by their association with it. While the Queen Street West scene has commercialized and evolved, it continues to offer an 'overproductive signifying community' with which groups such as KITH and venues such as the Rivoli can ground their alternative identities (Shank cited Straw 2004, p. 412).

Importantly, this association continues to frame narratives about the troupe. Even today, we see them linked with this 'scene' through references in interviews and reviews. The scene as creative origin is a dominant element of their official biography. This lends them a countercultural legitimacy, even when they are doing non-countercultural things, such as, for example, receiving a star on Canada's Walk of Fame, as they did in 2008. This is the kind of mainstreaming that has the potential to undermine their countercultural 'coolness'. Yet, even with this mainstream consecration, media discourses continue to privilege a linking of the performers with a legitimate, counter-cultural past rooted in a particular moment, in a particular cultural scene. While KITH were on their second reunion tour, in which they would play two shows at the prestigious Massey Hall in Toronto, journalist Adam McDowell says of the troupe:

> They've come a long way since their formative days working the backroom of the Rivoli on Queen Street West in the mid-1980s, but in the end, the Kids in the Hall are still five Canadian guys with a shared, twisted sensibility trying to make people laugh. (McDowell 2008, p. TO8)

This Rivoli name-dropping links the group with this original scene, and offers a legitimizing discourse. We are constantly being reminded of their 'cool' origins, and are invited to read their current success as a consequence of this positioning, rather than as a rejection of their original creative spirit – an assumption that KITH members expressed concern about as their careers began to take off in the early 1990s. Through a narrative link with the Rivoli, they keep one foot in an alternative scene, while also experiencing mainstream success and consecration. Indeed, while we carry with us a general capacity to identify a scene 'when we see it', it remains safest to define scenes in retrospect, as much of the sociocultural meaning that can be attributed to them is constructed in another time, through memory, nostalgia, and new position-takings or re-positioning made possible through the shift in the field which occurs around vibrant urban spaces.

Notes

1   For a critique of the uses, history and meaning of the term 'hip', see Henderson (2011, pp. 13–15).
2   The CBC is Canada's national broadcaster (French language version: Radio-Canada). It operates as a hybrid public/private broadcaster as it receives government funding and carries a mandate to produce distinctly Canadian programming, but is also obligated to obtain funds through commercial sponsorship.

Notes on contributor

Danielle J. Deveau is a Postdoctoral Fellow at Wilfrid Laurier University. She holds a Ph.D. in Communication from Simon Fraser University. She has published articles on comedy in *Feminist Media Studies*, *Topia: The Canadian Journal of Cultural Studies*, and *Humor: International Journal of Humor Research*. She is the Project Lead for Pop Culture Lab, a Kitchener-based, interdisciplinary research centre specializing in the areas of art, culture, media, and the creative economy.

References

Anne of Green Gables: The Sequel (1987) Video. Directed by Kevin Sullivan. Canada: CBC.

Atherton, T. (1990) 'The Kids in the Hall: comedy that can be shocking, offensive – and sensitive', *The Ottawa Citizen*, 23 September, p. E1.

Bacchus, L. (1989) 'CBC TV's new kids inspired', *The Province*, 28 September, p. 58.

Bourdieu, P. (1984) *Distinction: A Social Judgement of Taste*, Cambridge, Harvard University Press.

Bourdieu, P. (1993) *The Field of Cultural Production*, New York, Columbia University Press.

Brunt, S. (1982) 'Bernhard 'in love' with Jerry Lewis', *The Globe and Mail*, 28 August, p. E1.

Caulfield, J. (1994) *City Form and Everyday Life: Toronto's Gentrification and Critical Social Practice*, Toronto, University of Toronto Press.

Clark, A. (1996) 'The stand-ins step into moribund sketch scene', *Toronto Star*, 8 February, p. H8.

Comedy Gold: The Hilarious Story of Canadian Comedy (2005). DVD. Directed by Martha Kehoe. Canada: Insight Productions; CBC.

Cronin, J., McCarthy, M., & Collins, A. (2014) 'Covert distinction: how hipsters practice food-based resistance strategies in the production of identity', *Consumption Markets & Culture*, vol. 17, no. 1, pp. 2–28.

Dale, S. (1982) 'A conspiracy of words', *The Globe and Mail*, 29 May, p. F1.

Foley, D. (2007) *The Sound of Young America*, interviewed by Jesse Thorn [podcast], 21 February.

Gelder, K. (2007) *Subcultures: Cultural Histories and Social Practice*, London and New York, Routledge.

Ghomeshi, J. (2008) *The Kids in the Hall on QTV. Q* [online]. Toronto: CBC, 24 September. Available at: http://www.youtube.com/qtv (accessed 21 May 2013).

Henderson, S. (2011) *Making the Scene: Yorkville and Hip Toronto in the 1960s*, Toronto, University of Toronto Press.

Hesmondalgh, D. (2005) 'Subcultures, scenes or tribes?: none of the above', *Journal of Youth Studies*, vol. 8, no. 1, pp. 21–40.

Hume, C. (1989) 'Kids 'r' them', *Toronto Star*, 7 October, p. S4.

Hume, C. (2012) *Queen St.: Toronto's Urban Treasure*, Halifax, Nimbus Publishing.

Irwin, J. (1977) *Scenes*, Beverly Hills, CA, Sage.

Johnson, R. (1993) 'Editor's introduction: Pierre Bourdieu on art, literature and culture', in *The Field of Cultural Production*, ed. P. Bourdieu, New York, Columbia, pp. 1–25.

Kastner, J. (1996) 'The Rivoli's eclectic booker', *Toronto Star*, 29 April, p. C3.

Kates, J. (1984) 'On the menu: serving up drama a la carte', *The Globe and Mail*, 9 June, p. CL2.

Lacey, L. (1983) 'Underground pop is hopping again', *The Globe and Mail*, 3 October, p. 20.

Lacey, L. (1984) 'Underground bands rise to surface', *The Globe and Mail*, 17 January, p. 20.

Lacey, L. (1988) 'Doors starting to open for the Kids in the Hall', *The Globe and Mail*, 27 May, p. C9.

Lloyd, R. (2010) *Neo-Bohemia: Art and Commerce in the Postindustrial City*m 2nd edn, London, Routledge.

Mays, J. B. (1983) 'Drawing up new plans for new art', *The Globe and Mail*, 15 March, p. 20.

McDowell, A. (2008) 'The Kids in the Hall on the Kids in the Hall', *National Post*, 31 May, p. TO8.

Mietkiewicz, H. (1986) 'Intelligence and wit are kids' stuff', *Toronto Star*, 18 July, p. D13.

O'Connor, A. (2002) 'Local scenes and dangerous crossroads: punk and theories of cultural hybridity', *Popular Music*, vol. 21, no. 2, pp. 225–236.

Silver, D., Clark, T. N., & Yanez, C. J. N. (2004) 'Scenes: social context in an age of contingency', in *The City as an Entertainment Machine*, ed. T. N. Clark, Toronto, Rowman & Littlefield, pp. 241–272.

Straw, W. (1991) 'Systems of articulation, logics of change: communities and scenes in popular music', *Cultural Studies*, vol. 5, no. 3, pp. 368–388.

Straw, W. (2004) 'Cultural scenes', *Loisir et société* [*Society and Leisure*], vol. 27, no. 2, pp. 411–422.

Thornton, S. (1996) *Club Cultures: Music, Media, and Subcultural Capital*, Middletown, CT, Wesleyan University Press.

Van Eyk, M. (2010) 'The legacy of 48 Abell: tales from a gentrifying neighbourhood', Thesis (M.Arch.). University of Waterloo.

Kerryn Drysdale

WHEN SCENES FADE

Methodological lessons from Sydney's drag king culture

Every Wednesday night is Dyke Night in the small cluster of suburbs collectively referred to as Newtown, approximately 5 kms from Sydney's centre. Dyke Night's popularity is evidenced by the groups of women seen weaving their way through the congested sidewalks that link the numerous venues temporarily catering to queer patronage. Drag king performances – a subcultural phenomenon where women consciously perform masculinity before a primarily lesbian audience – became an integral part of the evening between 2002 and 2012, providing a highly visible spectacle that drew women to the series of events that came to designate Sydney's drag king scene. Set within the social life of Dyke Night, this decade-long scene provided the opportunity and justification for mid-week nights out with friends, lovers and fellow fans, as well as offering the potential to bind individuals to the shared pleasures of the performances. But what happens when this scene fades? Looking back on ethnographic research conducted in the moment of its decline, I explore the points of intersection between participants' ephemeral experiences of drag king events and the collective forms of investment that establish it as an intelligible social phenomenon. Data gathered from a series of group discussions reveals the work participants perform of looking backwards from their present position, suggesting that Sydney's drag king scene is only recognizable through anecdotal narration that generates shared meaning of the more mundane forms of sociality that took place. In offering the perspective of a contemporary social moment realized as an historical investment, this article highlights the particular temporal conditions that structure all scenes: their emergence through to their expansion or contraction and, inevitably, their fading.

As both a social practice and critical object drag kinging is located at the point of convergence between broader discourses on masculinity, performance and lesbian culture. Loosely defined, drag kinging is the performance of a consciously enacted masculinity by women (and sometimes trans men). Drag king performers argue for the uniqueness of their practices as distinct from other traditions of female performance and transgenderism including theatrical conventions of male impersonation (Senelick 2000, Torr and Bottoms 2010), masculinized lesbian identities such as the butch or stone butch (Rubin 1992, Maltz 1998), or passing women (Maltz 1998).

The critical scholarship on drag kinging has its genesis in Judith Halberstam's (1998) influential work *Female Masculinities*. Using Judith Butler's concept of performativity, Halberstam positions drag kinging as an embodied practice that challenges the primacy of masculinity and normative gendered identities. In her later work, Halberstam (2001, 2003, 2005) widens the critical framework to consider the subcultural context in which drag king performances occur. She highlights the strategic political potential of drag king subcultures as an alternative space in which masculinity can be remade. Halberstam's shift in emphasis from performance to subculture has found traction in a field that now reflects on a wider scale the two phases of her interpretative approach. At the risk of oversimplification, the field can be divided into those scholars who consider the practice of drag kinging as representative of gendered or sexual identity (Sennett and Bay-Cheng 2002, bradford 2002, Neevel 2002, Pauliny 2002, Schacht 2002, Shapiro 2007, Troka 2007) and those who concentrate on the subcultural context in which drag kinging is experienced (Koenig 2002, Patterson 2002, Surkan 2002, Braziel 2005, Kim 2007, Grey 2009, Gouweloos 2010, Escudero-Alías 2011). Unsurprisingly, these alternative approaches tend to depart from each other in terms of the emphasis they place on performer or audience.

In order to sidestep this now entrenched division, we might usefully reframe drag king cultures within the theoretical tradition of cultural studies. In particular, the work of Will Straw (1991, 2002, 2004) provides a conceptual framework through which we can respecify drag king culture as a scene rather than a performance. Where Straw initially conceptualized a scene as a range of practices within a 'bounded cultural space' (1991, p. 380), scene later developed into a transferable concept that could be used to describe the participatory nature of 'particular clusters of social and cultural activity' (2004, p. 412). According to Straw, the usefulness of the concept of scene lies in its flexibility and capacity to capture the peripheral energies and relationships that exist around visible subcultures, communities or neo-tribes. As Straw came to recognize, the expansive sociability of scenes fuels ongoing cultural innovation and experimentation within and against the rituals of everyday life. Scenes operate as highly localized and spatialized forms of sociality at the same time as they give unity and meaning to globalize practices (Straw 2002, p. 248, Straw 2004, p. 412).

The dual dimensions of scenes – their double-faced orientation to intensified experience and the mundane, their simultaneously local and global nature – present challenges for cultural analysis. How, for example, do we investigate scenes without flattening them into a single dimension? Ethnography provides a means of tracing the myriad forms of participation that coalesce around scenes in ways that allow everyday knowledges that arise to find expression. Rather than simply confirming a pre-existing theory of scenes and the way they work, the account that follows explores the way in which an ethnographic methodology has the capacity to advance our understanding of scenes' peculiar temporal qualities. Such an approach brings the lifecycle of scenes into focus: through the stories about them, we have the capacity to map their emergence, their expansion and, inevitably, their fading.

Sydney's drag king scene

Sydney's drag king scene revolves largely around Newtown, a small cluster of suburbs approximately 5 kms from Sydney's centre, Australia. Alongside the process of gentrification over the last few decades, the rising costs of rents have pushed the non-professional classes further westward. However, Newtown still acts as a social beacon for urban subcultures. In John Birmingham's popular history of Sydney, the transformation of Newtown is credited to a 'renovating class' led by 'fearless lesbians' (Birmingham 2000, p. 357). The area is now recognized as home to a large lesbian and gay demographic and presents a locally marked alternative to the international gay-tourist strip that is Oxford Street (McInnes 2001, p. 167). Every Wednesday night, Newtown hosts what is colloquially referred to as Dyke Night. Though there are few explicitly lesbian venues in Newtown, Dyke Night informally endorses a number of established venues that host lesbian-targeted events one night a week. Promoted through alternative media outlets and spread by word of mouth as events for queer- or lesbian-identified women, Wednesday night's popularity is evidenced by the groups of women who can be seen weaving their way through the congested sidewalks that link the numerous bars and pubs that cater to queer patronage.

Drag king performances form an integral part of Dyke Night. While there were one-off performances prior to 2000, the earliest regular drag king performances were originally associated with specific events, such as the Drag King of Sydney Quest (commonly referred to as DKSY) held at ARQ nightclub between 1999 and 2000, and Gurlesque, a monthly burlesque-themed event for women and trans-identified individuals that began in 2000. Circulating drag king events that shifted across a range of commercially unconnected venues were largely the tradition in Sydney until drag king performer Sexy Galexy established a weekly event in 2002. Called Kingki Kingdom, the event was hosted by the Sly Fox Hotel on Enmore Road and scheduled on Wednesday in order to draw on the established popularity of Dyke Night. With the departure of Sexy Galexy in 2005, Kingki Kingdom was renamed Queer Central and continued to run at the Sly Fox under the direction of a range of alternative event producers. A large and rotating cast of amateur and professional performers, producers and promoters has contributed to the development of

Sydney's drag king scene across time, but the Sly Fox Hotel stands out as its singularly enduring fixture.[1]

Straw's account of scenes provides a workable theoretical framework for analysing Sydney's drag king scene. The emphasis Straw places on the instrumental role of investments for a scene's emergence and vitality immediately suggests the importance of mapping the movement of material resources within the space of the Sydney drag king scene. Straw (2004, p. 413) argues that investments in physical spaces, such as the Sly Fox Hotel, are required to imbue urban culture with 'a set of institutions and textures' that marks the presence of a scene. These scene-related investments in a place produce complex infrastructures that generate ongoing engagement with economic interests, urban planning and policy. Rather than scenes being dependent on spaces for their existence, in other words, the emergence of scenes 'inscribe the broader history of social forms upon the geography of the city and its spaces' (Straw 2004, p. 414). Straw's account of the reciprocal investments made between scenes and venues is evident in the development of Sydney's drag king scene where particular pubs were designated LGBT-friendly by promoting and hosting drag king events. Unlike Oxford Street, where commercial venues are explicitly established for gay patronage, lesbian sites in Newtown are identifiable through events in a network rather than territorial model of spatial occupancy. While the Sly Fox Hotel does not promote itself as a lesbian venue and hosts drag king shows only once a week, it, nonetheless, appears in local and international guides to gay and lesbian nightlife in Sydney (Sapphic Sydney 2012, Time Out Sydney 2012). Rather than being the result of lesbian-specific venue management and promotion, the emergence of the Sly Fox Hotel as a drag king venue can be viewed as the result of a collateral investment in space made by the participants in the drag king scene.

Investments in scenes

What, then, are those collateral investments that enabled the Sly Fox Hotel to stand in for the complex relationship of people, places and practices that designates the presence of a scene? As the above account of how Sydney's scene developed suggests, investments in scenes and the returns given to participants are not solely economic or commercial. Perhaps more significantly, Straw's insistence that non-commercial investments in scenes are as important as commercial ones presents an opportunity to argue for the value of an ethnographic approach in tracing 'the role of affinities and interconnections which, as they unfold through time, mark and regularize the spatial itineraries of people, things and ideas' (Straw 2002, p. 253).

As the predominant drag king venue for over a decade, the Sly Fox Hotel consistently supported the full range of activities engaged by Sydney's drag king culture. The regular weekly event had an established format of two performance sets a night from which it rarely deviated except for special events such as Mardi

Gras or public holidays. At approximately 10:30 pm, women converged at the King Street end of Enmore Road for the walk-up to the Sly Fox Hotel. By 11 o'clock, the venue was full, with women massed in front of the stage and lined up along the bar area, making movement within the space difficult. Directed by an MC, who commonly performed a number, each set showcased at least one drag king and sometimes included drag queens, burlesque performers or striptease artists. The well-known resident DJs played dance music between sets and after the show when the stage became part of the dance floor. Though the second performance set was over by midnight, people often stayed to drink, dance and socialize until the venue closed at 3 am. Throughout the night, people spilled out of the pub onto the pavement for cigarettes and conversation. Each time the entrance door opened noise would be released into the neighbouring residential area. In order to comply with council restrictions, bouncers were engaged to contain the crowd within an area to one side of the hotel, though without much success

While the drag king performances took place inside, the range of practices associated with the event was not confined to the Sly Fox Hotel. As Straw (2004, p. 416) notes, scenes are not bounded by place but take place in relationship to 'the assemblages of things, places, technologies and artefacts along which people move and live'. The anticipatory, spillover and after-show routines generated around the drag king event are an example of what Straw describes as the 'excesses of sociability that surround the pursuit of interests' (Straw 2004, p. 412). These participatory routines are what scenes contribute as productive 'units of city culture', one of many 'event structures through which cultural life acquires its solidity' (Straw 2004, p. 413). Straw points out that a certain kind of labour is required to produce the social cohesion of scenes with their shared associations to place and time and unified relations of purpose. He cites Grossberg's point that the labour of scene-making involves personal, social and political investment in the idea of a connective phenomenon, a process that simultaneously realizes 'affective alliances' between the diverse participants in a scene (Grossberg 1984 cited Straw 1991, p. 374). The affective alliances associated with scene-making in turn become absorbed into the regularity of events and spread to other associated activities, like drinking, socializing and dancing. As with music scenes, associated practices involve much more than the symbolic marker of music participation. They also involve 'ongoing negotiation over the appropriate relations between speech and noise, noise and music, attention and distraction, human movement and the physical forms which enclose it' (Straw 2002, p. 247). This affective bleed extends the spatial reach of a scene across a range of sites and practices and, as Straw (2002, p. 255) notes, is often a sign of a scene's health and growth. The expansion of scenes engages regularizing and ritualizing itineraries of space so that new sites become collectively invested with established and evolving tastes and affinities (Straw 2002, p. 254). This accounts for the way in which full participation within the drag king scene extends to a range of sites and ritualized practices that may seem peripheral to its specified purpose, i.e. the showcasing of drag king performances.

Crucially, the affective spread of scenes disperses their 'spectacular' nature (Straw 2002, p. 255). As scenes increasingly partake of a ritualized regularity, the forms of visibility that would mark them as significant to outsiders diminish. Instead, within the scene, constant negotiations over relations between people, space and practice intensify. Through the process of ritualization, ethical protocols are elaborated over time and generate norms of behaviour that are embedded within itineraries of movement. These scene norms become integrated within mundane forms of everyday 'urban sociability' (Straw 2002, pp. 255–256). In my ethnographic research, I was interested to see how the connective effects or affective alliances generated around drag king performances become integrated into the everyday components of participants' lives. How do forms of investment become or remain meaningful beyond their original inception in spectacular moments of intensification, such as drag king performances provide?

Straw cites Shank's original work on the concept of scene in which he suggests that a scene is 'an overproductive signifying community' (Shank 1994 cited Straw 2004, p. 412). By referring to an 'excess of information' within scenes, he makes the claim that scenes are not meaningful solely through the function to which they are nominally attributed. Instead, scenes are difficult to decipher because they are produced by local energies generated through diverse forms of participation. Silver *et al.* (2010, p. 2297) argue further that this diversity suggests that 'scenes should be conceived as *places devoted to practices of meaning making through the pleasures of sociable consumption*' (emphasis in original). Viewed through this conception of a scene's purpose, the weekly trip up Enmore Road to the Sly Fox Hotel on Dyke Night becomes a ritual of social meaning-making crucially linked to drag king performances, though the precise nature of that relationship needs to be explored further.

Ethnography in scenes

Straw's account of the role of investments in scene formation allows us to see the drag king performances at the Sly Fox Hotel as a condensed metonym for a wider range of social interactions and rituals that are enhanced by their temporal and spatial proximity to the drag king event. How, then, do participants understand their experiences of the more widely dispersed rituals of drag king culture? Weeks *et al.* (2001) suggest it is 'the stories we tell each other' that give meaning to everyday lives, experiences and practices. In their study of non-heterosexual relationships and families, which involved in-depth interviews and group discussions, 'storytelling' emerged as a form of empirical data that reflected the full range of self-identifications engaged by lifestyle. Storytelling reveals both an individual's existing understanding of their life and their capacity to form new understandings of it as everyday experience is reordered in the development of new narratives (Weeks *et al.* 2001, p. 6, 206). Plummer (1995) argues that narrative truths are empirically valid when the content is analysed in connection to the circumstances of narration. Stories around the everyday sociality of participation may give expression to the negotiations between people, space and practices on which a scene depends for its ongoing viability.

The investigation of scenes highlights the individual and collective dimensions of narration in such a way that participants' stories are meaningful in connection to others. Using group discussions is an established approach designed to 'explore a people's view and experiences on a specific set of issues' (Kitzinger 1994, p. 103). The benefits of this type of ethnographic approach lie in both the quality of the data generated (see Merton 1987, Kitzinger 1994, Wilkinson 1998) and the use of groups' interactions in the generation of that data (see Morgan 1988, Kitzinger 1994). The emphasis on both content and context render group discussions as a mode of analysis, rather than simply a procedure for empirical data collection. However, these dual dimensions have not been frequently utilized in existing research, ignoring a valuable qualitative dimension of analysis in which group discussions emphasize 'the person as situated in, and constructed through, the social world' (Wilkinson 1998, p. 119).

My research design redresses this lack of attention by focusing on how social contexts construct meanings through interaction. Over May and June 2012, I conducted three group discussions with a total of 13 participants. One group of five and two groups of four met for discussions lasting between one-and-a-half to two hours. They progressed via the general themes of 'before a show', 'during a show' and 'after a show', with open-ended questions about past, present and potential future engagements with the scene. Questions around sights, smells and sounds prompted participants to narrate sensory recollections of events alongside other questions that encouraged more rationalized and systematically framed accounts. The verbal discussions were recorded on a digital recorder with non-verbal gestures and interactions manually noted at the time and later added to the verbal transcriptions.

The resulting transcriptions were coded through two simultaneous approaches. The first approach coded thematically, looking for group recurring patterns of participation in the content of the discussions. The second approach coded relationally, identifying where individual narration coincided with or was in conflict with collective sentiments in the interactions between participants, primarily attending to non-verbal social cues. This dual method allowed me to locate the points where 'the physicality of cultural politics (vocality, tactility, touch, resonance) exceeds the rationalized clarity of "system" and transcendent understanding' encouraged by conventional coding (Stewart 1996, p. 130).

The two coding approaches were then compared in order to identify how forms of interaction corresponded with thematic content. By comparing instances of coding, it became clear that conflict or disassociation between participants occurred largely over definitional concerns. These definitions included the taxonomical ordering of drag kings or audience, the terminology and politics between 'lesbian' or 'queer' representation and history and border maintenance or the policing of queer or women-only spaces. These moments of conflict were demonstrated by the presence of verbal forms of disagreement or silence from other participants that followed particular statements. Conflict was also reflected in participants' body language, such as drawing back from the table or from other people, head shaking or finger tapping, or in the raised or defensive tones participants used with each other at times. In contrast, social consensus often emerged around individual recollections that took a narrative form. Unlike the discussion of definitions, these stories tended to be historically framed accounts of particular moments or events: nostalgic recollections of experiences connected to specific venues, performances or songs or indications of regret around social behaviours, often in connection with other people. These moments of shared association were evident in the increased congeniality of the group, verbally indicated by exclamations of agreement and laughter and coupled with non-verbal actions that promoted closer group dynamics, such as when one participant would touch another for emphasis or turn to directly include them in their response. Over the course of the discussions, relations between participants oscillated. These changing alliances and dissolutions indicate that collective meanings did not precede the discussions but, rather, were the result of negotiations between participants as part of the group discussions.

The group participants revealed a reliance on anecdotes to facilitate the process of meaning-making. Participants related that the use of anecdotes was not restricted to the group discussions but occurred as a part of their everyday participation in the scene. For instance, all participants discussed how they would talk about the performances the next day in order to make sense of what they had witnessed. When asked if she thinks about drag king events the next day, Holly said:

> I think that I would. I would always discuss the performances, if they were worth it. Maybe with friends from that night or the next day.

Samantha extends the retrospective discussion from the performance to any significant event within the scene:

> I think so. I would do that same thing, if something stood out. If I saw someone the next day, once you've processed it, or process it with them.

The telling of anecdotes generated recognition from other participants, which then established the shared basis for further storytelling about Sydney's drag king scene. The meanings conveyed by stories were in part derived from their connection to the narration provided by other participants so that individual experiences were augmented by the collective consensus about anecdotal content. As Plummer (1995, p. 174) argues, communities are built through storytelling. By attending to the use of anecdotes within the group, I was able to map the emergence of shared meanings around the Sydney drag king scene. Further, the dynamic emergence of anecdotal knowledge reveals the individual and collective dimensions necessary for a scene to become an intelligible social event. Indeed, the ability to sustain the transmission of anecdotal knowledge may be the threshold criteria for the social coherence of any scene to endure as a meaningful cultural movement.

Temporalities in scenes

As a result of gentrification, Newtown's once-thriving live-entertainment precinct is now under pressure due to a succession of million-dollar developments that are steadily transforming local public houses into themed gastro-pubs. These remodeled venues, and the trendy fusion-food outlets that line the main drag of King Street, attract large numbers of non-residents to the area. This new pattern of patronage arguably refocuses the direction of the area's commercial sustainability. Given this changing economic context, it is perhaps not surprising that in September 2012, the Sly Fox Hotel ceased hosting weekly drag king performances. According to the venue's manager (personal communication, 9 November 2012), increased competition from newly established events targeting the 20-something girls who formed Queer Central's traditional market meant that the amount spent at the bar was insufficient to cover the fees paid out to the performers. Queer Central's diminished popularity is mirrored in the broader decline of drag king events in Sydney. Over a period of approximately 12 months, the promoters, organizers and performers upon whom the scene depended for its ongoing vitality had withdrawn. Less than three months after Queer Central's cessation, drag king events were no longer taking place in Sydney. My personal sense of loss at an unrecoverable social energy that accompanied this decline in drag king culture propelled me to re-examine the conditions under which the group discussions took place.

To begin with, the group discussions drew on pre-existing social alliances connected with the scene itself. All participants were recruited as self-identified fans of drag king performances as well as active participants in Sydney's drag king scene. One group was entirely comprised of participants who regularly socialized with each other prior to, during and after drag king performances. The remaining two groups included participants with some form of social familiarity with each other derived from the scene, though this familiarity did not extend to the same level that constituted the first group. Second, the group discussions were in spatial proximity to the drag king scene since the Sly Fox Hotel could be viewed from the room where the discussions took place. Third, on two occasions, the group discussions were held in temporal proximity to the scene when they were scheduled immediately prior to drag king events. At certain points in the three discussions, participants would point to the venue or the women on the street for illustration to their stories and some participants went on to attend the performances when the discussion had finished.

Unlike the temporal and spatial dimensions of 'normative ethnographic time', these aspects of proximity explicitly violate what Rooke (2010, p. 29) terms 'the fiction of the field'. Rather than keeping the field of observation at an illusory distance, Rooke (2010, p. 30) states:

> Producing ethnography requires a constant crossing between the 'here' and 'there', between the past, present and future: from being 'in the field' while thinking about the future point of writing up, to the point of writing and revisiting the 'ethnographic past'.

Her argument suggests that the field of any scene is never entirely separate from the ethnographic process of discussing it.

The generative effects of ethnographic proximity are supported by some of the statements made by participants about the drag king scene. This is evident in the use of the present tense in affective recollections of the scene. Brooke,[2] for instance, stated in response to Ruth's recollection of the social and sexual tensions that fueled the scene:

> Sometimes it's just a really lovely, lovely feeling of man, how great it is that there's this space where all of these people can do this. Can do these things and enjoy each other, enjoy each other's company [...]. Sometimes I just get really happy. Like, I just want to grin the whole time and be like, 'Isn't this nice! Look at us all! Yay us'!

Brooke's statement was met by corresponding grins and laughter from the others, with Ruth loudly exclaiming support. Samantha similarly recalled the affective dimensions of a past drag king performance in the present tense:

> I like, for me personally, while watching a show, I do like to watch and watch everyone else and then I'm watching the performer as well. And I like the sensuality. I like the play, the whole play of it. So for me, sometimes I find it very erotic, and I'm feeling very turned on, switched on, I'm buzzing because I'm watching this person doing this amazing, like having me feel amazing things in my body, you know?

At this point, Samantha gestured to herself and then widened the arc of her arm movement to include all participants at the table. Gillian and Samantha then continued to expand on their affective connections to some of the shows they had experienced. These brief excerpts demonstrate how relations of proximity to the drag king scene can facilitate an immediate response to the social energies produced by prior and current participation. While the group discussions existed outside of the scene itself, its ethnographic component – that which prioritizes participation through interaction – allowed participants to explore those moments within the scene together, engaged in the temporal and spatial movement between 'here and there', 'past and present' that Rooke identifies as part of the ethnographic process.

This review of the relations of proximity should not be taken to suggest that scene participation is synonymous with its description. Proponents of ethnographic methodology have long recognized impacted relations between experience and representation (see Geertz 1973, Clifford and Marcus 1986, Denzin 1997). For instance, Clifford (1986, p. 2) describes how writing operates as a process of mediation where ethnographic texts are concerned with the invention, and not the representation, of culture. Ethnography, then, is not separate from the means of communication in the use of metaphor, figuration and narrative – all these affect the ways cultural phenomena are registered (Clifford 1986, p. 4). Through anecdotal narration, scenes emerge through everyday processes of interpretation by the participants in the same process as their academic corollaries. These interpretations always contain a temporal dimension because the social moment is always a movement between the experience and the description of it. A description of the events immediately preceding the group discussions, and its impact on the way participants recounted their experience of these events, provides an example of how this relation of distance can manifest.

Although there was acknowledgement within the group discussion of the Sly Fox Hotel's decreasing popularity, Queer Central was still running at that time. Just prior to the group discussions, the venue had closed down for a fortnight for interior renovations. When it reopened, it was seen that management had replaced the old carpet, repainted the walls and installed new furniture, as well as having extended the stage area and improved the lighting and sound. The distance between the moment of social experience and the subsequent discussion of it was particularly relevant given these renovations. Participants recounted their experience of the renovations as a disruption to their established affective connection to the scene on two levels. The first level is based on disruption to the material conditions of the venue. Leonie recounted our first reaction to the renovations:

> Because I've been going there for so many years, from the time when it was the dance floor in the front [...] to the time where they've just re-laid the carpets. I remember when I was with you, Kerryn, the first night we were walking in there and we were like, 'What the hell has happened? This carpet is nice'. [...] But, when you first walk in you think, okay, this is the Sly Fox, it's going to be dirty, it's going to smell like stale alcohol, smell like lesbians.

The second level is based on the disruption to the immaterial conditions as determined by the loss of the material. Participants suggested that, in the process of renovating the Sly Fox Hotel, the management had intervened in the continuation of their historical experience. In speaking of their alienation from the gentrified site, the participants amplified their shared nostalgia for the scene. As Leonie said to Katie:

> I miss knowing that it's the Sly Fox and it will be the same every time you walk in, no matter who you go to see, no matter what shows are on. But, at the same time, they've gotten wall decals up, which [read] 'If in doubt, dance'! Dude, that's not the Sly Fox. That's not what I know as the Sly Fox.

This shared nostalgia motivated by both the material and immaterial changes to the venue can also indicate the presence of foresight into the scenes' anticipated dissolution. When questioned about why they would cease attending the Sly Fox Hotel, Amy and Leonie discussed the absence of drag kings performances as marking the end of the scene:

> The only thing that would stop me going is if they stopped the drag kings.
> [...]
> It would change our perspective if it starts bringing in just [drag] queens. [Amy]
> It wouldn't be the Sly Fox scene. [Leonie]

Yet, the passing of the scene has the potential to be reanimated through collective remembrance. Cate[3] discusses how the Sly Fox Hotel can still operate as the site of the drag king scene, even when it no longer hosts drag king performances:

> Which is still great, you know, in its own way, you know, as well, you know, to see. In five years' time, it might be, like, 'Oh I saw her at the Sly Fox when she was just starting out'.
> [...]
> If there are no other options on a [...] Wednesday night, or you know, out of some sort of going back to your lesbian roots or something. Like, 'Aw yeah! We'll go back to the Sly'! kind of thing.

Paradoxically, these comments highlighted how the historicized scene is affectively reanimated through, and in contrast to, its contemporary material passing.

This brief review of some of the statements made during the course of the group discussions highlights the peculiar temporal conditions that structure scenes. On the one hand, these discussions provided an opportunity for both participants and researcher to reflect on past forms of scene participation. But, on the other hand, they also reflect on the relation of scenes to their imminent passing. First, individual recollections of the Sly Fox Hotel enabled the work of collective scene-making. Through the process of anecdotal narration, the forms of everyday knowledge of the scene held by participants gave rise to collectively held meanings. This form of narration was produced as an immediate response to the context in which these discussions took place. Second, the anecdotal work of collective scene-making anticipates narrative retrospection. This temporal dimension is emphasized when we consider how meanings generated around scenes are organized by anecdotes. This revealed the work participants perform of looking backwards towards a historicized scene from their present position.

More than simply offering a description of Sydney's drag king scene in the moment of its decline, I suggest that the value of an ethnographic approach is the way it highlights the temporalities inherent in the process through which all scenes are rendered collectively meaningful. Sydney's drag scene is only recognizable *as a scene* through its community narration that provides meaning to those more mundane forms of sociality generated by the commercial and non-commercial investments in drag king culture. Without this retrospective narration, all that presents are a series of events identified by the more visible drag king performances.

Conclusion: enduring scenes

At the point where participants told stories about their past experiences at drag king events in Sydney, they were already engaged in a process of bringing this scene to life. As such, anecdotes capture the simultaneous ephemerality of social moments and their retrospective consolidation into collective forms of recognition. Why is it, then, that the affective bonds generated through participation, retrospectively realized, continue to bind people to the place and time of scenes long after that social moment has passed? The emphasis Straw places on the instrumental role of investments for a scene's emergence and vitality might also be enhanced by an understanding of their relation to the process of memorialization that accompanies narrative reactivation.

Straw (1991, p. 373) identifies two countervailing pressures within scenes, 'one towards the stabilization of local historical communities, and another which works to disrupt such continuities, to cosmopolitanize and relativize them'. He emphasizes the importance of the interaction between the globalized transform-ative force of particular agents and the localized reordering of social structures (1991, p. 375). The pull between the global and local produces a constantly shifting field against which scenes become metaphors for urban flux and excess. Experienced as ephemeral and effervescent, they operate as theatrical excesses outside the scope for any formal cultural policy (2002, p. 253, 254). A scene's temporal and spatial instability, Straw points out, constitutes the 'seductive sense of scenes as disruptive' (Straw 2002, p. 254). Part of a scene's instability is characterized by the way that it resists definition because it is moving in multiple directions. As Straw (2004, p. 412) argues, scenes move 'onwards, to later reiterations of itself; outwards, to more formal sorts of social or entrepreneurial activity; upwards, to the broader coalescing of cultural energies within which collective identities take shape'.

But, we might add, scenes also face backwards, anticipating their retrospective narration as socially intelligible moments. It is precisely by facing backwards that scenes produce the conditions of their own sedimentation. Consider Straw's anecdote of his experience at a dance club (1991, p. 379), which I quote in full:

> Several years ago, at the end of a conference held at Carleton University, I went with a number of academic colleagues to Hull, Quebec to dance. We ended up at the most explicitly 'underground' of the many clubs along Hull's main street (one whose recent history has been marred by door-admittance policies and changes in music style widely regarded as racist). As members of our group began to dance – with, in some cases, unexpected abandon – it was clear that the space of this club, like the act of dancing itself, evoked within many of them a sense of the eternal.

The sense of the eternal is produced by the way these scenes 'create grooves to which practices and affinities become fixed' (2002, p. 254). All it takes, Straw suggests (2002, p. 254), is a chance encounter for marginal knowledge to be reinvigorated and the peripheries of those social networks to be renewed. Each chance encounter acts like the analogy of uncovering archaeological artefacts or the endurance of architecture within urban spaces, so much so that 'the city becomes a repository of memory' (Straw 2002, p. 254). Straw's sense of the eternal is invoked when the moment of contemporary connection at the sites of historical instances of sociality is made meaningful through this anecdote. The sense of the eternal, then, is always accompanied by the recognition of the moment passing. In the process of retrospective scene-making through the stories they tell about past social moments, scene participants are simultaneously creating memories in the anticipation of its inevitable dissolution.

Sydney's drag king scene highlights the mode through which a contemporary social moment fades into a historicized scene. However, in offering the perspective of scene realized in the moment of its passing, this account also reveals its double-faced orientation – one that recognizes scenes as simultaneously moving forward at the same time as facing backwards. Paradoxically, the elusiveness of a scene prompts the process of memorization that guarantees its seeming solidity. The commercial and non-commercial investments in space made by participants in Sydney's drag king scene at the point of its emergence demonstrated their cognizance of its eventual fading. As the material infrastructure of scenes change, so too does other less-tangible investments, leading to either their expansion or their demise. Yet, scenes support forms of narration that give places historical depth and allow them to persist in personal and collective memory. The Sydney drag king scene is no longer found in the range of sites and practices that previously comprised it, and the Wednesday night slot at the Sly Fox Hotel held by Queer Central has been replaced by a live music night. However, through the stories told about it, the Sydney drag king scene endures through those invested relationships in time and space.

Notes

1   Other more recent events showcasing drag king performances in Sydney included The Pussycat Club, hosted by the Supper Club at the Oxford Hotel on Oxford Street, Darlinghurst from January 2010 to September 2011. This event was first billed as a night for women and trans* due to the venue management's planned marketing strategy, but the event organizers implemented and promoted it to 'All Queer Friends Welcome' door policy to encourage a non-gender-specific audience. However, the event was advertised as a queer performance night that featured drag king performers in the monthly line-up, rather than a 'drag' event or featuring drag performers predominantly. Other drag king specific events, like the ones produced by Nash Hill, were held roughly every three months at circulating venues. These were promoted as exclusively drag king events, but due to the production levels, high entry costs and upmarket venues, were structured conventionally as a performance and did not attract the same level of regularity as the weekly event at the Sly Fox Hotel.

2   Where participants gave authority for the use, first names are used to identify them. Otherwise, pseudonym is assigned to participants who wished to remain anonymous. The majority of participants opted to be identified on a first name basis.

3   A pseudonym.

Notes on Contributor

Kerryn Drysdale is a Ph.D. candidate in the Department of Gender and Cultural Studies at the University of Sydney. Her interests lie at the intersection of feminism, cultural studies and queer theory. Her doctoral research examines the Sydney drag king scene, with a specific focus on the relationship between individual and collective investments that cohere around drag king practices.

References

Birmingham, J. (2000) *Leviathan: The Unauthorised Biography of Sydney*, Sydney, Vintage.

bradford, k. (2002) 'Grease cowboy fever; or, the making of Johnny T', in *The Drag King Anthology*, eds. K. LeBesco, D. J. Troka, & J. B. Noble, New York, Harrington Park Press, pp. 15–30.

Braziel, J. E. (2005) 'Dréd's drag kinging of race, sex, and the queering of the American racial *machine-desirante*', *Women and Performance: A Journal of Feminist Theory*, vol. 15, no. 2, pp. 161–188.

Clifford, J. (1986) 'Introduction: partial truths', in *Writing Culture: The Poetics and Politics of Ethnography*, eds. J. Clifford & G. E. Marcus, Berkeley and Los Angeles, University of California Press, pp. 1–26.

Clifford, J. & Marcus, G. E. (1986) *Writing Culture: The Poetics and Politics of Ethnography*, Berkeley and Los Angeles, University of California Press.

Denzin, N. K. (1997) *Interpretive Ethnography: Ethnographic Practices for the 21st Century*, Thousand Oaks, Sage Publications.

Escudero-Alías, M. (2011) 'Ethics, authorship, and the representation of drag kings in contemporary US popular culture', *The Journal of Popular Culture*, vol. 44, no. 2, pp. 256–273.

Geertz, C. (1973) *Interpretations of Cultures*, New York, Basic Books.

Gouweloos, J. (2010) 'Social norms, what a drag: gender, sexuality and drag king communities', Thesis (M.A.), The University of Guelph.

Grey, L. (2009) 'Multiple selves, fractured (un)learnings: the pedagogical significance of drag kings' narratives', Thesis (Ph.D.), Georgia State University.

Halberstam, J. (1998) *Female Masculinity*, Durham, NC, Duke University Press.

Halberstam, J. (2001) 'Oh behave!: Austin powers and the drag kings', *GLQ: A Journal of Lesbian and Gay Studies*, vol. 7, no. 3, pp. 425–452.

Halberstam, J. (2003) 'What's that smell?: queer temporalities and subcultural lives', *International Journal of Cultural Studies*, vol. 6, no. 3, pp. 313–333.

Halberstam, J. (2005) *In a Queer Time and Place: Transgender Bodies, Subcultural Lives*, New York, New York University Press.

Kim, J. (2007) 'Performing female masculinities at the intersections of gender, class, race, ethnicity, and sexuality', Thesis (Ph.D.), The University of Texas.

Kitzinger, J. (1994) 'The methodology of focus groups: the importance of interaction between participants', *Sociology of Health and Illness*, vol. 16, no. 1, 103–121.

Koenig, S. (2002) 'Walk like a man: enactments and embodiments of masculinity and the potential for multiple genders', in *The Drag King Anthology*, eds. K. LeBesco, D. J. Troka, & J. B. Noble, New York, Harrington Park Press, pp. 145–159.

Maltz, R. (1998) 'Real butch: the performance/performativity of male impersonation, drag kings, passing as male, and stone butch realness', *Journal of Gender Studies*, vol. 7, no. 3, pp. 273–286.

McInnes, D. (2001) 'Inside the outside: politics and gay and lesbian spaces in Sydney', in *Queer City: Gay and Lesbian Politics in Sydney*, eds. C. Johnston & P. van Reyk, Annandale, Pluto Press Australia Limited, pp. 164–178.

Merton, R. K. (1987) 'The focussed interview and focus groups: continuities and discontinuities', *Public Opinion Quarterly*, vol. 51, no. 4, pp. 550–566.

Morgan, D. L. (1988) *Focus Groups as Qualitative Research*, Sage University Paper, Qualitative Research Methods Series, London, Sage.

Neevel, A. (2002) 'Me boy', in *The Drag King Anthology*, eds. K. LeBesco, D. J. Troka, & J. B. Noble, New York, Harrington Park Press, pp. 31–38.

Patterson, J. L. (2002) 'Capital drag: kinging in Washington, DC', in *The Drag King Anthology*, eds. K. LeBesco, D. J. Troka, & J. B. Noble, New York, Harrington Park Press, pp. 99–123.

Pauliny, T. (2002) 'Erotic arguments and persuasive acts: discourses of desire and the rhetoric of female-to-male drag', in *The Drag King Anthology*, eds. K. LeBesco, D. J. Troka, & J. B. Noble, New York, Harrington Park Press, pp. 221–248.

Plummer, K. (1995) *Telling Sexual Stories: Power, Change and Social Worlds*, London, Routledge.

Rooke, A. (2010) 'Queer in the field: on emotions, temporality and performativity in ethnography', in *Queer Methods and Methodologies: Intersecting Queer Theories and Social Science Research*, eds. K. Browne & C. J. Nash, Farnham, Surrey, Ashgate, pp. 25–40.

Rubin, G. (1992) 'Of catamites and kings: reflections on butch, gender and boundaries', in *The Persistent Desire: A Butch-Femme Reader*, ed. J. Nestle, Boston, MA, Alyson Publications, pp. 446–482.

Schacht, S. P. (2002) 'Lesbian drag kings and the female embodiment of the masculine', in *The Drag King Anthology*, eds. K. LeBesco, D. J. Troka, & J. B. Noble, New York, Harrington Park Press, pp. 75–98.

Senelick, L. (2000) *The Changing Room: Sex, Drag and Theatre*, London and New York, Routledge.

Sennett, J. & Bay-Cheng, S. (2002) '"I am the man!": performing gender and other incongruities', in *The Drag King Anthology*, eds. K. LeBesco, D. J. Troka, & J. B. Noble, New York, Harrington Park Press, pp. 39–47.

Shapiro, E. (2007) 'Drag kinging and the transformation of gender identities', *Gender and Society*, vol. 21, no. 2, pp. 250–271.

Silver, D., Clark, T. N. & Navarro Yañez, C. J. (2010) 'Scenes: social context in an age of contingency', *Social Forces*, vol. 88, no. 5, pp. 2293–2324.

Stewart, K. (1996) *A Space on the Side of the Road: Cultural Poetics in an "Other" America*, Princeton and New Jersey, Princeton University Press.

Straw, W. (1991) 'Systems of articulation, logics of change: communities and scenes in popular music', *Cultural Studies*, vol. 5, no. 3, pp. 368–388.

Straw, W. (2002) 'Scenes and sensibilities', *Public*, vol. 22/23, pp. 245–257.

Straw, W. (2004) 'Cultural scenes', *Society and Leisure*, vol. 27, no. 2, pp. 411–422.

Surkan, K. (2002) 'Drag kings in the new wave: gender performance and participation', in *The Drag King Anthology*, eds. K. LeBesco, D. J. Troka, & J. B. Noble, New York, Harrington Park Press, pp. 161–185.

Sapphic Sydney. (2012) *Queer Central*, [online] Available at: http://www.sapphicsydney.com.au/ (accessed 16 April 2013).

Time Out Group. (2012) 'The Sly Fox Hotel', *Time Out Sydney*, [online] Available at: http://www.au.timeout.com/sydney/gay-lesbian/venues/192/the-sly-fox-hotel (accessed 16 April 2013).

Torr, D. & Bottoms, S. (2010) *Sex, Drag and Male Roles: Investigating Gender as Performance*, Ann Arbor, The University of Michigan Press.

Troka, D. (2007) 'The kings of the Midwest: an oral history of three Midwestern drag king troupes', Thesis (Ph.D.), Emory University.

Weeks, J., Heaphy, B. & Donovan, C. (2001) *Same Sex Intimacies: Families of Choice and Other Life Experiments*, London, Routledge.

Wilkinson, S. (1998) 'Focus groups in feminist research: power, interaction, and the co-construction of meaning', *Women's Studies International Forum*, vol. 21, no. 1, pp. 111–125.

Kate Eichhorn

COPY MACHINES AND DOWNTOWN SCENES

Deterritorializing urban culture in a pre-digital era

In the early 1970s, as New York City was in an economic and social downfall, a vibrant downtown arts scene emerged in downtown Manhattan south of 14th Street. The scene's development is often attributed to the neighbourhood's at-the-time inexpensive rent, which permitted artists to live, work, and exhibit with low overhead. This article maintains that the scene's development was also contingent on the growing availability of a new medium: the copy machine. While xerographic copiers had been staples in office culture for 15 years, they were newly available to the general public in the early 1970s. This article examines how copy machines were used by artists and writers to produce and distribute works, to promote upcoming gigs of all kinds from drag shows to punk shows, and, eventually, to facilitate the downtown scene's migration into the suburbs and beyond through the production of mobile texts, including zines and mail art. Finally, this article asserts that as a media technology that is at once capable of intensifying the local and developing and sustaining non-local networks, copy machines were and remain uniquely situated to accommodate the inherent tensions and contradictions that define scenes.

In the early 1970s, as New York City was in an economic and social downfall, a vibrant arts scene emerged in downtown Manhattan south of 14th Street. From its onset, 'the downtown scene', as its members have always described it, was fully aware of its status as a bona fide scene. Over the next two and half decades, the scene gave rise to a generation of innovative artists, writers, and musicians, including David Wojnarowicz, Kathy Acker, and Thurston Moore. Yet, even though the downtown scene generated its share of art-world celebrities, the scene was always defined by a distinctly do-it-yourself (DIY) aesthetic and ethic. As Brandon Stosuy emphasizes in the introduction to *Up is Up, But So Is Down*, in the downtown arts scene, writers and other cultural producers 'took an active role in the production process, starting magazines, small and occasional presses, galleries, activist organizations, theaters and clubs', and this held equally true for the scene's celebrity artists as it did for cultural producers working in relative obscurity (2006, p. 20).

Like most scenes, New York's downtown arts scene was the result of a convergence of historic, economic, and technological factors. In many respects, the scene was an extension of an interdisciplinary arts scene that had flourished since the 1960s in and around several-storied institutions, including the performance space at Judson Church. Rather than continue to grow up around established performance spaces and galleries, however, artists connected to the downtown scene constantly sought to unmoor themselves from anything that carried even the faintest hint of establishment. As emerging artists actively sought out spaces to occupy rather than join, cheap rent emerged as a key factor in the downtown scene's development, and at the time, cheap rent was not difficult to find. In the 1970s and 1980s, many landlords south of 14th Street chose to abandon their buildings, believing that divestment was more economically viable than repairing old tenements in neighbourhoods with reputations for high crime (Mele 2000, p. 194). While some young artists, writers, and performers entrenched themselves in rent-controlled apartments, others squatted in empty buildings or became 'urban homesteaders' by striking deals with the city to bring abandoned buildings up to code over time (Mele 2000). At a time when living and exhibition and performance spaces often merged, the glut of available housing and gutted out loft spaces in SoHo and the Lower East Side played a major role in attracting young artists to the scene and, of course, shaped the type and scale of their work. But cheap rent was not the only factor driving the downtown arts scene. In many respects, it was also contingent on the growing availability of a new medium: the copy machine.

It is difficult to imagine the downtown arts scene without xerography. Copy machines were used to produce some of the scene's most memorable art works, to print and distribute publications by the scene's best and lesser known writers alike, and to promote upcoming gigs of all kinds, from drag shows to punk shows. Copy machines were also used to create zines, which in turn helped suburban kids know where to go when they got off the subway at Union Square to explore life below 14th Street. Copy machines not only helped to establish the scene and define its unique aesthetic but also eventually facilitated the scene's migration well beyond 14th Street. This is the story this article seeks to recount. It's the story of how one banal office technology helped to define the contours of a downtown art and music scene and then to deterritorialize the scene but without compromising its signature aesthetic or ethos. I maintain that copy machines – unlike other media, including current social media platforms – have a unique relationship to scenes. They have historically offered a way to publicize scenes both in and beyond their geographic points of origin but without necessarily making them vulnerable to the forms of overexposure that often result in their decline.

Defining the downtown scene

The Downtown Collection at NYU's Fales Library and Special Collections houses thousands of documents and artefacts connected to writers, artists, and performers associated with New York's downtown arts scene. If you are looking for a t-shirt worn by Richard Hell or a doll collected by David Wojnarowicz, this is where you'll find it. You will also find thousands of photocopied documents in the collection, from posters to fanzines.[1] Yet, however eclectic these objects may be, the collection is framed by a clearly defined understanding of the 'scene' in question, one that privileges its spatial and temporal boundaries. As the collection's description states, 'The Downtown Collection … is an attempt to document the downtown arts scene that evolved in SoHo and the Lower East Side during the 1970s through the early 1990s'.

Placed on a map, this locates New York's downtown arts scene in a tightly bound geographic area (see figure 1). If you take the broadest possible definition of the Lower East Side and include the East Village and Alphabet City, the scene

FIGURE 1 Approximate borders of New York's downtown scene.

in question was staged south of 14th Street from the East River to 1st Avenue and down to Canal Street and includes SoHo, which runs south of Houston down to Canal between Lafayette to West Broadway. Of course, over time, boundaries shift. What is clear is that the downtown arts scene did not happen above 14th Street or south of SoHo, and it was more of an East Village than West Village phenomenon. For at least some of the people who were part of the scene from the 1970s to 1990s, and perhaps especially for the people who are still there, the downtown arts scene was and is about geographic specificity. As every New Yorker knows, there are people who live below 14th Street and there are people who don't. However, the temporality of the scene is just as important as the geography. Writers, artists, or musicians who 'just arrived' (meaning they arrived any time since the mid-1990s) and who are willing to pay in excess of $2,500 a month for a studio apartment on Essex or Avenue B were, to be clear, never part of this scene and never will be. If you didn't live through the riots at Tompkins Square Park, or you've only experienced CBGBs as a palimpsest of photocopied posters and stickers on the otherwise pristine walls of the current John Varvatos store on the Bowery, this scene is not yours to claim.[2] Yet, however much we might like to confine scenes to a particular time and place, they are rarely so containable.

Scenes spill over and migrate. They may originate in the local but are often taken up around the world. Likewise, global scenes frequently take on a local specificity. That's why we can so easily talk about London versus New York punk or the Jamaican dance hall scene in Toronto. Scenes get inscribed in local geographies and re-inscribed in global ones. They are at once intensely local and always already prone to spectators, intruders, and enterprising parasites. As an example, consider the highly consumer-oriented and tourist-friendly scene that persists on St. Mark's Place in New York's East Village – on this heterotopic street block, various decades of the downtown scene appear to converge as tourists are given an opportunity to photograph and even try on everything from hippie beads to body piercings. Occasionally, scenes are also part of a collective imaginary – a sort of utopian longing powerful enough to bring fellow travellers together across eras, irrespective of whether they ever crossed paths in person. Writer Eileen Myles, a fixture in New York's downtown arts scene since the 1970s, explains that:

> For a while in New York when people would meet you, they'd say, 'Well, when did you come on the scene?' Sometimes it's gate keeping, but it's also about people's generosity, to even attribute to you things you weren't even there for … If they liked you, they saw you now and always as part of this scene. (Cooper and Myles 2006, p. 465)

In other words, according to Myles, scenes may be structured by a desire for recognition and belonging as much as they are by a shared geography.

Scenes are not only bound by space and time and sometimes their mutual collapse but also deeply entangled in the media. In the 1950s, celebrity gossip columns in local newspapers helped to foster scenes through their intense focus on the local (Straw 2001, p. 246). By contrast, today's scenes are more likely to be fostered through the careful management of mainstream media exposure. Scenes, in a sense, are produced through the media – scenes become scenes because they are publicized and publicity requires a medium – but a scene's death is also, more often than not, blamed on forms of media over exposure. When riot grrrl was still a group of friends plotting a punk feminist revolution in Olympia, Washington, and a few other small cities across North America, its core members were so virulently opposed to letting the media inside their scene that they created a 'media working group' – a few grrrls even called for a complete 'media blackout' (Marcus 2010, p. 200). Not surprisingly, when riot grrrl was eventually dragged out of the underground through a series of mainstream publications, the media was blamed for the scene's apparent sudden death. Yet, like most scenes, riot grrrl was also dependent on various forms of media: four-track players, audio recorders, letterset, typewriters, Fisher-Price video cameras, and, of course, copy machines. As a second-generation punk movement, however, the girls in this scene already knew a thing or two about the necessity of taking control of the media and the possibilities provided by accessible, cheap, and immediate media forms. Looking to New York's downtown art, activist, and punk scenes for guidance and inspiration, especially to the scene's queer and feminist icons – writers like Myles and Kathy Acker and artists like Carolee Schneemann – as well as the scene's many artistic and activist organizations, including ACT UP, the girls in Olympia realized early on that it is possible to make art without access to mainstream gallery spaces, publishers, or record labels and to publicize one's work without becoming subsumed by the mainstream media. They also recognized why managing the media had important political implications, and, like an earlier generation of writers, artists, and activists, they recognized copy machines as an invaluable tool in the struggle.

While copy machines would prove a ubiquitous feature of many late twentieth-century art and activist scenes, however, it is important to emphasize that this had nothing to do with the machine's original design. As the history of the copy machine reveals, these machines were engineered to reproduce exact copies of administrative documents – any creative or subversive uses of the copy machine have been by desire, *not* design.

From office culture to urban culture

By the time copy machines were commonplace in libraries and local bodegas and copy shops had started to appear around the edges of university campuses in cities across North America, most copy machines were based on a technology pioneered by Chester Carlson in his home laboratory in Queens, New York, in the late 1930s. Building on observations and discoveries dating back to antiquity, Carlson recognized that electrostatics could in principle be used as a method of print reproduction (Carlson 1965). Drawing on personal funds and largely working out of his kitchen, he set out to perfect a method of dry printing that would avoid both the mess and cumbersome equipment associated with photographic-based methods of reproduction and the invariable damage to original documents that occurred with other 'wet methods'. Suffice it to say that, between Carlson's initial discovery of electrophotography, a process that would only later be renamed xerography (a combination of the Greek words *xeros* – 'dry' – and *graphos* – 'writing'), and the launch of the first Xerox copy machine in the mid-1950s, his process would undergo a series of subsequent improvements. By the time Haloid Company, which eventually renamed itself Xerox Corporation, started to pitch its 'revolutionary, dry, direct positive xerography process' to thrifty executives, copy machines were able to prepare offset copies in a matter of minutes, enabling companies to reproduce hundreds of documents in house at great savings.[3]

Although the demand for efficient and affordable copy machines was first and foremost driven by the modern workplace's practical need to reproduce documents, the widespread popularity of copy machines coincided with a broader cultural shift in the mid-twentieth century. John Brooks's 1969 feature article on xerography in *The New Yorker* highlights the conditions under which the practice of making copies came to be considered a necessity. As he observes, in the 1950s, the 'raw, pioneering years of mechanized office copying', the market became flooded with new devices designed to reproduce documents without the use of a master page and at a much lower cost than earlier machines, such as those based on photographic methods (e.g. the Photostat). These machines:

> found a ready market, partly because they filled a genuine need and partly, it now seems clear, because they and their function exercised a powerful psychological fascination in their users. In a society that sociologists are forever characterizing as 'mass', the notion of making one-of-a-kind things into many-of-a-kind things showed signs of becoming a real compulsion. (Brooks 1969, p. 47)

In other words, copy machines not only realized a need that already existed in the workplace but also almost immediately impacted people's perception of what needs to be copied, should be copied, or might be copied. With the arrival of the Xerox 914, copying moved from a sometimes necessary task to a norm, explaining how the estimated number of copies made in the United States skyrocketed from 20 million in the late 1950s to an estimated 14 billion by 1966 (Brooks 1969, p. 47). As copy machines became increasingly accessible, rather than spend less time copying documents, people spent more time copying a wider range of documents.

By the late 1960s and early 1970s, copy machines were becoming a popular medium for artists and DIY publishers. At the Software Show, a groundbreaking new media art exhibit curated by the Jewish Museum of New York in 1970, Sonia Sheridan, a lab-coat–wearing artist-engineer from the School of the Art Institute of Chicago, invited visitors to interact with a rented colour copier. In a widely circulated newspaper article about the exhibit, the creative possibilities of copying machines are described:

> Bearded boys, girls in tie-dyed jeans and granny dresses, and many with bare feet said the whole thing was blowing their minds. Everyone was smiling, even the 3M technicians loaned to Miss Sheridan to keep the machines running. She photocopied hands, faces, designs and transferred them to T-shirts or heat-laminated them to paper in just a few minutes. ('Creative Office Workers Dig Electromagnetic Art' 1970).

The copy machine offered an instantaneous way to reproduce everything from bums to broadsides. While the colour copy machines used by Sheridan in the Software Show were costly and high maintenance, less expensive black-and-white Xerox machines were readily accessible by the early 1970s and began to transform how art scenes formed and thrived. As the authors of *Copyart*, a DIY guide to unleashing the creative potential of the copy machine, emphasize in their introduction, 'beyond its function as an "office tool", the copier has, for many people, become a means of self-expression' (Firpo *et al*. 1978). 'In some strange and mysterious way', they insist, 'the copier is a "magical machine". You will find that very often the "accident", the "unplanned", and the "unexpected" will produce results you could not even being to imagine' (1978). Noting that 'almost everyone who has been left alone with a copier has experimented with making copies of their face and hands', they offer a series of 'guidelines' on how to further exploit what may be best described as the art of self-copying (1978). Their guide book, however, is by no means limited to tips on how best to perfect such adolescent pranks. Interspersed with tips on copying everything from birth certificates to body parts are profiles of dozens of professional artists using copy machines in a wide range of disciplines from photography and animated film to performance art and visual collage.

Although copy art would ultimately remain a marginal artistic practice, copy machine-generated works would play an integral role in pushing art beyond the space of the gallery. Copy art, after all, could be easily and inexpensively reproduced and wheat-pasted onto the sides of buildings and scaffolding in highly visible public locations. Simultaneously, copy machines proved integral to the spread of micropress publishing initiatives. But this only partially explains their role in the development of downtown art scenes like the one that flourished in New York from the 1970s to the 1990s. Copy machines also functioned as a form of social media, predating contemporary social media platforms by several decades and in a form that is notably more material.

Xerography in the village

Before digital social media became integral to the development of local and global scenes, there was xerography. In many respects, one might even think about xerography as a form of pre-digital social media. 'Social media' usually refers to digital platforms that enable users to generate, share, and exchange information, often in collaborative ways and usually quickly and with little or no overhead. Beyond its obvious workplace applications, this is precisely why scenes valued xerography – it was a way to generate and circulate information quickly and inexpensively either independently or in collaboration with any number of users who may or may not already have face-to-face relationships. Of course, in contrast to contemporary social media platforms that can be accessed anywhere and anytime, copy machines were rarely found in private homes. Even if you could mock up a poster or fanzine or flyer in just a few minutes at home or in your studio, you had to go somewhere to reproduce it. As a result, the act of copying not only facilitated social interactions (e.g. by promoting upcoming gigs, readings, and rallies), it required even the most reclusive creators to get out of their apartments in search of a copy machine.

For a few decades, the Kinko's chain of copy shops capitalized on this need by providing people with a place to make copies all day and, more importantly, all night long. At its height of popularity between the late 1980s and mid-1990s, Kinko's outlets in urban centres across North America were catch basins for writers, artists, anarchists, punks, insomniacs, graduate students, DIY bookmakers, zinesters, obsessive compulsive hobbyists, scam artists, people living on the street, and people just living on the edge. Whether you were promoting a new band or publishing a pamphlet on DIY gynaecology or making a fake ID for an underage friend, Kinko's was the place to be. It is just such a scene that *New York Times* reporter Julia Szabo sought to capture in a 1994 article that ran under the headline, 'Copy Shop Stitches the Urban Crazy Quilt'. Focusing on a 24-hour Kinko's located on Madison Avenue at 34th Street, she observed:

> While the [...] upholstery may be strictly gray, there's nothing uniform about the clientele. Spotted over a week or so were these typical patrons: A Tomkins Square Park anarchist, who is a squatter from Avenue C, designing a poster [...]. Two staffers from *Mirabella* magazine's art department having a future cover sized. [...] A pierced club kid designing invitations to an event at the Pyramid. (paras. 2–3)

Later in the same article, Szabo cites conceptual artist Kerri Scharlin, who was a rising New York art star at the time. Scharlin confesses that she frequently collects fliers out of the Kinko's dumpster 'to use in her work', but also emphasizes that Kinko's is about more than copies: 'When you stand in line to pay and you look over your shoulder to see what the next guy was doing, 9 out 10 times it's interesting' (paras. 9–10). Hence, Szabo's suggestion that Kinko's is 'the forum in Marshall McLuhan's global village' (para. 8).

What Szabo was bearing witness to at the midtown Kinko's in 1994 was nothing more than an extension of a scene that had been well established below 14th Street since the 1970s. Emerging in the early 1970s just as copy machines started to move out of offices and libraries and into bodegas and copy shops, New York's downtown scene benefited from this new form of inexpensive print production from the outset: musicians without agents lined up at copy machines to turn out homemade posters advertising upcoming gigs; downtown artists embraced copy machines as a way to move their art out of the gallery and museum and into the street; and writers seized copy machines as a way to self-publish zines, broadsides, and even books. But xerography offered more than a means of production and distribution that bypassed the expectations and censorship imposed by promoters, curators, and publishers.

Any glimpse into the downtown scene's eclectic archive reveals that the media that Marshall McLuhan predicted would bring about 'a total revolution' in printing was an integral part of the downtown scene. As McLuhan observed, 'The highly centralized activity of publishing naturally breaks down into extreme decentralism when anybody can, by means of xerography, assemble printed, or written, or photography materials' (1995, p. 348). This is precisely what enabled DIY publishing to flourish in the downtown art scene. From the 1960s onwards, Fluxus members, like poet and composer Dick Higgins, were using copy machines to circulate individually authored and collective publications. For example, *The Fluxus Performance Workbook* (an ever-expanding, collaboratively authored encyclopaedia of Fluxus 'scores') was largely contingent on the growing accessibility of copy machines, which were used to reproduce and compile 'scores' for distribution amongst an ever-growing coterie of poets, artists, and performers (Friedman and Smith 2002, p. 1). By the 1970s, writers like Kathy Acker were also gravitating to copy machines. Acker, perhaps best known for her gritty novel-length cut-ups, used copy machines to collect materials, cut them up, and, early on in her career, to self-publish. Acker, of course, was by no means alone. The downtown scene she was part of revolved around copy machines and copy shops on many levels. Before Soft Skull Press went 'legit' and started publishing offset copies of perfect-bound books, its founding publisher Sander Hicks worked the graveyard shift at a Kinko's on 12th Street near University Place, turning out photocopied volumes of his own writing and that of his friends (Zaitchik 2010). As photographer, neighbourhood activist, and self-proclaimed community historian

Clayton Patterson (2007, p. 425) emphasizes, 'The Xerox machine became the printing press of this period'. However, Patterson appreciates not only that the copy machine was the scene's printing press but also that the copy machine was integral to producing and reproducing the aesthetic that came to mark the scene – an aesthetic rooted in punk and street art but by no means confined to the street.

In the 1970s and 1980s, walls of xeroxed posters and street art distinguished the downtown scene from other neighbourhoods by creating constantly changing and highly textured facades for the neighbourhood's crumbling architecture. The aesthetic was also re-circulated in much of the work produced by artists who were part of the scene. Soon after Jean-Michel Basquiat arrived in New York in the 1970s, he started appropriating techniques encountered in punk posters and publications to produce postcards and other small works. Basquiat reportedly copied his postcards on a colour copier at a photocopy shop on Prince Street in SoHo (Fretz 2010, p. 21). More accessible black-and-white copiers also found a place in the art world. One of David Wojnarowicz's most well-known series, *Arthur Rimbaud in New York*, features a photocopied cut-out of Rimbaud's face cast against various iconic locations around New York City. In the infamous series, the flimsy photocopied mask is repeated again and again, but in each photograph, the mask is attached to another body in another space – a gesture pointing to the ephemerality and mobility of the xerography and to the power of the multiple. While the Rimbaud series brought widespread attention to Wojnarowicz in New York and well beyond, for most artists in the downtown scene, the copy machine was less a medium of art than it was a means of communication and publicity (Carr 2012, pp. 133–136).

While xerography's gritty aesthetic was arguably one of the markers of New York's downtown arts scene, it also played a role in the scene's eventual deterritorialization. Although the downtown scene always remained defined by its geography, the scene was circulating well beyond its clearly defined urban boundaries through zines and mail art by the late 1970s. Initially, the scene's migration created an audience and income for local cultural producers, as young would-be East Village punks streamed down from the suburbs to attend shows and buy music and other products produced by local artists. Eventually, it meant that the downtown scene's aesthetic and approach to art making also became present in the suburbs and beyond, as some of these isolated punks started turning out their own fanzines and DIY recordings, realizing – long before the arrival of the Internet – the possibility of being part of a downtown scene without ever going downtown. Like social media platforms today, the copy machine opened up scenes to people, especially young people, who would otherwise never have had access. It offered them a medium through which they could access information about the scene and, more importantly, participate in its making.

In contrast to contemporary forms of social media, however, in which users can choose to take a relatively passive role (e.g. simply reposting texts and images from other sources), these uses of copy machines – to produce and circulate photocopied zines, for example – were active endeavours. To begin with, acquiring zines typically took considerably more effort than accessing social media sites. It meant going to a show or a used record store, which were among the only places you could find punk zines at the time. It also nearly always meant corresponding directly with other zine producers. This correspondence (usually handwritten notes and letters slipped into zines) was often intimate and personal, and it all happened in slow time with envelopes and stamps and the aid of the postal service. As a result, while copy machines may have played a role in the deterritorialization of the downtown art scene, perhaps specifically the punk scene that was so central to it, it is difficult and even misleading to suggest that this deterritorialization is comparable to the way a scene might become unmoored from its originary locale via contemporary social media platforms, such as Facebook. Indeed, although the scene became dispersed through the DIY forms of print reproduction facilitated by copy machine, the dispersal implicated participants in entirely different ways than today's social media. After all, as anyone who has spent time photocopying and distributing posters or zines knows, this is a qualitatively different activity from using digital social media. You have to find a copy machine – an affordable copy machine or, ideally, a free one. You have to fix its endless jams. You have to care enough to keep fixing these jams. In short, you have to be willing to do the work, deal with the jams, and take the time needed to put your work into circulation, and none of this has much in common with reposting slogans, photographs, or articles on Facebook or Twitter.

Viral reproduction

In Lizzie Borden's 1983 underground classic, *Born in Flames*, radical lesbian feminist vigilantes cruise the streets of the East Village on bicycles and in rented U-Haul trucks, taking on everyone from individual sexual harassers to the US Government. At the centre of Borden's feature length film is a radical critique of the mainstream media and a powerful parable about the power of underground forms of media production from pirate radio to photocopying and wheat pasting. While Borden's film is set in an imagined New York City – a city where an army of wheat-pasting lesbian feminists eventually manage to blow up the communications tower on top of the World Trade Center – by the late 1980s, the scene depicted in Borden's indie classic was the site of a highly politicized battle. In reality, however, the war staged in the downtown scene was not concerned with violence against women but rather with the systemic discrimination facing the queer community at the height of the AIDS crisis.

The impact of AIDS on the downtown scene was immediate and devastating. As Marvin Taylor, Director of the Fales Library and Special Collections, explains, even the Downtown Collection can be traced back to the AIDS crisis. By the early 1990s, it was becoming increasingly apparent that the material culture associated with the scene was rapidly disappearing. In some cases, artists' and writers' archives were being tossed away as family members showed up to clear out what remained of their apartments. In other cases, the materials were simply lost or dispersed. As result, as downtown scene artists, writers, and activists died, two decades of cultural production and community building were also at risk. The Downtown Collection emerged when it did to capture the scene's rich legacies of art and performance culture and politics and to keep these materials in the vicinity of the downtown neighbourhoods where the scene had historically flourished. (Fales Library and Special Collections is located at Washington Square on the New York University campus.) While some of the scene's artists who died, like Wojnarowicz and Keith Haring, were already well known at the time of their deaths, many more had yet to fully develop their careers or, like many downtown artists, were simply making art and music without widespread acclaim or the desire for it.

As much as the AIDS crisis threatened the downtown scene, it also galvanized the scene as downtown artists came together to raise awareness about the AIDS virus and put pressure on the City of New York and federal officials to respond to the crisis with increased aid for hospital beds and drug trials. Unsurprisingly, art-based forms of activism would prove to be a critical component in both the war on AIDS and the queer activism that came out of the downtown scene in the mid-1980s to mid-1990s, and copy machines were a favoured medium for the artist-activists collectives that formed during this period.

By the early 1990s, ACT UP was leasing a $10,000 a month copy machine that occupied the space of an entire room. The machine was capable of turning out professional quality posters, pamphlets, and banners, and by the 1990s, it had reproduced some of the late twentieth century's most iconic examples of art-based activism (Cohen 1998, p. 59). While the quality and quantity of posters produced by organizations like ACT UP were on a scale unavailable to most activist organizations, the aesthetic and mode of distribution was inspired by the street-based art scene that had existed before the community found itself at the centre of an epidemic. For example, while Gran Fury, an artist collective that grew out of ACT UP in the late 1980s, primarily worked on large-scale public awareness campaigns, its tactics and aesthetic were consistent with the type of art that had been produced by downtown scene artists throughout the 1970s and 1980s. Named after the model of car used the New York City Police Department at the time, Gran Fury was about policing – in this case, public opinion – and the work they produced, inspired by everything from street art to agitprop, reflected the urgency of the era. Its iconic 'Read My Lips' poster campaign included two gender-specific posters – one of two sailors kissing and another of two women from the 1920s about to kiss (Meyer 2002, pp. 227–228). Thanks to photocopiers, these posters, originally produced for a day of action against homophobia in 1988, were not only widely distributed at the time but continued to circulate for years after the event. In the mid-1990s, blurry reproductions of these same posters were still being reproduced in queer community centres and on college campuses across North America.

Yet, the scale of Gran Fury's ACT UP–sponsored activism was not necessarily the norm for the artist-activist collectives that grew out of the downtown scene in the late 1980s and early 1990s. In contrast to Gran Fury, the Lesbian Avengers encouraged its members to reproduce the movement's posters and pamphlets on copy machines in their own workplaces. In their 1993 handbook, free photocopying is repeatedly cited as a critical resource: 'Find out who has access to free xeroxing at their offices, or a fax machine. Someone may be willing to do legal support or design flyers or just wheat-paste'. In the same handbook, they reiterate, 'There are Avengers who work in corporations with massive xerox possibilities. But they need ample advance warning and assistance transporting the guerrilla copies' (Lesbian Avengers 1993). The viral nature of xerography – its ability to reproduce itself with limited skill and even limited money – was pivotal to the Avengers' impact.

In the midst of the AIDS crisis, the inexpensive reproduction of posters and pamphlets was one of the ways the downtown art scene expressed its rage and ultimately, one of the ways the scene survived. The copy machine helped downtown artists and activists take their local crisis out of the village and into the rest of the city. Quite literally, it helped them go viral with a series of urgent messages designed to raise awareness about the AIDS virus, expose how local, state, and federal levels of government were complicit and complacent in the management of the epidemic, and fight back against escalating homophobic attacks. Because copy machines could produce professional quality graphics (if you had access to the type of machine being leased by ACT UP) or quick, cheap DIY pamphlets (if you only had access to the type of copy machine you typically find at your local bodega), the medium was open to creative exploitation on an ambitious scale but also effectively levelled the playing field between professional artists and anyone else with a message. Of course, no single tool was powerful enough to save the downtown scene. As Sarah Schulman (2008, p. 7) emphasizes, the AIDS crisis permanently altered the scene on myriad levels:

> My communities – the community of innovative artists, and the community of gay people willing to take action for social change [...] located in Manhattan's East and West Village in the 1980s and 90s – had such high death rates the infrastructures and cultural ways of these groups were basically destroyed.

But just as copy machines had played a pivotal role in defining the scene in the 1970s and early 1980s, the same DIY media proved critical to the scene's self-preservation during the years of the AIDS crisis.

There is a tendency to think about scenes as more deterritorialized today than they were prior to the mid-1990s, when the widespread arrival of the web began to radically restructure everyday life and communications on a local and global level. After all, scenes now frequently develop with little or no connection to street life at all. Using New York's downtown scene as an example, this article suggests that the unmooring of scenes from local geographies was already well under way in the 1970s and 1980s, as the printed ephemera produced on copy machines created the groundwork for networks rooted in but by no means confined to local scenes. Yet, as emphasized throughout, copy machines also have a unique relationship to scenes. On the one hand, this banal office technology brought people together in common spaces (as demonstrated by the scenes that once thrived around 24-hour Kinko's outlets) and helped local scenes demarcate their boundaries (e.g. by creating temporary facades on existing architecture and public works). On the other hand, copy machines were deployed to create dispersed networks through which highly localized scenes were nonetheless able to include the participation of social actors living far beyond the scene's geographic boundaries. As much as copy machines can be said to have intensified the local, then, they have also played a historically pivotal role in the migration of scenes. Scenes are difficult to capture precisely because they so often point simultaneously to local clusters of activity and dispersed practices, sounds, styles, and attitudes (Straw 2001, p. 248). As a media technology that is at once capable of intensifying the local and developing and sustaining non-local networks in ways that do not undermine the primacy of the local scene's sensibility and style, copy machines are and remain uniquely situated to accommodate the inherent tensions and contradictions that define scenes.

Notes

1   For details, see *The Downtown Collection Finding Aid* (Fales Library and Special Collections 2011).
2   Following the widely mourned closing of CBGBs in 2006, John Varvatos, a high-end men's apparel company, moved into the former CBGBs location on the Bowery. Today, t-shirts with a 'preworn' appearance, black leather jackets, and designer jeans as well as so-called 'business casuals' are sold alongside memorabilia connected to CBGBs. A few sections of wall still contain palimpsests of the store's previous occupants, who were not known for their 'business casuals'.
3   Display advertisements for the Haloid Company's new XeroX machine started to appear in papers, such as *The New York Times*, in the mid-1950s. The earliest

advertisements invited executives to send away for a free 12-page illustrated report that 'shows how your company can simplify and speed paper work – and cut costs!'

Notes on Contributor

Kate Eichhorn is Assistant Professor of Culture and Media Studies at The New School University in New York City. She is the author of *The Archival Turn in Feminism: Outrage in Order* (Temple UP, 2013) and *Adjusted Margin: The Copy Machine and the Making of Public Cultures* (forthcoming from the MIT Press) and numerous articles and book chapters on late twentieth-century to early twenty-first century radical print cultures.

References

Born in Flames. (1983) Dir. Lizzie Borden, USA.

Brooks, J. (1969) 'Xerox Xerox Xerox Xerox', *The New Yorker*, 1 April, pp. 46–90.

Carlson, C. (1965) 'History of electrostatic recording', in *Xerography and Related Processes*, eds. J. H. Dessauer & H. E. Clark, London, The Focal Press, pp. 15–42.

Carr, C. (2012) *Fire in the Belly: The Life and Times of David Wojnarowicz*, New York, Bloomsbury.

Cohen, P. F. (1998) *Love and Anger: Essays on AIDS, Activism, and Politics*, Binghamton, NY, Haworth Press.

Cooper, D. & Myles, E. (2006). 'Afterword: the scene: a conversation between Dennis Cooper and Eileen Myles', in *Up is Up, but So Is down: New York's Downtown Literary Scene, 1974–1972*, ed. B. Stosuy, New York, New York University Press, pp. 463–482.

'Creative office workers dig electrographic art' (1970) *Chronicle-Tribune*, 25 November.

Fales Library and Special Collections (2011) *Downtown collection finding aid*, [online] Available at: http://www.nyu.edu/library/bobst/research/fales/downtown.html (accessed 1 July 2013).

Firpo, P., Alexander, L. & Katayanagi, C. (1978) *Copyart: The First Complete Guide to the Copy Machine*, New York, Horseguard Lane Productions for R. Marek Publishers.

Fretz, E. (2010). *Jean-Michel Basquiat: A Biography*, Santa Barbara, CA, Greenwood.

Friedman, K. & Smith, O. (2002) 'Introduction to the Fortieth Anniversary Edition of the *Fluxus Performance Workbook*', in *Fluxus Performance Workbook: A Performance Research E-publication*, eds. K. Friedman, O. Smith, & L. Sawchyn, Aberystwyth, UK, Centre for Performance Research, pp. 1–2.

The Lesbian Avengers. (1993) *The Lesbian Avenger Handbook: A Handy Guide to Homemade Revolution*, [online] Available at: http://www.lesbianavengers.com (accessed 1 June 2013).

Marcus, S. (2010) *Girls to the Front*, New York: Harper Collins.

McLuhan, M. (1995) 'The emperor's new clothes', in *The Essential McLuhan*, eds. E. McLuhan & F. Zingrone, Toronto, ON, House of Anansi Press, pp. 339–356.

Mele, C. (2000) *Selling the Lower East Side*, Minneapolis, University of Minnesota Press.

Meyer, R. (2002) *Outlaw Representation: Censorship and Homosexuality in Twentieth-century Art*, New York, Oxford University Press.

Patterson, C. (2007) *Resistance: A Radical Social and Political History of the Lower East Side*, New York, Seven Stories Press.

Schulman, S. (2008) *Rat Bohemia*, Vancouver, BC, Arsenal Pulp.

Straw, W. (2001) 'Scenes and sensibilities', *Public*, vol. 22/23, pp. 245–257.

Stosuy, B., ed. (2006) *Up is Up, but So Is Down: New York's Downtown Literary Scene, 1974–1972*, New York, New York University Press.

Szabo, J. (1994) 'Copy shop stitches the urban crazy quilt', *New York Times*, [online], 3 July. Available at: http://www.nytimes.com/1994/07/03/style/copy-shop-stitches-the-urban-crazy-quilt.html (accessed 1 July 2013).

Zaitchik, A. (2010) 'The lonely truth quest of Sander Hicks', *The New York Observer*, [online], 21 February. Available at: http://observer.com/2010/07/the-lonely-truth-quest-of-sander-hicks (accessed 1 July 2013).

Sara M. Grimes

LITTLE BIG SCENE

Making and playing culture in Media Molecule's *LittleBigPlanet*

Drawing on an on-going, multi-method investigation into Media Molecule's popular LittleBigPlanet video game franchise and its ever-growing network of games, players, activities and events, this paper seeks to explore how the notion of 'cultural scene' might be used to better understand and analyse games-based, collaborative cultural activities. The discussion begins with a description of LittleBigPlanet, its contents and history, and the various actors involved in the social shaping of its wide-reaching community. The focus then shifts to identifying some of the ways in which LittleBigPlanet might be understood as functioning as (or at least akin to) a 'cultural scene', as well as to exploring those facets of LittleBigPlanet that challenge previous interpretations of this concept and its underlying assumptions. Particular attention will be given to the ways in which the LittleBigPlanet scene reflects, extends and deviates from the geographically situated notions of the cultural scene found in previous works in this area. An argument is made that understanding examples such as LittleBigPlanet as cultural scenes requires more than a shift in our notions and experience of locale, but also necessitates a renewed foregrounding of lingering questions relating to power and privatization within both traditional and digital cultural practice.

In Fall 2008, Media Molecule, a British independent game design company, released *LittleBigPlanet* for the Sony PlayStation 3 video game console system. The game was highly anticipated, heavily promoted and quickly drew both strong sales and near unanimous critical acclaim. Unique in its incorporation of extensive yet highly accessible user-generated content (UGC) and 'do-it-yourself' (DIY) game creation tools, LittleBigPlanet[1] has since evolved into a wildly successful cross-platform game series and media brand. It has concurrently become something of a poster child for various government- and industry-led initiatives focused on promoting technical skill development and STEM[2] learning among children and teens. Perhaps even more significant, however, is that the game sustains a vibrant community of player-creators, followers and fans who to date have produced and published over 8 million UGC game levels, as well as innumerable player-made objects, stories and other content (Isbell 2013).

From this larger group of players and activities, a new sort of 'cultural scene' has emerged, out of which shared forms of cultural expression, social norms and expectations continually unfold. This scene, in turn, has significantly shaped the broader LittleBigPlanet community, influenced industry design decisions, and contributed to the movement towards DIY and UGC currently found throughout gamer culture. While the concept of 'cultural scenes', as used by Straw (1991, 2004), Stahl (2001), Shank (1994) and others, describes particular networks of cultural activities, collaborative meaning-making practices and social 'happenings' associated with specific geographical (predominantly urban) locales, the term's emphasis on a shared temporal and spatial 'place' suggests that it might also be useful for analysing digital examples such as the LittleBigPlanet community. After all, LittleBigPlanet is similarly comprised of unbounded sociocultural practices, which are situated in and around the virtual – yet also fundamentally material – 'location' of a digital game system.

The game as artefact, or system, supplies the underlying infrastructures, tools and content upon which the majority of player activities are based. It plays a uniquely powerful role in making the scene manifest, by providing it with the materials, the (virtual) stages and shared forums, as well as the very network through which players interact, congregate, share content and construct meaning. The LittleBigPlanet scene is furthermore tethered to a particular brand of console systems, and a significant amount of its members' interactions occur through the system's sole communication network, both of which are owned and controlled by a handful of commercial entities. Yet, LittleBigPlanet's players also extend their activities across a range of informal spaces, domestic and material contexts. Within this dynamic, the player-creators' complex relationships with creativity, production, prosumption and play – along with the underlying corporate and legal structures that mediate these relationships – unfold in a constant state of negotiation, reproduction and occasional subversion.

Drawing on an on-going, multi-method investigation into LittleBigPlanet and its ever-growing network of games, players, activities and events, this paper seeks to explore how the notion of 'cultural scene' might be used to better understand and analyse games-based, collaborative cultural activities. The discussion begins with a description of LittleBigPlanet, its contents and history, and the various actors involved in the social shaping of its wide-reaching community. The focus then shifts to identifying some of the ways in which LittleBigPlanet might be understood as functioning as (or at least akin to) a cultural scene, as well as to exploring those facets of LittleBigPlanet that challenge previous interpretations of this concept and its underlying assumptions. Particular attention will be given to the ways in which the LittleBigPlanet scene reflects, extends and deviates from the geographically situated notions of the cultural scene found in previous works in this area. An argument is made that understanding examples such as LittleBigPlanet as cultural scenes requires more than a shift in our notions and experience of locale; it also necessitates a renewed foregrounding of lingering questions relating to power and privatization within both traditional and digital cultural practice.

Little big deal

Over the past 5 years, LittleBigPlanet has expanded from a single, original title exclusively made and sold for the Sony PlayStation 3 console system, into a highly popular game series. The series includes the original *LittleBigPlanet*, released in 2008, a sequel (*LittleBigPlanet 2* 2011), two mobile versions (*LittleBigPlanet* (2009) for the PlayStation Portable and *LittleBigPlanet PS Vita* (2012) for the PlayStation Vita), a spin-off title (*LittleBigPlanet Karting* 2012), and an expansion (*LittleBigPlanet 2 Move Pack* 2011). The games themselves are dynamic and continuously evolving, with new downloadable content (DLC) released on a regular basis. Combined, these titles have sold over 11 million copies to date,[3] over half of which were purchased outside of North America (VGChartz 2013). It is rated 'E for Everyone' by the US-based Entertainment Software Ratings Board, rated 'ages 7 and up' by the Pan European Game Information ratings board, and is available in over 13 languages. While demographic details about LittleBigPlanet users have not been released, small-scale studies, marketing rhetoric and corporate presentations all suggest that the game attracts players of various ages, including both children and adults. Moreover, a number of K-12 targeted educational programmes based on LittleBigPlanet games have emerged over the past few years, and in 2011 Media Molecule even released an official 'Teacher Pack' for using *LittleBigPlanet 2* in the classroom.

Making games in LittleBigPlanet

LittleBigPlanet is noteworthy for its integration of sophisticated yet easy-to-use tools and templates that enable players to design their own mini-games or levels. These tools include a wide variety of digital stickers, 'paints' and other materials that can be used for aesthetic customization; virtual cardboard that can be 'cut' into almost any shape; and a range of distinct 'actions' (such as jump, patrol or electric shock) that players can assign to objects in order to create interactive elements and obstacles. Players use a standard PlayStation 3 controller to scroll through and select from this extensive menu of customization options, as well as to resize and position the objects they have made. These objects are then used not only to decorate each level but also to construct the space, objectives and challenges that make up a game level.

Pre-made objects and many of the materials made available to players share the same 'arts and crafts' aesthetic. As a result, most LittleBigPlanet creations have a 'handmade' look and feel. LittleBigPlanet's creation tools and templates are remarkably flexible, enabling players to produce highly original and innovative creations. The games also contain dozens of interactive tutorials that coach players through every step of the progressively complex design process – from customizing a colour scheme, to programming 'end-boss' antagonists. In addition, there are hundreds of thousands of user-made 'walkthroughs'[4] and instructional videos published on YouTube and other forums.

LittleBigPlanet not only supplies players with tools for creating UGC levels but also provides them with an easy-to-use system for sharing their creations with each other. The game comes with its own, LittleBigPlanet-specific (and Sony PlayStation 3–specific) network where players can publish their UGC levels, which allows them to be seen and played by other LittleBigPlanet players from around the world. So far, LittleBigPlanet players have produced and shared over 8 million UGC levels (Isbell 2013). Media Molecule representatives claim that the majority of active players have at some point uploaded UGC to the LittleBigPlanet network.[5] Players also actively engage with each other's creations, by leaving comments and ratings on a significant proportion of the levels published. Following the standard web 2.0 business model, UGC content produced by other players is free to play and access. Instead, revenue is derived from retail purchase of the LittleBigPlanet games themselves, as well as from add-on DLC sold through the 'LBP Store' – an in-game store where users can buy additional tools, costumes and materials for real-world money.

Social features and fan activities

In addition to creating UGC levels, many players contribute to online forums, participate in events (such as contests) and engage in various fan activities. The games' publisher (Sony Computer Entertainment) runs a social networking site called LBP.me, where players can share new project ideas and discuss the finer points of LittleBigPlanet with other players.[6] Social interaction is also a core feature of the games themselves (Grimes 2013). Players are repeatedly invited to explore other players' creations. They are also encouraged to rate and 'heart' (the equivalent to Facebook's 'like' feature) UGC levels, comment on them and (in some cases) remix them. While it is unclear what actual percentage of the overall player base engages in the social aspects of LittleBigPlanet, the LBP.me forums are noticeably active, and there is ample evidence of activities such as 'hearting' and commenting on player-made levels.[7] Such evidence can be thought of as 'networking residues', which Grimes and Fields (2012, p. 43) define as 'traces of one's social connections to other users on a site' that work to 'establish and reify connections' between players in visible ways. In addition to indicating the level of social interaction unfolding within a particular game or forum, networking residues work to foster a sense of 'copresence' (Zhao 2003), shared experience and collaborative interaction among users.

As mentioned, LittleBigPlanet also extends far beyond the confines of its official spaces and networks, and has inspired various forms of fan participation (Jenkins 2011). In addition to the many player-made instructional videos and walkthroughs mentioned above, players have created vast amounts of fan fiction, LittleBigPlanet websites and wikis, digital artwork and machinima. With its 'handmade' arts and crafts aesthetic, LittleBigPlanet has also inspired a remarkably steady supply of 'ludic artefacts', which Tolino (2009, Para. 4) defines as 'player-created content' that is 'inspired by video games and posted on the Internet', but is largely 'generated or used outside the confines of the game itself'. For instance, fans have produced numerous handcrafted 'Sackboy'[8] (the name given to LittleBigPlanet avatars) dolls and DIY knitting patterns, images of which they have subsequently posted and shared online. Such activities not only help extend gameplay but also produce 'paratexts' which in turn help 'shape the reader's experience of a text' and 'give meaning to the act of reading' (Consalvo 2007, p. 9).

While many of these fan activities are technically unsanctioned, occurring outside of the official game space and social network, LittleBigPlanet's corporate owners have been incredibly proactive in keeping track of such activities and occasionally re-appropriating them. A key example can be found in Media Molecule's reaction to the aforementioned player-made Sackboy dolls. Rather than attempt to quelch the practice, LittleBigPlanet's developers quickly teamed up with a celebrity knitter to release an 'official' version of the Sackboy knit pattern, which was made available online for free. To some extent, Media Molecule (and now Sony) has also actively encouraged players to build their own LittleBigPlanet fan sites, by providing a corporately sanctioned 'Fansite Kit', which can be downloaded from the company's blog. On the other hand, both instances also function to extend corporate influence over fan activities, by providing sanctioned, standardized templates out of which player-made, yet brand-consistent, ludic artefacts and paratexts might emerge.

Previous literature

Despite its popularity and unique attributes, there has been surprisingly little critical scholarship examining LittleBigPlanet to date. A notable exception is Sotamaa's (2010) early analysis of *LittleBigPlanet*'s (the original title) commercial and technological infrastructures, and their (then as yet) potential impact on player innovation. Focusing on the game's seamless integration of play and production, Sotamaa suggests that while there are clearly important opportunities for player appropriation and unanticipated uses within and around *LittleBigPlanet*, there is also palpable evidence that these occur in constant dialogue with the commercial interests of the game's corporate owners, which may ultimately take precedence. Pointing to the multi-levelled control LittleBigPlanet's corporate owners exert over the games' contents and system, Sotamaa (2010, under 'Conclusion') argues, 'While the potential for transformation and controversy is obviously not entirely erased, the room for altering the rigid structure defined by the platform manufacturers seems somewhat limited'.

A handful of other works have recently emerged, shifting the focus more intently on player agency and cultural dimensions. For instance, Westecott's (2011) discussion of *LittleBigPlanet*'s game design and semiotics posits that the game's extensive creation tools reveal important linkages with contemporary DIY and maker movements, while its handmade-craft aesthetic opens up game creation to a wider range of non-expert users. At a recent games conference, Robinson and Simon (2013) applied and dismissed a political economic critique of LittleBigPlanet's web 2.0 business model, in which the game's mobilization of UGC might be seen as an exploitation of players' immaterial labour. They argue that the players' contributions to LittleBigPlanet cannot be understood as labour because even pro-am (a contraction of professional-amateur) players do not describe their activities as work. Instead, players report a sense of reciprocity vis-à-vis LittleBigPlanet's corporate owners, feelings of creative engagement and a 'sense of value and purpose that is not tied to capital'.

Both sets of arguments, Westecott's and those advanced by Robinson and Simon, are compelling and present important insight into the potential for LittleBigPlanet to serve as a forum for cultural engagement, empowerment and meaning making. Conversely, both are perhaps overly dismissive of the imbalance of power and control that exists between players and producers within this particular community. While LittleBigPlanet might *look* handmade, players are prevented from accessing, let alone modifying or contributing to, the game's underlying code and mechanics – a key requirement of DIY and maker movements. Similarly, no matter what terms the players use to describe their relationship to LittleBigPlanet, the games' corporate owners clearly benefit from players' participation in UGC creation. They also structure player participation to align with corporate priorities, for instance through pro-grammed design limitations that work to sustain the common look and feel found in many UGC levels, as well through the restrictions found in the games' terms of service contracts relating to how players may draw on copyrighted content.

While uncovering the cultural dimensions of LittleBigPlanet is clearly crucial to understanding its significance, the fact that players' activities and perspectives are largely unfolding within a highly corporately controlled space should not be overlooked. Indeed, rather than focus on *either* commercial structures *or* player agency, Sotamaa points out examples such as LittleBigPlanet require 'more nuances and less dichotomous models'. A more balanced approach would be one that considers *all* of these facets and seeks to understand how they function (and sometimes malfunction) in concert.

From prosumption to 'cultural scene'

In recent years, the notion of *prosumption* has been used by various scholars as an entry-point for collapsing such dichotomies, particularly within studies of digital technologies and practices that, as in LittleBigPlanet, blur processes of production and consumption, work and play (Herman *et al*. 2006, Ritzer and Jurgenson 2010). The term not only describes the conflation of production and consumption but also seeks to understand how this conflation occurs within spaces and activities that in turn create a bridge between practices of distributed agency and commercial imperatives (Ritzer and Jurgenson, 2010). Contrary to the critique advanced by Robinson and Simon, various scholars aligned with the political economy of communication approach have used prosumption and other, similarly nuanced analytic tools to understand how users' participation in commercial processes can concurrently function as both a highly personal, affective and deeply meaningful experience *and* as a type of labour that is mobilized and monetized by corporate entities. Key examples of this include Pybus' (2007) analysis of 'lovemarks', Herman *et al*.'s (2006) discussion of 'distributed agency', as well as Hardt and Negri's (2004) iteration of 'immaterial' and 'affective' labour.

Then again, political economic frameworks are indeed often limited by their origins in economic theory, particularly in terms of their ultimate preoccupation with the sublimation of individual meaning making by commercialization processes. As argued elsewhere, the term prosumption carries its own set of pre-emptive politics, in that it too often frames user experiences in industrial terms from the outset (Grimes 2011). Despite their intended emphasis on constructing a dual-level critique, concepts such as lovemarks and affective labour are predominantly used to analyse the commercial processes and labour relations found within prosumption spaces. Moreover, beyond the production of use value, cultural dimensions are frequently downplayed within many of these discussions.

This is evident in the emphasis that is frequently placed on measurable outcomes within the scholarly work in this area, through which user participation is linked up with identifiable market transactions, such as data-mining users' data in order to design targeted advertising or develop new products. By focusing on the point at which use value is transformed into exchange value, such works are able to uncover historical precedents and the 'hidden' politics of commercial sites and systems, as well as contribute to longstanding Marxian critiques of late capitalism and social rationalization. However, as Westecott, Robinson and Simon demonstrate, there are myriad other experiences and transformations that also unfold within these spaces – many of them extra-economic or otherwise resistant to commercial appropriation – that become overlooked in the process.

A compelling alternative may be found in the growing number of studies that have revived and adapted the term 'cultural scene' as a framework for investigating the range of relationships, movements and activities involved in complex, bounded, cultural phenomena. Straw's (2004) approach is particularly promising for constructing an analytic framework that not only enables equal consideration of user perspective and corporate processes but also of the various *other* elements and events involved in the social construction of specific sociocultural happenings. Straw outlines a number of characteristics that may be seen as typical of a cultural scene: that they are localized, that their boundaries are difficult to trace, that they incorporate a cluster of activities that feed into one another, and that they include commercial aspects and some relationship with the very 'mainstream' they seem to operate in contrast with.

Arguably, versions of each of these characteristics can also be identified in LittleBigPlanet. For one, LittleBigPlanet is largely virtual but it is also localized. To use Zittrain's (2008) term, the games are 'tethered' to a particular set of technological artefacts, in that they are exclusively available on Sony PlayStation video game consoles. The various ancillary activities described above, such as participating in the LBP.me network, producing fansites and other ludic artefacts, are also 'tethered' to this system, in terms of their aesthetics and intertextuality, as well as their source materials. LittleBigPlanet players, while physically located all around the globe, similarly interact and perform their participation within the tethered spaces of the games and online forums. Some situate their participation within 'real world' locales even further by creating LittleBigPlanet-inspired crafts and ludic artefacts. Located simultaneously in both the virtual and the real world, the players work to expand and remap the LittleBigPlanet network as a hybridized space, at once digital and material. The fact that many players access LittleBigPlanet from domestic settings – homes, bedrooms and dorm rooms – further complexifies the 'territory' through its transgression of traditional public/private divides.

Another feature that LittleBigPlanet shares with cultural scenes such as Straw's (1991) music scene, Atkinson and Young's (2001) body modification scene, Perrone's (2010) dance club scene and Woo's (2012) nerd-culture scene, is that its boundaries are difficult, perhaps even impossible, to trace. LittleBigPlanet is made up of a complex cluster of activities that shape and feed into one each other. Across a wide range of artefacts, events and practices, players, fans and developers engage in a highly iterative, intertextual and mutual shaping of the LittleBigPlanet space and what goes on 'there'. While proprietary software and corporately operated networks link up many of these activities at the infrastructural level, a significant part of what makes LittleBigPlanet a unique, meaningful and engaging cultural experience arguably derives from the collaborative, affective and largely extra-economic dialogue that continuously unfolds between the various actors and artefacts involved. This dialogue takes place on multiple levels – from the social and material, to the discursive and aesthetic.

Although difficult to delineate, LittleBigPlanet's seemingly innumerable spaces, texts and activities are nonetheless distinguished by a particular 'genre of cultural production which gives them coherence' (Straw 2004, p. 412). In addition to the coherence provided by the games' underlying corporately owned infrastructure, things and spaces related to LBP are visually and thematically linked by a shared 'handmade' aesthetic. As Westecott (2011, pp. 94–95) describes, LittleBigPlanet 'shrieks craft throughout its construction: felt, sack, fabric, cardboard, hand drawn sketches, the textures that wallpaper the world, are all built from digital copies of analogue materials'. Indeed, the games' developers describe purposefully giving it a 'handmade look to celebrate imperfection' (Ettourney cited Things to make and do in *LittleBigPlanet* 2008, p. 3), in order to make players feel more comfortable about sharing their own imperfect creations. Accordingly, many of the tools, templates and materials that are made available to players for their UGC creations afford the same, handmade aesthetic. Thus, both the official games and the player-made UGC levels of LittleBigPlanet tend to evoke semiotic and ideological associations with broader DIY and Arts and Crafts movements (Cumming and Kaplan 1991, Greenhalgh 1997).

The 'handmade look' that characterizes the official game spaces of LittleBigPlanet also appears in a significant proportion of player-made ludic artefacts, fansites and paratexts. An illustrative example of this tendency can be found in an award-winning, player-made short film released in 2010 (*Last minute big planet* 2011). The film, which depicts an analogue recreation of a LittleBigPlanet-esque game level, uses actual cardboard and hand-drawn signs, and features an *a cappella* cover of a song from the official LittleBigPlanet soundtrack. Such artefacts do not merely reproduce the aesthetic (i.e. handmade) 'genre' engendered within the LittleBigPlanet game space, but advance and expand, remix and transform it in both tangible and immaterial ways.

Meanwhile, the games' developers have been remarkably savvy in their approach to 'synergizing' such activities. They have been particularly adept at identifying and celebrating ludic artefacts that not only cohere with the games' intended DIY ethos and handmade aesthetic but also appear to resonate with a large cross-section of the LittleBigPlanet playerbase. Their re-appropriation of the fan-made Sackboy knit patterns is but one among many examples of Media Molecule's on-going engagement with player-made artefacts and player-driven initiatives. As a result, even the most corporate facets of LittleBigPlanet represent a combination of official and unofficial, developer-made and player-made, digital and analogue.

LittleBigPlanet's underlying business model similarly reflects a heavy investment in supporting players' involvement in fan activities. The promotional materials and developer blog posts that have been released over the past few years have often showcased 'homages' – player-made levels that seek to reproduce well-known games or create innovative remixes of beloved media tropes and characters. Significantly, the 'LBP Store' features a growing number of DLC packs and 'add-ons', which players can purchase (using real-world money) in order to acquire exclusive access to additional stickers, costumes, sets and other customization tools. Many of these packs feature popular media brands, such as the Disney Princesses, Thatgamecompany's *Journey*, and Marvel's *X-Men*. Increasingly, many of these branded DLC packs appear in cross-promotional coincidence with the release of a new film, video game or toyline associated with the same media brand. These DLC packs can thus be seen as serving a promotional function, one which is further amplified when players actually use them to create and publish content.

As is the case with many corporately owned web 2.0 platforms, LittleBigPlanet's commercial mechanisms are fuelled by the affective labour of its users, and many of its features are intentionally designed to inspire and channel player engagement in order to maximize profits and build brand identity. Within Straw's (2004) framework, commercial processes such as these are approached as often-integral components of the cultural scene, rather than as separate, invasive or necessarily exploitative forces. Cultural scenes involve 'levels of consumption and spending' (p. 415), are practices that '"work" to produce a sense of community' (Straw 1991, p. 373), attract commercial investment and mainstream appropriations, and are thereby implicated in a range of market relations and infrastructures.

Scenes, Shank (1994, p. 122) explains, contain 'far more semiotic information … than can be rationally parsed'. Straw (2004, p. 412) expands upon this argument, describing the volume and complexity of the 'information' generated by a cultural scene as 'forever in excess of the productive ends to which it might be put'. At the same time, Straw points out that outside attention – from the cultural industries, popular press and mainstream culture – can itself play a role in establishing a particular cultural moment or set of activities as a 'scene'. The notion that the economic, the commercial and even the 'mainstream' can play important roles in the social shaping of a cultural scene invites a deeper consideration of the presence of branded DLC within LittleBigPlanet. For instance, it might be understood as an iterative response to existing player practices, or as a means of extending creative activity through the regular introduction of new, topical design elements.

On the other hand, LittleBigPlanet also diverges significantly from the cultural scenes found in previous works in this area. At the most basic level, LittleBigPlanet's born-digital status may be seen as problematic given the centrality of geography and place within scene theory. Indeed, Shanks, Straw and others utilize the cultural scene framework first and foremost as a way of 'accounting for' the enduring relationship between practice and place, and much of the work in this area is focused on situating activities, interactions and events within their specific geographic, largely urban locales. In contrast, the spaces, people and technologies that make up the LittleBigPlanet scene may appear as *de*-situated – as generating a non-place (Augé 1995, Mortensen 2003) or third-place[9] (Oldenburg 1989, Putnam 2000) that works to transcend, homogenize and subsume geographic locales within a shared virtual experience.

Much has already been written about the place-ness of virtual environments and online worlds. While early works sought to first draw and then deconstruct boundaries between the virtual and the material, contemporary scholarship has largely moved away from such dichotomous ways of understanding digital culture. As Mortensen (2003, under 'Creating history') argues, 'Remediation, the act of translating or transferring content from one medium to another does not create a non-place'. Moreover, although LittleBigPlanet may challenge traditional notions of space, it is nonetheless located and locatable. It emerges out of the particular geography and infrastructure provided by the LittleBig-Planet game software and the Sony PlayStation Network. It inhabits and is sustained by millions of console systems and home Internet connections. It is enacted and performed by hundreds of thousands of flesh-and-blood players and fans, by dozens of developers, and an unknown number of community managers and content moderators, each of whom is located somewhere. By applying an expanded notion of 'geography', the complex, mediated-yet-situated relationships between practice and place within LittleBigPlanet can still be accounted for. As Straw (2004, p. 412) admits, the notion of cultural scene often requires that the researcher consider 'kinds of activity whose relationship to territory is not easily asserted'.

A much more compelling set of questions arise when we set aside old debates about the place-ness of virtual environments, and instead delve into the particular breed of place that LittleBigPlanet both generates and occupies. For if LittleBigPlanet is a scene, it is one in which the majority of activities, creative outputs and interactions emerge out of 'private' spaces – namely, the home(s) of the players and the Sony-controlled infrastructure. First, since a significant amount of console gaming takes place in the home, the users' bodies, actions and interactions can be understood as partially situated within domestic, 'private sphere' contexts – a realm of activity that is rarely considered within the cultural scenes literature. Second, the commercial and technical mechanisms through which much of the LittleBigPlanet scene is articulated are privately owned and operated, subject to the whims and agendas of a small collection of corporate entities who exert an enormous amount of control over the scene and its participants. The LittleBigPlanet scene is inseparable from this institutional infrastructure, whereas other cultural scenes are characterized in no small part by an ability to remain autonomous from the cultural institutions they are engaged with. Together, these contexts place LittleBigPlanet in stark contrast to the public (urban city streets) and quasi-public (dance halls and comic book stores) spaces usually associated with cultural scenes. The remainder of this article considers these issues and their implications for the current discussion.

From cityscapes to bedrooms

The domestic plays a myriad of roles in the shaping and maintenance of the LittleBigPlanet scene. As mentioned, the players' bodies and much of the hardware they use to generate LittleBigPlanet's digital contents and social interactions are often situated within the living rooms or bedrooms of the players' homes. In addition, the LittleBigPlanet games contain numerous discursive and material linkages to the 'home' – both as place and as an abstract concept. For example, upon commencing the game, each player is automatically given a 'Pod', a personal space within the game that they can decorate and to which they can invite other players for a visit, much like a 'home'. The 'Pod' also functions as a hub or 'homebase' from which players can transport themselves to other 'worlds' (i.e. game levels). The Pod thus recreates and, to some extent, provides a virtual extension of contemporary 'children's bedroom culture' – the multi-purpose, heavily mediated space for leisure, autonomy, social interaction and cultural engagement discussed by Bovill and Livingstone (2001), Kearney (2007) and others.

The emphasis placed on the player's in-game Pod as a personal, customizable space reflects the symbolic value that is often associated with children's real bedrooms. In addition to becoming more heavily technologized, children's bedrooms have come to function as key spaces for the consumption and display of commodities (Cook 2004), a reflection of the ever-deepening association between identity and consumer practice found throughout contemporary society. Of course, links between consumption and the domestic sphere extend far beyond children's bedrooms. As Mortensen (2003) writes, in Western culture the 'home can be said to be less where the heart is and more where we store our favourite possessions' (under 'My home is my airport'). Writing about another form of personalized online space, Mortensen suggests that it is through the collection and display of virtual possessions that players develop a 'sensation of having a "home away from home"'. The ability to engage in virtual versions of domestic consumption activities may thus compensate to some extent for the lack of 'physical definition' found in virtual environments.

Whereas domestic space takes on a unique primacy within LittleBigPlanet, urban geography predominates much of the previous work on cultural scenes, from Straw's description of the Montreal discothèque scene to Woo's examination of nerd culture in 'a Canadian city'. Even within studies of scenes that traverse multiple geographic locations (e.g. Atkinson and Young's exploration of body modification practices in Calgary and Toronto, or Perrone's observations of drug/club culture in four US cities), the emphasis on cities and urban spaces remains. As Straw (2004, p. 412) suggests, the very term ('scene') can be understood as a 'way of speaking of the theatricality of the city – of the city's capacity to generate images of people occupying public space in attractive ways'. Conversely, however, Straw also points out that the cultural scenes approach 'invit[e] us to map the territory of the city in new ways' (2004, p. 412). Just as there is room within cultural scenes theory for virtual place-ness, the framework can surely be further expanded to accommodate a more deliberate consideration of the role of the domestic within cultural practice.

Indeed, McRobbie and Garber's (1976) identification of a comparable oversight within the early works on youth subcultures eventually led to a crucial shift in the ways in which issues of space and gender were approached within cultural studies research. It also led to the formulation of a valuable new analytic concept ('girls, bedroom culture') for investigating the role of the domestic within cultural experience. Moreover, cultural theorists have long argued that much of the work that goes into the development and maintenance of cultural norms, trends and capital, happens 'behind the scenes' or 'back stage'. For instance, Goffman (1959) argues that, much like food, bodies are predominantly 'prepared' (cleaned, primped, cooked, etc.) in the backstage spaces of the bedroom and the bathroom, before they are displayed and performed in social contexts.

It is reasonable to think that domestic spaces may fulfil a similar set of functions within cultural scenes. After all, domestic spaces, such as bedrooms, basements, garages and home offices, are frequently appropriated for various forms of cultural practice and production. They provide safe spaces for learning and rehearsing cultural repertoires. They provide creative spaces for producing a range of cultural texts and artefacts, from paratexts and DIY projects, to many of the songs, games, comics and artwork that fuel and stoke cultural movements. They also provide crucial intermediary spaces for testing out, performing and negotiating new ideas, styles and appropriations among friends and other sub-groups. A similar argument can be made when it comes to domestic consumption practices, through which commodities are acquired and displayed in ways that embed the home within a broader, shared culture. It is likely that many activities and outputs that initially unfold in domestic contexts will eventually contribute in some way to shaping the 'frontstage' of a cultural scene. The domestic facets of LittleBigPlanet should thus not be seen as incongruous with cultural scenes theory, but rather as an opportunity to rethink and expand the standard urban-centric framework to better account for the (potential) roles of domestic contexts within the construction and reproduction of cultural groupings.

Tethered spaces and LittleBigEdges

As discussed in previous sections, a key strength of the cultural scenes approach is that it affords a dual-level critique in which both production and consumption practices are considered, and in which contemporary cultural experience and political economic processes are understood as functioning in a dialectical relationship. However, unlike other cultural scenes, LittleBigPlanet emerges out of a particularly wide-reaching infrastructure of commercial relationships and corporately controlled processes. Although the cultural scenes examined by Straw and others do contain commercial elements, industry involvement and interactions with market forces, scenes are conventionally understood to be much more than the sum of their commercialized parts. Cultural scenes may unfold with and alongside commercial enterprise and exchange, but they also operate outside and at the edges of corporate (or other forms of institutional) control.

Although the boundaries of any cultural scene are unclear and continuously shifting, one of their core attributes is the presence of 'edges' (see also Gaonkar and Povinelli 2003). The edges not only work to distinguish a 'scene' from the cultural mainstream but also provide crucial spaces for the creation of surplus 'expressive energy', ephemera and liminal practices. These in turn enable scenes to maintain a certain level of independence from the cultural institutions and commercial processes that might otherwise seek to absorb them. Despite the strong presence and obvious influence of the various player-driven initiatives, ludic artefacts and spontaneous interactions within the LittleBigPlanet scene, there is also much to suggest that LittleBigPlanet's 'edges' do not function in quite the same way.

For one, the LittleBigPlanet scene is not only rooted in Media Molecule's proprietary software (i.e. the official game titles, tools and content) but also firmly entrenched in Sony's 'digital locked' hardware and exclusive online network. It is through the Sony infrastructure that players are able to access LittleBigPlanet's main spaces and contents (including their own UGC), and connect with other players. It fuels the LBP.me online social networking platform with data drawn from the console systems, providing players with more sophisticated ways of creating, connecting and making-sense of the multiple 'clusters of social and cultural activity' (Straw 2004) that are involved. As the user community changes and grows, hired moderators and heavy-use players collaborate to identify and re-incorporate particularly noteworthy trends. The LittleBigPlanet scene may unfold across multiple forums, in other words, but it is the Sony-managed infrastructure that supplies the scene's map and navigation system – linking console to computer, public to private, commercial to domestic, social to creative, grassroots to branding.

The depth of corporate involvement found in LittleBigPlanet is made possible by a number of factors – from broader trends found throughout digital

culture (Mosco 2004) to established industry norms around the commercialization and control of users within web. 2.0 platforms (Côté and Pybus 2007,
Cohen 2008). The fact that most of LittleBigPlanet's content and activities are
only accessible through a PlayStation 3 console is also significant. As Zittrain
(2008, p. 8) describes, 'centrally controlled devices' such as console systems
are 'tethered' appliances that encourage 'users away from a *generative* Internet
that fosters innovation and disruption, to an *appliancized* network that
incorporates the most powerful features of today's Internet while greatly
limiting its innovative capacity [italics in original]'. While Sotamaa proposes that
examples such as LittleBigPlanet challenge Zittrain's assessment of consoles as
inherently uncreative, the notion of a 'tethered' network nonetheless provides
an apt description of the LittleBigPlanet 'scene'.

Of course, the argument can be made that LittleBigPlanet's Sony-managed
infrastructure functions in much the same way that city streets and urban
infrastructures do in traditional cultural scenes. While controlled and managed
by municipal governments, business associations, social norms and legal
requirements, public urban spaces can nonetheless afford and at times even
foster the emergence of vibrant cultural practices. Indeed, the cultural scenes
framework encourages a middle ground or 'betwixt and between' approach to
understanding cultural participation within late capitalist societies, wherein
multiple outcomes and meanings are given equal weight and consideration.
Recent works examining cultural scenes draw attention to the frequent slippage
that occurs between traditional categories (producer/consumer, professional/
amateur, mainstream/marginal), and the potentially transformative dimensions
of such slippages and the collaborations they, at times, enable. They allow for
the possibility of what Feenberg (1999, p. 310) calls the 'margin of
manoeuvre', within which groups or interests otherwise subordinated by
traditional power hierarchies can mobilize to 'support conscious cooperation in
the coordination of effort and creative user appropriation of devices and
systems'.

In LittleBigPlanet, however, the 'tether' does not merely tie the players to
a particular technology or business model. It also works to embed and integrate
the player-generated cultures and autonomous player practices back into the
LittleBigPlanet brand. It works to either appropriate or efface that which *would*
make up the 'edges' of the LittleBigPlanet scene. These processes are even
partially acknowledged within the games' official corporate discourses and
marketing materials, for they also represent some of the primary ways in which
Media Molecule and Sony have formed a responsive and collaborative
relationship with a large segment of the player community. Examples include
hiring leading amateur designers to join the development team, supporting
amateur podcasters, sponsoring game design competitions for children and re-
appropriating fan appropriations (such as the Sackboy knit pattern).

Through such high-profile examples of user engagement, LittleBigPlanet has associated itself with a DIY-*esque* ethos. It exhibits many of the same features and follows many of the same trajectories found in grassroots online fan communities. LittleBigPlanet's corporate owners have adopted a relatively user-friendly approach that appears to promote participatory culture and support ancillary ideas and activities. In so doing, they are able to represent LittleBigPlanet as an assemblage of cultural and social activities drawn together by a common interest in creating and sharing adorable, handmade-like digital playthings. Although there is clear evidence that not all ideas are supported (e.g. claims of unfair corporate censorship of player-made levels abound), and that not all forms of fandom are deemed acceptable, LittleBigPlanet nonetheless manages to evoke a sense of boundless-ness, diversity, mutability and liminality.

Although LittleBigPlanet may look and feel a lot like a cultural scene, however, this too can be understood as a fabrication or product. Crafted by a small group of independent game developers, now operated by a monopolistic corporation, LittleBigPlanet is largely generated by a core network of commercial interests, spaces and commodities. Whereas cultural scenes emerge out of the edges or margins of cultural institutions, the LittleBigPlanet phenomenon can be understood as emerging out of this corporate core. Here, the dissenting and potentially subversive voices that might otherwise make up the edges of LittleBigPlanet are not merely marginalized, but can be disconnected from the core as required, or in some cases forcibly shut down. LittleBigPlanet is thus perhaps not so much a new form of 'cultural scene' as it is a corporately controlled appropriation of a cultural scene.

Conclusion: from digital scene to non-scene

Ultimately, LittleBigPlanet presents a compelling yet somewhat contradictory case study for developing an adapted version of the cultural scenes framework. On the one hand, focusing on a cultural phenomenon that predominantly unfolds within digital contexts has enabled a crucial revisiting of the ways in which cultural scenes are commonly imagined and situated. The current discussion suggests that analysing a digital cultural scene not only requires an expansion of traditional notions of 'locale' to include virtual spaces and online geographies but also necessitates a re-examination of the persistent influence of power relations and public/private divides within our conceptions of practice and place. Specifically, analysing LittleBigPlanet has raised important questions about the role of domestic contexts within cultural scenes and highlighted a potentially problematic gap within the existing literature. Future applications of the cultural scenes framework are thus invited to pay greater attention to the home as a potential space of learning, performing and producing one's membership to, and understanding of, scenes and other forms of cultural participation.

On the other hand, the scope of LittleBigPlanet's corporately controlled infrastructure distinguishes it from other cultural scenes. The absence of 'edges', along with the near ubiquitous involvement of the games' corporate owners in everything from interpersonal interactions to collaborative fan practices, conflicts too heavily with accepted criteria for what makes a scene a scene. The scene-ness of the LittleBigPlanet phenomenon manifests in numerous ways, but many of these are highly manufactured. At the same time, most players and fans are likely unaware of LittleBigPlanet's commercial under-pinnings. Unless they happen to break one of the rules, players evidently experience a relatively wide range of autonomy and sense of agency as they collaborate in the mutual shaping of the games' designs and discourses. Significantly, the tethered and commercially manufactured facets of LittleBig-Planet do not negate the cultural, experiential and affective dimensions of this vibrant and complex cultural assemblage. In fact, the former thrives on the latter.

How then are we to seek to understand examples such as LittleBigPlanet, which lack the type of extra-economic 'commons' found in city-based cultural scenes, but nonetheless generate comparably meaningful, seemingly boundless, multi-modal genres of cultural production and social interaction? While it is beyond the scope of the current discussion to consider this question in adequate detail, the answer may lie in a further exploration of cultural scenes and other contemporary theories relating to shifting notions of space. For example, the disappearing edges of LittleBigPlanet share many commonalities with other heavily commercialized, 'de-situated' cultural places such as shopping malls and theme parks. As theorized by Augé (1995), such places – or rather 'non-places' – evoke a contradictory sense of familiarity and strangeness, intimacy and distance. They are at once culturally meaningful and profoundly alienating for, as Bolter and Grusin (2000, p. 177) propose, their accommodation of cultural production and social activity is contingent upon the whims and interests of their corporate owners:

> Non-places, such as theme parks and malls, function as public places only during designated hours of operation. There is nothing as eerie as an airport at three o'clock in the morning, or a theme park after closing hours. When the careful grids of railings and ropes that during the day serve to shepherd thousands of visitors to ticket counters or roller coasters stand completely empty. Such spaces then seem drained of meaning.

Much like Augé's non-place, LittleBigPlanet may best be understood as a non-scene: a cultural scene that only functions as such when it falls within the parameters set by its (corporate) operators. It is an amalgam of non-public, private, commercial and commercially informed spaces that aims to foster DIY-inspired forms of cultural participation, in the interests of generating brand loyalty and identity. As such, it is part of a genre of cultural production that does not emerge at the edges of cultural institutions, but is rather born inside of them. The non-scene is informed by commercial interests that do not merely seek to appropriate and monetize grassroots cultural activities, but instead work to build sustainable, embedded networks through which surplus creative production (not to mention immaterial labour and use value) can be continuously generated, identified, amplified or discarded as required.

An amalgam of cultural scenes theory and Augé's notion of non-place is just one possible avenue that future work in this area might explore. The important takeaway here then, is that further exploration is indeed required. Examples such as LittleBigPlanet highlight a growing need for new frameworks for thinking about the deepening relationships between cultural movements and commercial processes – as well as for understanding how individuals' experience, agency and cultural participation are transformed by such relationships. The shift to digital spaces and contents has greatly facilitated the spread of the cultural industries into new areas of everyday life, while amplifying their ability to observe and influence cultural trends as they emerge. However, it is not enough to simply label the outcomes of this shift as commercial, tethered sources of immaterial labour and exploitation, or to exclude them outright from existing cultural studies frameworks. The challenges such examples present to existing models may reveal important ways in which these models might yet be revisited, adapted and expanded to better account for current political economic and cultural conditions.

Funding

This research was partially funded by GRAND, the Graphics, Animation, and New Media Network of Centres of Excellence, as part of the DigiKidz project.

Notes

1   Herein, unless otherwise specified, LittleBigPlanet will be used to refer not only to the original game title *LittleBigPlanet* but also to its sequels, spin-offs, community of players, development team and the various actors involved.
2   STEM is a widely used acronym, particularly within education circles, that refers to Science, Technology, Engineering and Math.
3   This number excludes the unknown number of free downloads of LittleBigPlanet titles that have been distributed by Sony to players through special promotions (e.g. at various times, the games have been included 'free' as part of a console purchase package). Notably, LittleBigPlanet titles were among those offered to players as a free reward following the high-profile hacking and interruption of service the PlayStation Network suffered in 2011.

4   A game walkthrough video consists of a detailed, step-by-step, often unedited demonstration of how to progress through a particular game or level.

5   In a recent interview, the company's co-founder, Alex Evans, was quoted saying, 'Basically, everybody publishes a level' (Gaston 2011).

6   Notably, the development of newer LBP titles has shifted out of the hands of the game's original creators, Media Molecule, to various other small development firms partnered with SCE, while Media Molecule focuses on its next Sony-exclusive UGC game title, *Tearaway*. While, the company maintains links to the game's management, spin-off designs and surrounding player community, it has distanced itself over the past few months. For instance, there have been no LBP-related posts on the Media Molecule blog since late 2012.

7   It should be noted that a certain amount of interaction is now enforced by the game design. For instance, in recent years, after players finish a UGC game, they are not able to return to the menu until they have rated and tagged the level by selecting from a collection of pre-approved keywords.

8   Despite the default masculine designation, player avatars in LBP are in fact fairly malleable and explicitly described by the game narrative in androgynous and gender-inclusive terms as 'Sackboys', 'Sackgirls' or 'Sackthings' (for players who would prefer not to assign a static gender to themselves and their avatars).

9   Of course, postmodern theorists have suggested that cities themselves can now be understood as sorts of 'third spaces' (Soja 1996).

Notes on Contributor

Sara M. Grimes is an Assistant Professor with the Faculty of Information, University of Toronto, and Associate Director of the Semaphore Lab. She teaches and researches primarily in the areas of children's digital culture, digital games and critical theories of technology. She is currently Principal Investigator of the Kids DIY Media Partnership, a transnational, cross-sector research collaboration investigating the opportunities, challenges and politics associated with children's DIY media creation within commercial, online contexts. She has published in *New Media & Society*, *Information Society*, and *Communication, Culture & Critique*, and her current manuscript, *Digital Playgrounds*, will be published by the University of Toronto Press.

References

Atkinson, K. & Young, M. (2001) 'Flesh journeys: neo primitives and the contemporary rediscovery of radical body modification', *Deviant Behavior*, vol. 22, no. 2, pp. 117–146.

Augé, M. (1995) *Non-places: Introduction to an Anthropology of Supermodernity*, trans. J. Howe, London, Verso.

Bolter, J. D. & Grusin, R. (2000) *Remediation, Understanding New Media*, Cambridge, The MIT Press.

Bovill, M. & Livingstone, S. (2001). 'Bedroom culture and the privatization of media use', in *Children and their Changing Media Environment: A European Comparative Study*, eds. S. Livingstone & M. Bovill, London, Lawrence Erlbaum Associates, pp. 179–200.

Cohen, N. S. (2008) 'Valorisation of surveillance: towards a political economy of Facebook', *Democratic Communique*, vol. 22, no. 1, pp. 5–22.

Consalvo, M. (2007) *Cheating: Gaining Advantage in Videogames*, Cambridge, The MIT Press.

Cook, D. T. (2004) *The Commodification of Childhood: The Children's Clothing Industry and the Rise of the Child Consumer*, Durham, Duke University Press.

Côté, M. & Pybus, J. (2007) 'Learning to immaterial labour 2.0: MySpace and social networks', *Ephemera: Theory & Politics in Organization*, vol. 7, no. 1, pp. 88–106.

Cumming, E. & Kaplan, E. (1991) *The Arts and Crafts Movement*, London, Thames and Hudson.

Feenberg, A. (1999) *Questioning Technology*, London, Routledge.

Gaonkar, D. & Povinelli, E. (2003) 'Technologies of public forms: circulation, trans-figuration, recognition', *Public Culture*, vol. 15, no. 3, pp. 385–398.

Gaston, M. (2011) '1.5m new LittleBigPlanet players since PSN outage', *Videogamer.com* [online] 20 July. Available at: http://www.videogamer.com/ps3/littlebigplanet_2/news/1_5m_new_littlebigplanet_players_since_psn_outage.html (accessed 14 August 2013).

Goffman, E. (1959) *The Presentation of Self in Everyday Life*, Garden City, NY, Doubleday.

Greenhalgh, P. (1997) 'The history of craft', in *The Culture of Craft: Status and Future*, ed. P. Dormer, Manchester, Manchester University Press, pp. 20–52.

Grimes, S. M. (2011) *Children's Virtual Worlds, Bedroom Culture and the Preemptive Politics of Prosumption*. Canadian Communication Association Annual Conference at Congress, 1–3 June, Fredericton NB, University of New Brunswick.

Grimes, S. M. (2013) 'Child-generated content: children's authorship and interpretive practices in digital gaming cultures', in *Dynamic Fair Dealing: Creating Canadian Culture Online*, eds. R. J. Coombe, D. Wershler, & M. Zellinger, Toronto, University of Toronto Press, pp. 336–345.

Grimes, S. & Fields, D. (2012) *Kids Online: A New Research Agenda for Understanding Social Networking Forums*, New York, The Joan Ganz Cooney Center at Sesame Workshop.

Hardt, M. & Negri, A. (2004) *Multitude: War and Democracy in the Age of Empire*, London, Penguin.

Herman, A., Coombe, R. J. & Kaye, L. (2006) 'Your second life?: Goodwill and the performativity of intellectual property in online digital gaming', *Cultural Studies*, vol. 20, no. 2–3, pp. 184–210.

Isbell, S. (2013) *LittleBigPlanet* update: 8 million levels! *PlayStation Blog* [online] 1 July. Available at: http://blog.us.playstation.com/2013/07/01/littlebigplanet-update-8-million-levels/ (accessed 1 July 2013).

Jenkins, H. (2011) 'DIY media 2010: video and gaming culture (part two)', *Confessions of an Aca-fan: The Official Web-log of Henry Jenkins* [online], 14 January. Available at: http://henryjenkins.org/2011/01/diy_media_2010_video_and_gamin_1.html (accessed 5 August 2013).

Kearney, M. C. (2007) 'Productive spaces: girls' bedrooms as sites of cultural production', *Journal of Children and Media*, vol. 1, no. 2, pp. 126–141. doi:10.1080/17482790701339126

Last minute big planet (2011) Video [online]. Directed by David Hall and Shaggy Shanahan. Themis Media, USA. Available at: http://www.mediamolecule.com/blog/article/escapist_recreates_littlebigplanet/ (accessed 14 August 2013).

McRobbie, A. & Garber, J. (1976) 'Girls and subcultures', in *Resistance through Rituals: Youth Subcultures in Post-war Britain*, eds. S. Hall & T. Jefferson, London, HarperCollins, pp. 209–222.

Mortensen, T. (2003) 'The geography of a non-place', *Dichtung Digital: A Journal of Arts and Culture in Digital Media* [online], 4/2003 (30). Available at: http://dichtung-digital.de/2003/issue/4/mortensen/index.htm (accessed 14 August 2013).

Mosco, V. (2004) *The Digital Sublime: Myth, Power, and Cyberspace*, Cambridge, The MIT Press.

Oldenburg, R. (1989) *The Great Good Place: Cafés, Coffee Shops, Community Centers, Beauty Parlors, General Stores, Bars, Hangouts and how they Get you through the Day*, New York, Paragon House.

Perrone, D. (2010) 'Gender and sexuality in the field: a female ethnographer's experience researching drug use in dance clubs', *Substance Use and Misuse*, vol. 45, no. 5, pp. 717–735.

Putnam, R. D. (2000) *Bowling Alone: the Collapse and Revival of American Community*, New York, Simon & Schuster.

Pybus, J. (2007) 'Affect and subjectivity: a case study of Neopets.com', *Politics and Culture* [online], (2). Available at: http://www.politicsandculture.org/2009/10/02/jennifer-pybus-affect-and-subjectivity-a-case-study-of-neopets-com/ (accessed 1 June 2013).

Ritzer, G. & Jurgenson, N. (2010) 'Production, consumption, prosumption: the nature of capitalism in the age of the digital 'prosumer'', *Journal of Consumer Culture*, vol. 10, no. 1, pp. 13–36.

Robinson, W. & Simon, B. (2013) *Meaningfulness in Digital DIY: Creative Labour in LittleBigPlanet*. International Conference on Japan Game Studies at Ritsumeikan, pp. 24–26, May, Kyoto: University in Kyoto.

Shank, B. (1994) *Dissonant Identities: The Rock'n'roll Scene in Austin, Texas*. Hanover, NH, Wesleyan University Press.

Soja, E. W. (1996) *Thirdspace: Journeys to Los Angeles and other Real-and-imagined Places*, Malden, MA, Blackwell.

Sotamaa, O. (2010) 'Play, create, share?: console gaming, player production and agency', *The Fibreculture Journal* [online], 16. Available at: http://sixteen.fibreculturejournal.org/play-create-share-console-gaming-player-production-and-agency/ (accessed 25 May 2013).

Stahl, G. (2001) 'Tracing out an Anglo-Bohemia: musicmaking and myth in Montréal', *Public* [online], 22–23. Available at: http://pi.library.yorku.ca/ojs/index.php/public/article/view/30328 (accessed 7 May 2013).

Straw, W. (1991) 'Systems of articulation, logics of change: communities and scenes in popular music', *Cultural Studies*, vol. 5, no. 3, pp. 368–388.

Straw, W. (2004) 'Cultural scenes', *Loisir et société* [*Society and Leisure*], vol. 27, no. 2, pp. 411–422.

Things to make and do in LittleBigPlanet (2008). *EDGE Online* [online], 5 August. Available at: http://www.edge-online.com/features/things-make-and-do-littlebigplanet/ (accessed 10 July 2013).

Tolino, A. (2009) 'Beyond play: analyzing player-generated creations', *Gamasutra* [online], 14 May. Available at: http://www.gamasutra.com/view/feature/4008/beyond_play_analyzing_.php (accessed 16 May 2009).

VGChartz (2013) *Video Game Charts, Game Sales, Top Sellers, Game Data*. [Online Database] Available at: http://www.vgchartz.com/gamedb/?name=little bigplanet (accessed 30 May 2013).

Westecott, E. (2011) *Crafting play: Little Big Planet. Loading…: the journal of the Canadian Game Studies Association* [online], 5 (8), 90–100. Available at: http://journals.sfu.ca/loading/index.php/loading/article/view/99 (accessed 2 April 2013).

Woo, B. (2012) 'Alpha nerds: cultural intermediaries in a subcultural scene', *European Journal of Cultural Studies*, vol. 15, no. 5, pp. 659–676. doi:10.1177/1367549412445758

Zhao, S. (2003) 'Toward a taxonomy of copresence', *Presence: Teleoperators and Virtual Environments*, vol. 12, no. 5, pp. 445–455.

Zittrain, J. (2008) *The Future of the Internet – and How to Stop It*, New Haven, CT, Yale University Press.

Shams Bin Quader and Guy Redden

APPROACHING THE UNDERGROUND

The production of alternatives in the Bangladeshi metal scene

This article aims to shed light on how and why the underground urban metal scene in Bangladesh came into existence, and why it takes the forms it takes in this post-colonial country. Consistent with much recent work about alternative rock, it is argued that the concept of scene is helpful in this task because it allows a framework through which to understand how multiple elements come together but never fully cohere into a unified subcultural whole that has a 'straightforward' relationship with a cultural locality. Based on interviews with key figures in the scene, ethnographic observation and textual analysis, the article proposes that urban youths' frustration with the poor state of conditions in the country is channelled into a passion to build an alternative space. The exploration of foreign musical styles and the fantasy worlds of metal allow participants to occupy 'another place'. While participants assert the distinction of their music from mainstream rock and pop, one of the main findings is that they are not much concerned about the idea of selling out to the corporate music industry if they become popular. Rather, translocal connections with other underground scenes existing elsewhere are emphasized in a local scene that remains tied to the activities of a largely middle-class, part-time, male population of artists who share particular social and economic resources. These resources afford their participation in the metal scene. The findings lead to questions about the extent to which the scene reproduces alternative rock discourses about authenticity and implicit critiques of capitalism, and also whether its transnationalism contributes to the hybridization of global cultural forms.

One hot Friday afternoon in January 2012, in the Agargaon area of Dhaka, the parking lot of a very drab venue, The National Library Auditorium, attracts a few dozen teenagers and 20-something guys, the majority dressed in black, with

Iron Maiden, Megadeth, Metallica, Slayer and Slipknot T-shirts, long hair, piercings, cigarettes and skull neck chains and rings scattered across their bodies. The parking lot soon fills to a throng of over a hundred, all of whom eventually shift inside to hear the distinctive, growing riff of Metallica's 'Enter Sandman'. Most of the audience rush to the front of the stage and start head banging and shouting out loud while interacting with the performers onstage in a mix of immense intensity. As band after band takes to the dark stage, cheap lights, sound system and dry ice combine with the wall of sound to smother time and everyday. Enter night, off to never-never land.

Such a mix of sweat, distortion and visceral release has been much repeated in alternative metal and punk scenes around the world. However, such acts also come in multiple variations. In this article, we examine what might be distinctive about one such variant – the Bangladeshi underground metal scene – in light of the now considerable cultural studies literature regarding alternative youth collectivities centred on popular music.

The concept of subculture holds a key position in the history of cultural studies. The Birmingham School's work in the area in the 1970s provided a model and impetus for a new generation of scholars who have since identified distinctive domains of youth cultural practice across popular culture, such as the style and culture of teddy boys, mods, skinheads and punks (Clarke *et al*. 1976, Hebdige 1979, Hall and Jefferson 1993, Colegrave and Sullivan 2001, Simonelli 2002, Clark 2003, Hodkinson and Deicke 2007, Williams 2007). Early on in this research, working-class youth rebellion expressed through musical style was not only taken to indicate the homology between cultural form and social grouping (Willis 1978), but also the promise of a kind of popular resistance in youth's everyday practices.

By the 1990s, however, subculture would be displaced from its position as the central concept in research about the music-related cultures of young people (Hesmondhalgh 2005, Bennett 2011). In stressing stylistic clarity, unity of purpose and relatively stable meanings and working-class identities, subculture seemed to lack the explanatory power necessary to address the complex field of cultural practices, and symbolic and material resources characteristic of youth lives. Bennett (2011) affirms as much, noting that the 'post-subcultural turn', was a consequence of:

> a general postulation [that] held that youth identities – and indeed social identities per se – had become more reflexive, fluid and fragmented due to an increasing flow of cultural commodities, images and texts through which more individualized identity projects and notions of self could be fashioned. (p. 493)

For scholars working in the tradition of cultural studies, it thus no longer made sense to think of specific youth cultures as distinct constellations or as practices that operate separately from mainstream culture, in a relationship of binary opposition.

Instead, Maffesoli's (1996) concept of the 'neo-tribe' was one alternative concept used to capture the looser affiliations of young people who are inclined to move between and identify with a range of cultural styles available to them (Bennett 1999). Meanwhile, as neo-tribes emphasized elective participation and the instability of personal identity, Will Straw (1991) revisited the idea that musical cultures are linked to place by theorizing the term 'musical scene', which he defined as 'cultural space in which a range of musical practices coexist, interacting with each other within a variety of processes of differentiation, and according to widely varying trajectories of change and cross-fertilization' (p. 371).

Questions remain about how these concepts intersect and overlap with each other and the degree to which scene, neo-tribe and subculture raise different possibilities for empirical inquiry by suggesting certain recurring relationships that can be mapped across contexts. For instance, the neo-tribes approach raises the possibility that musical cultures are related to broader developments in consumer culture and late modernity, which have arguably loosened how structural conditions related to ethnicity and class influence young people's cultural practices. The scenes perspective, on the other hand, draws attention to cultural geography and the interpretation of localized musical forms and questions about the nature of place in a world where the social space in which youth culture emerges is increasingly a 'product of relations and interconnections from the very local to intercontinental' (Massey 1998, p. 125).

In this article, we draw selectively from these debates in order to frame and develop an empirical study of a musical culture that appears to have characteristics associated with both subcultures and scenes. The Bangladeshi underground metal scene is distinguished from the mainstream by its participants and involves expressions of resistance. It is also, however, a product of global cultural flows, one consequence of which is that the scene lacks clearly defined boundaries in relation to genre and style. Nonetheless, we seek to understand the emergence of a nominally subcultural music scene centred on international metal genres in the distinctive locale of a post-colonial developing country, where the musicians responsible for production express sentiments towards local situations through the global cultural resources available to them. A central concern in our discussion is to assess both the usefulness and the limitations of theoretical models largely developed in Western and Anglophone countries in explaining the distinctive configurations of symbolic, social and economic elements mobilized in a particular post-colonial scene that our findings reveal to be shaped by both local and translocal interconnections of specific kinds.

For this study, a total of 14 participants involved with the scene were interviewed in 2012 (13 men and 1 woman) using a semi-structured format with open-ended questions about how the informants became involved in the scene, their views on it and the ways they participate in it. All of them are either musicians or music enthusiasts who took on roles as organizers of the gigs and recordings through which the scene is formed. Only one of the participants derived their principal income from the underground music scene. Ten participants had jobs in various media industries (including marketing and business communications), while three participants were students at universities. Based on their parents' professional and business occupations and areas of residence, the majority of the participants come from middle-class or upper middle-class backgrounds in Dhaka, the capital city of Bangladesh. A summary of the details of these participants anonymized by pseudonyms can be found in table 1. Participant observation was also undertaken at five alternative scene gigs and five mainstream[1] gigs, and public documents including album artwork were collected as part of the research.

Bangladesh and the formation of the alternative

Bangladesh is a post-colonial country occupying the eastern part of the territory historically known as Bengal. It was part of the British Empire until 1947 when Bengal was divided into East Bengal and West Bengal to separate Hindu and Muslim populations, respectively. In 1955, it became part of the state of Pakistan (as the region of East Pakistan) because of its Muslim majority, despite being located over 1,000 km from the rest of the country and no strong ethnic links existing between the areas. Bangladesh became a country within the lifetime of many of its living adults through the Liberation War in 1971. Since this time, the country has experienced political unrest, widespread corruption, lack of infrastructural development, crippling inflation, poverty and frequent changes of government, as well as large-scale flooding due to cyclones. The major cities of Bangladesh, like Dhaka, enjoy comparatively better transport and utility infrastructures, such as roads and electricity. They are also hubs for primary, secondary and tertiary educational facilities. The population of Dhaka has a greater concentration of the educated middle class and upper middle class, whereas the population of the rural areas of Bangladesh is predominantly less-educated agricultural workers (Wahid 2006, Hamid 2010).

Given Bangladesh's recent history, it is perhaps not surprising that there is no academic work of note in English about popular music in the country. Ethno-musicological literature in English is more often concerned with Bengali folk music than with Bangladeshi music (for instance, in the *Cambridge Encyclopedia of Music*). There is a small literature about popular music practices among the Bangladeshi diaspora (Huq 2006, Quader 2009), but much of the focus is on how Bangladeshi elements form part of hybrid genres such as Bhangra, created by youth of South Asian origin in the UK. Given the paucity of academic literature about contemporary Bangladeshi rock music, in what

TABLE 1 Summary of details of the participants.

	Pseudonym	Age	Sex	Occupation outside scene	Occupation in scene	Class of family	Years in scene
1	Tariff	28	M	Marketing strategist at music company	Front man of popular underground metal band	Middle	9
2	Ridwan	36	M	Business	Drummer; owner of a mid-level record label and sound system company	Upper	25
3	Zakaria	20	M	Student	Guitarist of a new underground metal band	Middle	3
4	Mahbub	28	M	Musician, head of PR at music company	Front man of popular underground band	Middle	8
5	Ismail	28	M	Creative professional	Guitarist of mid-level underground rock band	Middle	10
6	Ranjib	29	M	Graphics designer	Owner of indie record label and manager of online promotions for bands	Middle	5
7	Alisha	25	F	Freelance music journalist	Freelance drummer; gig organizer	Middle	7
8	Nuruddin	38	M	Producer, TV channel	Organizer of mixed albums	Middle	13
9	Hasib	31	M	Business	Drummer of disbanded veteran underground metal band	Upper middle	16
10	Adil	34	M	Senior creative director	Front man of popular underground metal band	Upper middle	20
11	Kamran	17	M	Student	Guitarist of new underground metal band	Middle	9
12	Amer	21	M	Student	Drummer of mid-level underground rock band; producer in scene; gig organizer	Middle	10
13	Mostafiz	26	M	Musician, bank officer	Drummer of mid-level underground rock band; gig organizer	Middle	6
14	Jahangir	25	M	Music promoter	Owner of underground gig organizing company	Middle	15

follows, we depict the underground and mainstream music scenes mainly through our fieldwork findings.

According to Graham (2010), underground music is a practice and cultural philosophy that exists outside the mainstream. Musicians, music critics and music-related online sites often refer to underground music as music that is not corporately sponsored, by choice. 'Underground' is also sometimes combined with the concepts of independent music, counterculture and subculture. Bangladeshi commentators have come to use the term to denote a scene dominated by heavy rock and metal, providing, in the words of a sympathetic anonymous journalist for the English-language newspaper, *The Daily Star*, an 'outlet through which to channel the frenetic nervous energy of teenagers'. Among the hallmarks of underground music are an 'emphasis on originality' and the freedom of 'bands to shine in their preferred styles, without having to conform much to suit the mainstream'. For this journalist, the underground scene is also marked by 'great camaraderie' and 'an openness and inclusiveness that is sadly lacking from many other spheres of life in this country' (STS 2010).

Although 'underground' appears to be a term of convenience that is interchangeable with synonyms like 'alternative', those active in the scene generally concur with these sentiments. Research participant Jahangir states:

> From my perspective, the underground is something that has not been endorsed, that is something that nobody has looked into or cared for, and something that comes from different set of audience who find their own niche in music. They try to find this sort of music out, they try to build communities around it, and they are not into media coverage or gaining mainstream popularity.

When the participants of this research were asked what the underground means to them, the most common responses highlighted the non-commercial focus of the bands, their creative independence from a mainstream audience and industry demands, and the fact that they produced music for themselves. Jahangir explains that it is about audiences and musicians who converge around different, 'non-endorsed' music and then 'try to build communities around it' rather than seeking 'media coverage or gaining mainstream popularity'. The scene originated in the 1980s but really gathered momentum in the early 2000s. Mahbub explains:

> It all started in Bangladesh [with] some bands who started covering bands like Metallica, GNR [Guns 'N' Roses] and other rock and alternative bands. We used to go to the shows to see bands like Sellout, Breach, Nemesis, Artcell. Then some heavy bands came out like 666, Kral, Aurthohin, your own band … – even a huge band like Aurthohin started off from this UG [underground] scene. The main idea was that doing a different kind of music [*sic*], not sounding commercial. People who are inspired and influenced by foreign bands used to organize shows and play covers of their favourite bands. Then these musicians started to compose their own music as well, with heavy influences from the foreign bands.

Long-timer Ridwan reflects on how in the late 1980s bands like Warfaze and Rockstrata started covering hard rock and metal songs – a sound that was completely new at that time in Bangladesh – resulting in a new community of kids running weekly gigs in small venues (e.g. local schools), using music gear purchased by their families. It was not until the late 1990s, however, that the music of local underground metal and alternative rock bands became an identifiable presence in the local recording market. The compilation album *Chcharpotro* was released in 2000 by the record label, G-series (an upcoming major record label at that time). Many agree that this album, which was the first of several similar discs, announced the birth of the underground scene in a form that is still recognizable today. Before this, in Nuruddin's words, 'The people of Bangladesh didn't even know that there were bands here who were playing metal, hard rock, alternative rock and also composing with Bengali lyrics'.

Most informants said that metal genres were the basis of the scene. However, nobody expressed any hard and fast rules about styles of metal or even the fact that metal or hard rock is compulsory. Variations mentioned included heavy metal, thrash metal, death metal, grunge rock, psychedelic rock, punk rock, progressive rock, alternative rock, jazz and folk fusion amongst others. For Tariff, 'Underground music comprises a range of different musical genres that operate outside of mainstream culture'. Ismail talks of:

> the commercial or mainstream being populated with pop or rock genres, and the alternative scene with so much more diverse genres … Now we have a lot of bands playing different genres of music, but I believe that they are trying different things on their own, sort of like the DIY philosophy of punk.

It seems then that independence from mainstream styles is the main criterion of underground status, rather than a substantive definition of musical style based on permitted genres. With this in mind, in the next section, we turn to the cultural ethos of the scene before considering the social, technological and economic processes that make its expressive forms possible.

The alternative ethos

While musical genre may be flexible in the underground scene, one of the key themes running throughout the interviews was a sense of distinction the participants made between the underground and more mainstream cultural and political norms. As suggested above, however, the distinctiveness of the underground is due less to the fact that it has a thought-out platform and more to do with opening up alternative spaces of apparent freedom and creativity. According to our research participants, the history of the scene's development is linked to a whole range of bands identified as local pioneers and/or influences that come from abroad. The scene is more a matter of 'family resemblances' and contingent social links among a 'community of the different', as opposed to a fixed canon or code. For instance, Ridwan recounts how he once discussed the scene's origins with a sound engineer who had acquired some new amps from the USA in the 1970s and loaned them to young artists, including Miles (now considered mainstream Bangla rock by most), for gigs and jamming sessions in small venues. It was the mere fact of having a new focal point, a togetherness borne of doing something different that seemed most important. Indeed, Ridwan notes further that the draw of a new focal scene that stood apart from traditional or mainstream music was key:

> I believe that whatever socio-historical or political issues are there in a country, and especially at a time when the country just survived a war of nine months [Liberation War], music is something that heals the people and brings them together. So I think, at this critical time of our social and cultural history, the UG scene as it became known … was born. People involved with this scene were young musicians trying new sounds, new western influences and had a passion for trying something different.

In an important sense then, members of the scene define it in terms of a freedom from aesthetic and commercial constraints. This in turn allows members to do what they wish, rather than adhering to a fully thought-out alternative to which all must conform or belong. When asked what people get from the scene, there is often the suggestion that the compulsion to seek out alternatives is influenced by the social environment in which young people grow up. For instance, according to Nuruddin, those youth who became part of the metal/alternative rock scenes were looking for an outlet and a space to express their thoughts and emotions. He says:

> The political situation in our country has been quite poor for the past 15–20 years. So there may have been a frustration amongst the youth. They didn't have much scope to do anything so maybe they took up these foreign genres of music and wanted to express their creativity in a new space.

A number of respondents also agreed that these developments were made possible because the mainstream music scene in the late 1990s did not provide enough innovation and novelty to satisfy urban youth. At the same time, playing foreign genres like heavy metal and hard rock and covering songs from Metallica and Megadeth were taboo in the homes of many youth. Parents did not understand this music, in part because playing the guitar and being in a band was not considered the proper thing to do. These activities were instead associated with abusing drugs, and thus parents, schools and professional musicians were wary of the emerging sounds and practices linked to metal.

As a result, a sense of rebellion surrounded the playing of metal in Bangladesh during the late 1990s. Research participant Hasib, for example, explains:

> Socially, this sort of music was not accepted. Garage bands were not allowed. We got a lot of complaints. So playing this genre of music [metal and rock] became a rebellious thing, because all our parents and neighbours hated that we did this.

The youth were also inclined to play metal because the local mainstream music scene was dominated by pop and folk music, which was 'not enough'. Research participants Ranjib and Alisha explain:

> This death or thrash metal has become so popular with the youth maybe because we had that sense of rebel and fighting back in all of us, and this sort of music just allowed us to go there and find some peace in expressing ourselves.

While 1980s bands paved the way by playing metal, by the late 1990s, with access to cable TV (music channels) and the Internet, youth discovered new and different genres, which would come to be focal points for their rebellion against the mainstream and the problems of Bengali society as a whole. For Jahangir, this new music included a combination of playing distorted guitars and 'talking about political issues, the youth and their frustrations'. Such themes could not be aired through love songs, and so aesthetic and social rebellion combined together in a cocktail of distortion, energy and politics. The creative space of underground gigs and jam pads allowed young people, principally men, to express their anger about the numerous problems of society[2] since there was little censorship involved here. While many of the bands write lyrics 'about political problems, aggression, frustration and rebelling against the downfalls of our society' (Ranjib and Alisha), the fantasy lyrical worlds of metal also allow indirect and figurative ways of expressing the frustration. So while research participant Amer explains 'With my band, we write about social problems, problems faced by our youth etc.', it is also true that 'My band's songs and music always ha[ve] metaphorical meanings'. Likewise for research participant Mostafiz, social commentary merges with the more affective and indirect possibilities of darkness: 'We write about political problems, love and even hate. Especially amongst the metal bands, the themes [of] hate, darkness, satan worship, anti-god etc. are quite popular'.

In an important way then, the scene involves patterns of symbolic resistance that bear similarities to other rebellious musical movements like punk (Colegrave and Sullivan 2001, Gimarc 2005) or grunge (Strong 2011). Metal has also been linked with rebellion in other developing Asian countries. For instance, according to Baulch (2003), the death/thrash metal scene in Bali came into existence in the early 1990s and served as a critique of the accelerated tourism development of the country. In this context, the aesthetic qualities of metal also served as a means of protest against other more popular genres of music like reggae, which was associated with tourism. These metal artists showed their disapproval of rapid tourism development and its impact on local cultures and heritage, but they did so in complicated forms of symbolic expression that were neither wholly critical of the government nor the capitalistic youth ideology evident in Bali (Baulch 2003). Unlike the Balinese death/thrash scene, however, the metal scene in Bangladesh did not come into existence as a movement against a particular service or industrial sector. Rather, the Bengali scene included a kind of generalized resistance to commercial mainstream music and social issues associated with political unrest, which we would link to an ethos documented in early work on subcultures in the UK (Hebdige 1979, Clarke 1981, Hall and Jefferson 1993). Having said that, however, the Bengali metal scene is also less organized than some other more explicitly politicized underground scenes evident in Russia (Orlova 1991), Hungary (Szemere 2001) or even within British anarcho-punk (Gosling 2004) communities, where stronger levels of exclusivity and shared philosophies are in evidence.

Affording the alternative

Having examined the rationale for participation, the question arises, how does one become a participant in this scene? On what terms and using what resources are people able to create that which is culturally alternative?

The underground is a small-scale but intense environment in which audience members and performers invest a great deal of energy and time. There is basically no expectation that playing in the scene is a matter of making money. The majority of mainstream artists are also full-time musicians, making an earning from their music careers. The artists in the underground scene, however, are generally not full-time musicians. They have separate careers and they do not usually make money off their music. Indeed, informants describe what might be understood as a break-even economy which includes personal investment in equipment, recording studios, practice pads and gig slots in the hope that sufficient financial return will help to sustain further involvement in the scene. As Ranjib explains, 'What happens here is that a few friends usually get together, make a band, do a few shows. Then if they become a bit popular, they look for promotion, interviews and try to land slots at bigger shows' – where they are more likely to earn a decent fee rather than have to 'push sell' – that is pay for gig and record slots in order to gain exposure. The costs of participation can be defrayed by taking on additional organizing roles in the scene, including gig promotion and volunteering during gigs. However, the most common element that enables bands to sustain activity amid the vagaries of uncertain returns is the effective subsidy from their own careers outside the scene. As research participant Adil explains:

> So either you have to be a music director, or you have to have a job and music has to be your hobby. Otherwise you are finished. (Laughs) If you want to do UG music in this country, then you have to be extremely passionate about it, and accept the fact that you won't make any money from this; it can't be anything more than your hobby.... [W]hatever money we make, we invest it back on the band.

Although money is seen as a constant challenge and not as the intended reward, the flip side of this is that artists/participants are limited to those who can afford to subsidize involvement in a pro-am model by bringing pre-existing social and economic resources to it. In the early days, according to Hasib:

> We organized our own shows, sold our own tickets to our families, made them come to our concerts, and actually forced them. (Laughs) We didn't even know that we [were] labeled as the underground scene. We were just doing our own thing. This was in the '90s. So some people, rich people, this is the demographic that I'm talking about, could actually afford to buy the guitars, ... could afford to listen to foreign music, ... [and] had access to these things.

While Hasib is unusually frank about wealth, others also mention how its affordances underlie the mobilization of the scene. The most important site for the formation of bands was English medium schools, prestigious institutions where students learn in English as the medium of instruction. Not only does an English-language school education ensure that one has the linguistic ability – educational capital – to consume and learn to produce international music styles, but it also allows for networking with those of like mind. In the 1990s, the students of many English medium schools gained access to cable TV and started to watch and be influenced by foreign music and genres through MTV and other similar music channels. Some of these kids also had the opportunity to travel abroad, and bring back with them cassettes and eventually CDs of foreign artists, which they shared with their friends and classmates. Many of them started to learn different Western instruments, from a handful of music schools that taught these skills, formed bands and even played a few gigs in their school fields and basketball courts.

The economic conditions of possibility of the scene are thus twofold. On the one hand, to become part of the scene, one has to have a way to cover the costs, including those associated with renting and using shared practice and performance spaces. On the other hand, more than money, key social networks that link to influential cultural intermediaries (Bourdieu 1984, p. 16) in the scene are also important for access to shared spaces and potential collaborators. Who you know and who approves of your music are important to be a successful member of the scene. The most influential people are often called *Murubbis* (a Bengali term which translates roughly to mean, veterans) or *Boro Bhais* (another Bengali term translates to mean, big brothers). Alisha explains:

> When a young guy wants to start doing music, he has to start from the underground scene. But there are a number of challenges he faces. He needs family support, monetary support to buy gear and take classes. Then if he is good, and if he gets in a band, ... his band also has to have connections with the organizers. Otherwise they won't get any shows. There is a lot of lobbying involved. The concept of big brother, *Murubbi*, is a moderator, gate-keeper, very influential person. They are usually the band members of big bands in the underground scene like Cryptic Fate, Powersurge, Mechanix, Severe Dementia, Aurthohin, etc. They have a lot of power ... to decide who plays and who doesn't in a concert, who gets a slot in a mixed album and who doesn't, etc. Most importantly, they have a power over the organizers because they are usually the headlining bands.

Research participants Amer, Kamran and Mostafiz take this notion a step further, noting that there are different big brothers depending on a band's level of success and the areas where they operate in Dhaka city. For example, if a band is coming from a Scholastica school (a renowned English medium school in Dhaka) and is trying to break into the underground scene, they would need support from other Scholastican bands.

On *not* not selling out

One of the key findings of the research is that participants do not talk about 'making it' as such, beyond the idea of becoming established in the scene. They tend to use a highly affective vocabulary about passion and freedom to describe the intrinsic rewards of being involved. This appears consistent with findings of other studies of 'indie' and 'underground' scenes where a key aspect of the ethos is that one should not compromise aesthetic autonomy and integrity by seeking mainstream or commercial success. Claims of authenticity which separate music with value from that with no value are normal in rock culture, and they centre on how ethical judgments are made about music 'in relation to ideas about the workings of a capitalist system', as represented by the mainstream music industry (Keightley 2001, p. 111). Accordingly, in Western rock and punk movements, the issue of becoming popular after having enjoyed alternative or indie status can be fraught and met by charges of selling out (Frith 1996, 2004a, 2004b) as in the cases of grunge superstars Nirvana (Azzerad 1992) and the Sex Pistols in punk (Adams 2008). What is distinctive in this scene, however, is not that participants repeat familiar underground and indie positions about maintaining artistic integrity while eschewing a discourse of intentionally 'making it'. Rather, while giving lip-service to this view, the vast majority of bands in the Bengali metal scene actually have little ethical problem with the idea of becoming commercially successful. Research participants Tariff, Mahbub, Zakaria and Ranjib note, for instance, that the underground scene in Dhaka can be used by some artists as the first step towards mainstream popularity. As Alisha puts it:

> All the bands that are doing well right now in Bangladesh, they were all underground at one point. Because before this niche crowd was very small, but it has grown a lot in the last 10 years and bands like Cryptic Fate and Artcell are really huge, even though they started from the underground scene.

Research participant Jahangir notes that it has been all too typical for bands to lose some of their underground fans in order to gain broader validation and move into the mainstream:

> You take some of these amazing UG bands to the media, they would take them to the audience, that would create a demand for this sort of music and then you would bring more and more bands from the UG to the mainstream. Some bands have actually done this like Artcell, Black, Cryptic Fate, Shunno, Bohemian, Nemesis etc. They have all successfully made this transition.

Given this pattern, it seems to be the case that the underground scene, is above all else, that place where musicians can experiment without fear of compromising their commercial standing. New fresh sounds have arisen as a consequence; alas when a band finds this new sound, they risk becoming popular in the underground scene and thus susceptible to mainstream success. Adil explains:

> I think there is a connection between the underground scene and the mainstream scene. The underground is where you experiment. The underground is where you do a lot of different things, which you are not afraid to sound bogus or really good. As you experiment, you hit something which is so fresh and so new, and that it can connect with the mass crowd. That is when the crossover happens.

It is in this sense that the underground metal scene in Dhaka is a kind of incubator for the new. Increased popularity is thus taken as a by-product of the development of innovative sounds that inevitably shape the popularity of particularly bands. Some stress that after a band gets popular and more seasoned in the scene, they may decide to break into the mainstream music scene *or* remain in the underground where they can cater to their core audience. But sometimes, bands apparently do not choose to cross over to the mainstream, it just happens due to the popularity of their music. As Amer and Kamran say of Artcell:

> I don't think they even dreamed that their songs would become such a hit to the mainstream audience. They created their metal songs for the UG crowd, but the mainstream crowd loved them as well. As a result, they became really huge both nationally and internationally.

Overall, 'making it', in the sense of becoming popular with audiences who do not frequent the scene, is not opposed. However, it is treated in a fatalistic and relatively disinterested way. Those artists who succeed by *exclusively* playing commercial pop, rock or folk *have to* cater to the mass crowd; they are seen as not being free to experiment with their music and are limited to a proven formula. But for most of the participants interviewed for this study, there does seem to be room enough for a transition from underground to mainstream recognition, particularly if audiences sense that key aesthetic principles are not compromised.

It is a rather strange situation for a scene labelled underground *not* to have specific ethical codes about selling out. The only time the concept was mentioned by any of the informants was when Adil was discussing a professional musician known to him, who makes a living from music. According to Adil, this full-time performing and recording musician 'suffers because he cannot always make the kind of quality of music he wants to. He has to sell out sometimes to cater to the commercial market and the mainstream audience'.

The translocal turn

At the same time, it is quite clear that, for most participants, this historical development towards the potential mainstreaming of artists is not killing off the underground. Almost all regard the future of the scene as bright. Before *Chcharpotro*, bands used to do more cover songs, but from the 2000s onwards, they started doing a lot more originals, still heavily influenced by foreign music. In many ways, the existence of a scene revolving around international genres depends on facility with English that many participants developed at English medium schools. However, the ability of artists to switch between English and Bengali has played an important role in allowing the development of a local audience in Bangladesh. Back in the early 2000s, the dominant language in the emerging underground scene was English. It provided an easily distinguishable boundary line with the mainstream scene, where the dominant language was obviously Bengali. By the mid-2000s, after the release of *Chcharpotro* and other similar albums, the majority of the bands started writing in Bengali, but their music still drew heavily on Western influences – very different from the music compositions and genres of the mainstream scene. Nowadays, a lot of underground bands write their own material in English because they want to distribute their music via foreign channels. It depends on the bands, their genres and their beliefs about which artistic trajectory they want to take. Mainstream artists have no choice (and many with no linguistic ability) to 'code switch' between languages in this way. They have to sing in Bengali, and they have to stick to lyrical themes that are relatable to the majority of people.

The bright future identified by most is often linked to the new possibilities of the Internet which promises a virtual hub for the local scene and a new kind of translocal dimension that is not confined to artists consuming foreign music and recreating its styles, but involves them sharing music in regional and global scenes. As Mahbub puts it, 'Internet is all we have. That is our lifeline. Without this, there would be no UG scene'. Ismail and Mostafiz believe that with English lyrics, great compositions and good production quality, artists can successfully relate to the international underground scenes. Bangladeshi bands such as Severe Dementia and Orator have released albums with foreign underground labels and have performed in underground concerts in other Asian countries. Ismail explains:

> Also, nowadays a lot bands make music for the international scene. My band for example, if we have two fans in Dhaka, we have two in Kuala Lumpur, two in Delhi, two in Bangkok. They are keener to listening to a new sound from a different country. If our music industry grows, I think we have a huge chance of taking our alternative scene to the globalized scenes.

This kind of synchronicity is possible currently in Bangladesh due to the urban middle-class youth's access to the Internet and social network sites (especially Youtube), not to mention the accessibility of cable television and the availability of pirated foreign music in local stores. In the 1980s and 1990s, there was a certain lag between the kinds of globally popular music and the music performed by cover bands in the underground scene. For example, in the 1990s, some of these bands would cover Deep Purple, Led Zeppelin, Scorpions, Iron Maiden, etc. There may have been a lag of about 10 years, due to lack of accessibility. However, now the Internet forms the basis of informants' optimism about the future as it allows real-time connection and a sense of being contemporaries with peers in other places. There is recognition that the Internet makes piracy easier, especially in a country without significant services for downloading paid-for musical content. As research participant Zakaria puts it, 'Over here, you get downloads for free. And no one is complaining. We don't have the proper legal systems at work, protecting the copyrights of artists'. Adil affirms 'I think piracy is a way of life. (Laugh)', while noting it has destroyed the careers of professional musicians. However, in the underground, most do not depend on income from music careers to live anyway. According to Mahbub:

The record labels are doing nothing. They will offer a deal. You give me a certain amount of money, I will publish and distribute your album all over Bangladesh. Nothing to do with royalty or copyrights. Whatever money is made from digital and CD sales of my music, will be kept by the record labels. What do I get out of this? My music will be out there. My CD will be available in the music stores.

Following this logic, the new possibilities for distributing music on the Internet mean at least there is no financial or geographical limitation on who the music can reach in an environment where significant earnings from music are unlikely. The Internet is also the primary media for the scene, at least in part because it allows for promotion and distribution that can otherwise require significant financial investment and labour.

It seems then that the online and transnational possibilities for the scene act as an outlet through which its integrity can be maintained. However, it is possible for artists to become more popular in Bangladesh and not be seen as selling out if this does not also involve aesthetic compromise. Above all, the Internet allows an extension of the scene via connection with like-minded peers working in similar experimental ways elsewhere. This signals a key difference from mainstream Bangla rock, which is also influenced by Western artists and sounds. The mainstream version of rock – practised by artists like Ayub Bacchu (from LRB), James (from Nagar Baul) and Habib, Fuad and Bappa (from Dal Chut) – is more clearly a cultural hybrid, an indigenized or localized form where the music, tonality, composition, arrangements and song structures are a fusion of English and Bengali song traditions, with the lyrics in Bengali. Such localized versions of global rock can also be found within the music of various artists around the world (Regev 2007). Similar to the Cantopop club and electronic music scene in Hong Kong, where the local DJs rewrite lyrics of popular tracks into local languages and dialects (Chew 2010) to form one instance of unique cultural hybridization, some Bangladeshi mainstream artists also rewrite lyrics and improvise music arrangements of popular English songs into Bengali and local styles. Examples include the track 'Bhule Gechi Kobe' (Ark 2008) by the mainstream popular band Ark (where the frontman is Hasan) which is a Bengali version of Starship's 'Nothing's Gonna Stop Us Now' (Starship 1987). However, the translocalism evident in the underground, which now extends to playing for non-Bangladeshi audiences, suggests that creating indigenized versions of Western genres is not the point of the scene.

Placing the Bangladeshi underground

Is the 'underground' perhaps simply a term of convenience or a misnomer that really only represents the process of rock entering the nation from abroad and becoming mainstream? It could be that the Bangladeshi case is similar to the way the term was used in Iran, where Nooshin (2005) argues that it was the label given to the music of artists who had yet to gain recognition in the public sphere. This would help to explain the most surprising finding of the research that participants in this underground scene largely think it possible to become popular without selling out.

However, taking this position would not explain clearly the characteristics that demand closer consideration, including the significance that international cultural forms can have when they are taken up in particular places. Indeed, the informants *also* have very little interest in intentionally 'making it' through the music industry. They want their music to be recognized by their international underground peers while at the same time maintaining the local space through non-professional, part-time cultural production.

The full set of characteristics of the Bangladeshi underground metal/ alternative rock scene is fully explained by neither subculture nor scene models, but each seems to have some purchase. It is quite clear that the scene involves particular signs of opposition in which aesthetic distinctiveness tends to be linked to alternative forms of social commentary directed towards the surrounding social environment. Although the notes of resistance do not cohere into anything programmatic, the clear alternative aesthetics and politics are consistent with what has traditionally been linked to the ethos of subcultures. Meanwhile, the tolerance of aesthetic diversity within discursive limits of rock genres deemed alternative, and the ongoing openness to international links suggest dynamics compatible with those accounted for in scene approaches. In other words, it is still useful to ask whether this is a 'subculture or scene?' because this question enables certain repeated dynamics of musical cultures to be highlighted even when no single type is confirmed. This failure to fully explain all aspects of actually existing cultures does not signify the redundancy of typological theories. Rather, it suggests both that interpretation of the overall logic of combined elements needs to recognize contextual factors, which is also to question underlying theoretical approaches regarding their power to explain distinctive relationships between social, cultural and economic elements evident on the ground.

Along these lines, some of the subcultural resemblances of the scene seem to make more sense when the post-colonial situation of Bangladesh is considered. Clear homologies of working-class resistance through aggressive aesthetic forms cannot convincingly be deduced, nor can middle-class versions of rock authenticity, despite concern with the integrity of the alternative in the Bangladeshi underground. Metal in the West has previously been considered to appeal to white suburban male youth who lack economic, social and physical power because it allows them compensatory expressions of rebellion and empowerment (Horrocks 1995). In this case, however, participation is allowed by social and economic affordances, and any disenfranchisement is not based on class marginality.

Rather it would appear that in the Bangladeshi underground, general dissatisfaction of educated, world-weary young men – and also their enthusiasm and passion – is channelled into a compensating experimental space that is distinctly other from local traditions, representing a fantasy release from social realities of an extremely difficult post-colonial nationhood while sometimes tackling issues 'head on' in lyrics. With recalcitrant economic and environmental realities underlying the situation and both major political parties who would promise a better future at each other's throats, it is no wonder that youth symbolic resistance is sublated into a broader alternative aesthetic of freedom and integrity rather than channelled into a clear activism that offers specific answers. For example, the cover of Cryptic Fate's album *Danob* (CrypticFate 2006a) shows faceless army figures with fire coming out of their heads, and the album name *Danob* when translated into English means 'Monster'. The lyrical themes of the whole album revolve around social injustice, oppression by the government on the general people, violence and aggression. The album features songs such as 'Raag' and 'Danob'. 'Raag' (CrypticFate 2006b) when translated into English literally means anger, and the lyrics of the song talk about grotesque violence and the act of murdering someone with one's bare hands. 'Danob' (CrypticFate 2006a) talks about a monstrous oppressive government regime which is greedy for money and power and will do anything necessary to the general people to get what they want. Other examples include Artcell's song 'Chilekothar Shepai' (Artcell 2004), which in English means, 'Soldier of the Attic'. The lyrics of this song talk about a man's (referred to as a soldier or fighter) struggle to survive in a corrupt and unjust society suffering from political disarray. This soldier is comfortable with the darkness but afraid to face the light outside because he knows that as soon as he ventures outside, his dreams and aspirations will be torn to shreds by society.

The lack of concern with selling out while maintaining such an alternative ethos also makes more sense when the situations of the participants are considered. The concept of selling out is a dimension of a broader rock discourse of authenticity which stresses the originality of rock (or punk) against generic and formulaic kinds of music (Keightley 2001). Yet the Bangladeshi underground was only possible because of cover bands playing already-existing music. It is the newness of the styles to the context that is more significant. In this light, we suggest that integrity is a better term to describe the concern for aesthetically creative and experimental work based on reworking imported resources. As Hibbett (2005) notes, rock authenticity derives from a long-standing romantic mass culture critique in which original music is seen to embody the imaginative virtues that capitalist industrialization destroys and which mass music commodities exemplify. However, while industrialization throws up its own issues (mainly experienced by rural to urban migrant labourers who are not involved in this scene), highly developed industrial or corporate capitalism is not among the principal problems in Bangladesh, nor singled out as significant targets of resistance in the scene. Given this and the privileged socio-economic status of participants, it makes less sense for those in the scene to resist 'the machinations of late-capitalist culture' as Overell (2010, p. 82) finds of the Melbourne grindcore scene, or to fixate on a particular sector of 'runaway capitalism' such as the tourism sector in Bali.

On a more practical level, the participants can only be active if they have money from elsewhere, including family wealth and careers in the mainstream cultural industries. The financial rewards of being a mainstream artist in Bangladesh are neither attractive nor worth the loss of integrity. Distinctive elements of the context – including widespread piracy and the relative modesty of rewards on offer in mainstream music careers compared to middle-class professions – mean that the choice between being a part-time or full-time musician with potential to garner a mainstream audience does not present itself as a major contrast between remaining authentically underground and selling out to corporate capitalism. Participants can afford to become and remain alternative, which is a chosen cultural position defined by aesthetics that neither entails structural social marginality in the sense identified in classical subculture theory nor its 'betrayal' in selling out. Nonetheless, our findings also suggest that the scene is far from being adequately characterized by post-subcultural concepts that stress temporary affiliations of participants among multiple fluid and unstable sociocultural groupings. Neo-tribes and similar theorizations that see contemporary youths as patrons of a 'supermarket of style' (Polhemus 1998) have little power to explain the network of committed organizers and small-scale collectives that endures into its third decade. More broadly, such concepts do not travel well to Bangladesh as the kind of extensively pluralized youth consumer culture they assume does not exist in the country.

Yet this should not be taken as an argument that ultimately the form in which the Bangladeshi underground exists can be explained purely by undifferentiated 'local factors'. This is where the concept of scene is especially pertinent. Hesmondhalgh (2005) notes that it is often used, without engaging its potential theoretical richness, to denote musical practices around a genre in a particular place. It is certainly true that, as Bennett and Peterson (2004, p. 4) note, 'local scenes develop in local ways with local sensibilities'. However, for present purposes, we argue that the value of the concept lies in raising critical issues about locality that militate against a latter-day interpretive essentialism of the local.

As Connell and Gibson (2003, p. 90) explain, there are clearly connections between popular music and place that are expressive of 'specific socio-economic and political contexts'. However, they are careful to specify the forms that music takes are not simply reflective of contexts as such but 'the positions of writers and composers within those contexts'. People are located in local space in certain ways that depend on specific sets of relationships with other actors, some of whom are in 'local' places and some in 'non-local' places. It is because of the positions and resources afforded to given actors that a distinctive scene can form. It is all too easy, as Hesmondhalgh (2005) fears, to lose the explanatory power of the concept by reducing 'scene' to a byword for purely local arrangements. The reality is more complex. The form of the Bangladeshi underground is intimately tied up with the particular positions of the middle-class young men in their local environment, and a key aspect of that positioning is distinctive relationships within and beyond Bangladesh. A cultural practice of reading the local and finding alternatives to it is afforded by international connections and a post-colonial context where middle-class status, educational networks, geographic mobility and facility with English allow participants to access transnational cultural forms that may be accessed/exist on different terms elsewhere.

By way of a final point, we would like to take this argument one step further in a context of musical and cultural globalization. As Bennett and Peterson (2004) note, many local scenes involve using 'music appropriated via global flows and networks to construct particular narratives of the local'. The combined local/transnational orientation of the contemporary cultural produc-tion in the Bangladeshi underground scene places it in relation to regional and global underground metal scenes. However, these days it is only minimally true that the Bangladeshi underground scene takes cultural resources from elsewhere and 'localizes' them. There may be cases in which this way of thinking about the localization of transnational cultural flows may be warranted. For instance, there is a great deal of work on hip hop that shows how its codes are adapted, mixed with local culture and enrolled into social commentary in various places outside of North America (Forman and Neal 2004, Alim *et al*. 2008). Yet, while their scene may have origins in covers of foreign bands, Bangladeshi underground artists today, assisted by the real-time translocal alliances possible through the Internet, see themselves as contributing to regional and global scenes that cut across places and do not reduce to a logic of primary centres of production and secondary sites for the reworking musical styles in the image of a receiving culture. There is little in underground practices that suggests participants are concerned with fusing international musical styles with distinctively local musical and lyrical traditions as might be the case say with mainstream 'Bangla rock'. Following O'Connor's (2002) critique of hybrid-ization theory in popular music studies, in which he argued punk scenes have characteristics that do not reduce to being variants of cultural forms from elsewhere, the translocal relations of production, consumption and affiliation of Bangladeshi underground artists complicate quite commonplace assertions that global flows of music get indigenized resulting in hybrid forms that mix local and global elements. Rather, participating in global genres in their own right and associated translocal networks would seem to form an important aspect of the local scene's displaced utopian and often escapist politics of moving beyond the travails and confines of a particular place.

Consequently, if scene is a good concept for raising the question of place regarding cultural formations in which various kinds of alliances across and between places are evident as originally proposed by Straw, it also supplies no specific theory of place as an answer. This is where both ongoing empirical work and theorization remain important.

Notes

1 All the informants of this study agreed that there are two main scenes in the Bangladesh music industry, namely the mainstream and the alternative scene. The mainstream artists cater to the mass public, so their songs, compositions, lyrics and genre are more suited towards this audience, as oppose to the alternative artists who cater to the niche crowd, whose orientations are much more international and niche crowd based. The majority of the artists of the mainstream scene of Bangladesh are full-time musicians making an earning from their music careers.

2 Including widespread corruption, lack of jobs and economic opportunities, social injustice, poor safety and security conditions, lack of infrastructural development, crippling inflation, as well as frequent natural disasters.

Notes on Contributors

Shams Bin Quader is a Masters of Philosophy candidate at the Department of Gender and Cultural Studies at the University of Sydney, where his thesis is about the alternative music culture of Bangladesh. He has more than six years of experience teaching at the university level at multiple universities in Bangladesh, and his research interests include popular music, cultural identity, diaspora, migration, new media and *online* SNS.

Guy Redden is a Senior Lecturer in the Department of Gender and Cultural Studies at the University of Sydney, where he was also Convenor of the Master of Cultural Studies by coursework programme for four years. His research concerns the intersections of culture and economy, with particular emphasis on media, organisational and alternative cultures.

References

Adams, R. (2008) 'The Englishness of English punk: sex pistols, subcultures, and nostalgia', *Popular Music and Society*, vol. 31, no. 4, pp. 469–488.

Alim, H. S., Ibrahim, A. & Pennycook, A. (2008) *Global Linguistic Flows: Hip Hop Cultures, Youth Identities, and the Politics of Language*, New York and London, Routledge.

Ark (2008) *Bhule gechi kobey* [I almost forgot] [online] Available at: http://www.youtube.com/watch?v=u-RgH90wZ2k (accessed 25 August 2013).

Artcell (2004) 'Chile Kothar Shepai', *Maxi Lyrics* [online] Available at: http://www.maxilyrics.com/artcell-chile-kothar-shepai-lyrics-ea22.html (accessed 12 May 2013).

Azzerad, M. (1992) 'Inside the heart and mind of Nirvana', *Rolling Stone*, 16 April, pp. 6–28.

Baulch, E. (2003) 'Gesturing elsewhere: the identity politics of the Balinese death/thrash metal scene', *Popular Music*, vol. 22, no. 2, pp. 195–215.

Bennett, A. (1999) 'Subcultures or neo-tribes? rethinking the relationship between youth, style and musical taste', *Sociology*, vol. 33, pp. 599–617.

Bennett, A. (2011) 'The post-subcultural turn: some reflections 10 years on', *Journal of Youth Studies*, vol. 14, no. 5, pp. 493–506.

Bennett, A. & Peterson, R. A., eds. (2004) *Music Scenes: Local, Translocal and Virtual*, Nashville, TN, Vanderbilt University Press.

Bourdieu, P. (1984) *Distinction: A Social Critique of the Judgement of Taste*, London, Routledge and Kegan Paul.

Chew, M. M. (2010) 'Hybridity, empowerment and subversiveness in Cantopop electronic dance music', *Visual Anthropology*, vol. 24, no. 1–2, pp. 139–151.

Clark, D. (2003) *The Death and Life of Punk, the Last Subculture*, New York, NY, Berg.

Clarke, G. (1981) 'Defending ski-jumpers: a critique of theories of youth subcultures', in *On Record: Rock, Pop, and the Written Word*, eds. S. Frith & A. Goodwin, London, Routledge, pp. 68–80.

Clarke, J., Hall, S., Jefferson, T. & Roberts, B. (1976) 'Subcultures, cultures, and class', in *Resistance through Rituals: Youth Subcultures in Post-war Britain*, eds. S. Hall & T. Jefferson, London, Routledge, pp. 9–74.

Colegrave, S. & Sullivan, C. (2001) *Punk*, New York, NY, Thunder's Mouth Press.

Connell, J. & Gibson, C. (2003) *Sound Tracks: Popular Music Identity and Place*, New York, NY, Routledge.

CrypticFate (2006a) 'Danob', *Music News* [online] Available at: http://musicbd-news.blogspot.com.au/p/cryptic-fate.html (accessed 12 May 2013).

CrypticFate (2006b) 'Raag', *Bangla Geetibitan* [online] Available at: http://lyricsbanglasong.wordpress.com/2011/09/07/rag%E0%A6%B0%E0%A6%BE%E0%A6%97-by-cryptic-fate-from-the-album-danob/ (accessed 12 May 2013).

Forman, M. & Neal, M. A. (2004) *That's the Joint! The Hip-hop Studies Reader*, New York and London, Routledge.

Frith, S. (1996) *Performing Rites*, Cambridge, MA and Oxford, Harvard University Press/Oxford University Press.

Frith, S. (2004a) 'What is bad music?', in *Bad Music*, eds. C. Washburne & M. Darko, New York, NY, Routledge, pp. 15–38.

Frith, S. (2004b) 'Why does music make people so cross?' *Nordic Journal of Music Therapy*, vol. 13, no. 1, pp. 64–69.

Gimarc, G. (2005) *Punk Diary: The Ultimate Trainspotter's Guide to Underground Rock, 1970–1982*, San Francisco, CA, Backbeat Books.

Gosling, T. (2004) '"Notfor sale": the underground network of anarcho punk', in *Music Scenes: Local, Translocal and Virtual*, eds. A. Bennett & R. A. Peterson, Nashville, TN, Vanderbilt University Press, pp. 168–181.

Graham, S. (2010) 'Where is the underground? in an age when music is available anywhere, anytime, where do you find the underground and what defines it?' *Journal of Music*, 1 August [online] Available at: http://journalofmusic.com/article/1187 (accessed 6 May 2013).

Hall, S. & Jefferson, T. (1993) *Resistance through Rituals: Youth Subcultures in Post-war Britain*, 2nd ed., London, Routledge.

Hamid, S. (2010) *Bangladesh and the United Nations*, Dhaka, The University Press Ltd.

Hebdige, D. (1979) *Subculture: The Meaning of Style*, New York, NY, Routledge.

Hesmondhalgh, D. (2005) 'Subcultures, scenes or tribes? None of the above', *Journal of Youth Studies*, vol. 8, no. 1, pp. 21–40.

Hibbett, R. (2005) 'What is indie rock?' *Popular Music and Society*, vol. 28, no. 1, pp. 55–77.

Hodkinson, P. & Deicke, W., eds. (2007) *Youth Cultures: Scenes, Subcultures and Tribes*, New York, NY, Routledge.

Horrocks, R. (1995) *Male Myths and Icons: Masculinity in Popular Culture*, London, Macmillan.

Huq, R. (2006) *Beyond Subculture: Pop, Youth and Identity in a Postcolonial World*, New York, NY, Routledge.

Keightley, K. (2001) 'Reconsidering rock', in *The Cambridge Companion to Pop and Rock*, ed. S. Frith, Cambridge, Cambridge University Press, pp. 109–142.

Maffesoli, M. (1996) *The Time of the Tribes: The Decline of Individualism in Mass Society*, London, Sage.

Massey, D. (1998) 'The spatial construction of youth cultures', in *Cool Places: Geographies of Youth Cultures*, eds. T. Skelton & G. Valentine, London, Routledge, pp. 122–130.

Nooshin, L. (2005) 'Underground, overground: rock music and youth discourses in Iran', *Iranian Studies*, vol. 38, no. 3, pp. 463–494.

O'connor, A. (2002) 'Local scenes and dangerous crossroads: punk and theories of cultural hybridity', *Popular Music*, vol. 21, pp. 225–236.

Orlova, I. (1991) 'Notes from the underground: the emergence of rock music culture', *Journal of Communication*, vol. 41, no. 2, pp. 66–67.

Overell, R. (2010) 'Brutal belonging in Melbourne's grindcore scene', *Studies in Symbolic Interaction*, vol. 35, pp. 79–99.

Polhemus, T. (1998) 'In the supermarket of style', in *The Clubcultures Reader: Readings in Popular Cultural Studies*, eds. S. Redhead, D. Wynne & J. O'connor, Oxford, Blackwell, pp. 199–219.

Quader, S. B. (2009) 'Impact of the British Bangladeshi musicians of London', *The Bangladesh E-journal of Sociology*, vol. 6, pp. 83–97.

Regev, M. (2007) 'Ethno-national pop-rock music: aesthetic cosmopolitanism made from within', *Cultural Sociology*, vol. 1, no. 3, pp. 317–341.

Simonelli, D. (2002) 'Anarchy, pop and violence: punk rock subculture and the rhetoric of class, 1976–78', *Contemporary British History*, vol. 16, no. 2, pp. 121–144.

Starship (1987) *Nothing's Gonna Stop Us Now* [online] Available at: http://www.youtube.com/watch?v=bBQVrCflZ_E (accessed 25 August 2013).

Straw, W. (1991) 'Systems of articulation logics of change: communities and scenes in popular music', *Cultural Studies*, vol. 5, no. 3, pp. 368–388.

Strong, C. (2011) *Grunge: Music and Memory*, Burlington, VT, Ashgate.

STS (2010) 'Underground music', *The Daily Star Newspaper* [online] Available at: http://archive.thedailystar.net/lifestyle/2010/10/03/centre.htm (accessed 28 April 2014).

Szemere, A. (2001) *Up from the Underground: The Culture of Rock Music in Post-socialist Hungary*, University Park, PA, Penn State University Press.

Wahid, Z. H. (2006) 'Middle class paradox and the problem of National Identity in Bangladesh', *Journal of the Asiatic Society of Bangladesh (HUMANITIES)*, vol. 51 [online] Available at: http://www.asiaticsociety.org.bd/journals/vol%2052/MIDDLE%20CLASS%20PARADOX%20AND%20THE%20PROBLEM%20OF%20NATIONAL%20IDENTITY%20IN%20BANGLADESH.html (accessed 15 July 2014).

Williams, J. P. (2007) 'Youth-subcultural studies: sociological traditions and core concepts', *Sociology Compass*, vol. 1, no. 2, pp. 572–593.

Willis, P. E. (1978) *Profane Culture*, London, Henley & Boston, Routledge & Kegan Paul.

Daniel Silver and Terry Nichols Clark

THE POWER OF SCENES

Quantities of amenities and qualities of places

This paper elaborates a general theory of scenes as multi-dimensional complexes of meaning embedded in material, local practices. It outlines techniques for measuring scenes empirically and shows how certain types of scenes provide environments in which new social movement (NSM) organizations (like human rights and environmental groups) tend to thrive. However universal and cosmopolitan the content of NSM goals, they appear to get much of their energy and support from the qualities that inhere in concrete local contexts.

We have worked with the concept of 'scene' for about a decade as members of 'The Cultural Amenities Project' with the University of Chicago Cultural Policy centre and subsequent research that has generated six monographs, papers and a major book (*Scenes: Culture and Place*, University of Chicago Press).[1] The concept emerged for us as a solution to a specific research problem. Our question was: how and why do amenities – operas, art galleries, restaurants and the like – influence community and urban development?

To answer this question, we downloaded data on hundreds of amenities for every US zip code, primarily from the US Census' ZIP Business Patterns and online business directories (yellow pages), as well as other sources. It quickly became clear, however, that it would be a mistake to focus too heavily on any single amenity. What mattered more than a contemporary art gallery, yoga studio or body-piercing studio in isolation was the overall picture they all generate together. This in turn suggested a different way of regarding places, one we analogize to *taking the scenic route*. On the scenic route, one does not simply go from point A to B as quickly as possible. Instead, one tunes into the qualitative character of the passing scenery: an awesome coastline, a quaint village, a foreboding mountain range.

'Scenic' thinking shifted our analytical approach to cities and neighbourhoods. The goal became understanding the styles of life they evoke. Instead of simply counting churches, for instance, we now were asking to what extent tradition formed the basis of legitimacy in a given scene. Churches certainly could feed into this type of legitimacy, but so could classical ballet companies or etiquette schools. The question for each amenity then became: 'To what kinds of scenes does it contribute?' And our descriptions of these scenes began taking forms like: 'one that tends to anchor legitimacy in personal self-expression, favor a transgressive style of theatricality, and attack the authenticity of the corporation'. Looking for scenes meant looking for the holistic but differentiated meanings of places.

The attraction of the concept lies in its grounded mobility. This twinning of seeming opposites is one of the centrepieces of Will Straw's (2001, p. 248) version of the concept: '"scene" seems able to evoke both the cozy intimacy of community and the fluid cosmopolitanism of urban life'. A similar sentiment informs our approach. When we describe a place as a scene, we are trying to capture the experiential attractions rooted in the on-going public life of its businesses, people, places of worship, activities – in the particular mix of concrete practices happening *here*. At the same time, these meanings are not exclusive to this place; we can find them elsewhere, even if to different degrees and in different combinations. To investigate scenes, in our conception, is to ask what is in the character of *this particular place* that may speak to *broader and more universal* themes?

This paper elaborates how these principles feed into our theory of scenes as multi-dimensional complexes of legitimacy, theatricality and authenticity that are embedded in material, local practices (Section 1). We then (Section 2) describe in somewhat more detail one key dimension of scenes – self-expressive legitimacy – and discuss techniques for locating scenes empirically (Section 3). We highlight self-expression because self-expressive scenes provide environments in which new social movement (NSM) organizations such as human rights or environmental groups tend to thrive (Section 4). Joining our amenities data with Census information, we find that NSMs tend to be located in distinctive places: dense, walkable neighbourhoods with more college graduate and non-white residents, higher crime, and, significantly, with amenities that evince the legitimacy of self-expression. There is, moreover, a strong interaction effect between walking and self-expression whereby self-expressive scenes strengthen the correlation between walking and NSMs. However universal and cosmopolitan the *content* of NSM goals, they appear to get much of their energy and support from the qualities that inhere in concrete local contexts. We conclude with a brief summary of on-going scenes analyses internationally and the prospects this research offers for humanistic social science.

1. A theory of scenes

While the concept has been loosely used by art and music critics for decades, academic researchers have focused on 'scenes' in multiple research traditions: to trace the role of national theatres and lifestyle communities in modernization processes; as niches for urban belonging in the metropolis that do not require nostalgia for the pre-modern village; or as linked to 'youth' as a specific phase of the life-course (Irwin 1977, Straw 2001, Blum 2003, Hitzler *et al.* 2005). Others feature specific genres, such as the jazz scene or the theatre scene (Bennett and Peterson 2004, Lena and Peterson 2008), or investigate how scenes sometimes gather around and animate social movements in bars and cafes (Haunss and Leach 2007). Still others highlight specific neighbourhoods or types of places: the Camden Town scene or the Haight-Ashbury scene or the Beach scene. In contrast to these, our usage emphasizes the styles of life these neighbourhoods support – 'neo-bohemian' or 'hippie', 'surfer' or 'spring break' – and how these might be similar or different in other locales [Silver *et al.* (2010) reviews these and other uses].

These works are not exactly a 'literature' in the sense of the product of an inter-connected research community cumulatively pursuing a scientific pro-gramme: they have largely emerged independently and in ignorance of one another. Still, our review helped in formulating our conception of scenes as the meanings expressed by the people and practices in a place [Haunss and Leach's (2007) review produced a similar result]. Our multi-dimensional theory of scenes incorporates some of the main themes stressed by others, such as exhibitionism and transgression (Blum 2003), local authenticity (Zukin 2009), among others. But we sought to place them in a more comprehensive and integrated framework.

Scenes analysis as we typically practice it revolves around several key premises. We stress *neighbourhoods*, rather than cities or nations, to capture local differences within and across these larger units; highlighting *physical structures*, such as dance clubs or shopping malls, roots scenes in concrete, identifiable gathering places; and including *persons*, described according to their race, class, gender, education, occupation, age and the like, captures the fact that a scene is defined not only by what is there but also who is there. At the same time, distinctive combinations of people, physical structures and places are articulated through particular *activities* (e.g. young tech workers attending a local area punk concert), and accounting for how they are joined together helps us generate a more refined picture. These combinations express *symbolic meanings* that define what is important about the experiences on offer in a place. In particular, we highlight meanings such as legitimacy, defining a right or wrong way to live; theatricality, an attractive way of seeing and being seen by others; and authenticity, a real or genuine identity. Finally, scenes have *publicness* and are available to passersby and deep enthusiasts alike.

While scenes may emerge and grow spontaneously, politics and policy influence them as well, especially those that take scenes as their objects: through debates about how to shape, sustain, alter or produce a given scene, how certain scenes attract (or repel) residents, firms and visitors, or how some scenes mesh with political sensibilities, voting patterns and specific organized groups, such as NSMs. These foci are part of a more general effort to retain the sensitivity to local complexity characteristic of ethnographers but disciplined by comparative methods. No single point is original to us, but joining these elements adds new insights bridging quantitative and qualitative traditions of social and cultural analysis.

1.1. Scenes as multi-dimensional complexes of meaning

'Scene' is a powerful conceptual tool for discerning the range and configurations of expressive meanings evinced in various places, for seeing the locatedness of cultural life. For the concept of scene nicely directs our focus, not at 'common values' or 'ways of life' hermetically sealed from 'other cultures', but rather at multiple, loosely binding, more flexible arrays of local meanings. People can choose to enter or leave different scenes; scenes facilitate more choices than primordial characteristics like race, class, national origin and gender. The concept is sufficiently open to include marginal as well as less transgressive configurations – not 'ways of life' or 'conditions of life' but looser 'styles of life' make the scene.

At the same time, 'scene' facilitates cross-case comparison. The concept focuses on the range of cultural meanings expressed in many activities and people that define the lifestyle of a place, including, but not restricted to, ethnic or class labels. This focus on lifestyle distinguishes 'scene' from 'milieu', as in the 'student milieu', which says little about the difference between frat party and vegan co-op. And because the cultural elements of a scene – glamour, corporateness, formality, charisma and the like – can be found in many places, we can pinpoint the precise character of one scene versus another by comparing how they combine these elements.

Take, for instance, three coffee shops in three different neighbourhoods. In the first, in a well-established, working-class classic ethnic neighbourhood, old men are sipping cappuccinos outside a café while their younger fellows play pool inside. Nearby, shoppers sift through baskets of zucchini and peppers at an outdoor fruit and vegetable market, and an afternoon mass is letting out at the church down the block. In the second, on a trendy, 'neo-bohemian' strip, young people sip coffee on an outdoor patio, typing on laptop computers or scribbling in Moleskine notebooks while indie rock floats through the air. In the third, located on the first floor of an office tower in a downtown financial district, professionals in power ties and pin-stripe suits are power lunching; beeping smartphones are slipped out of expensive handbags, and stock prices scroll along the television, which is tuned to Bloomberg TV. In each of these scenes, people are drinking coffee, and yet this mundane activity means something very different in these qualitatively different settings.

The challenge is to map and analyse how they differ. To do so, we translate these general ideas about scenes into an analytical model that can answer the question, 'What kind of scene is this?' in terms of both objective characteristics and symbolic meanings. Creating this model involves three major orienting assumptions for scenes analysis: holism, multi-dimensionality and combinatorial thinking.

1.1.1. Holism. We cannot look to any one type of amenity or activity to define the scene. Many neighbourhoods have some restaurants, shops, music venues and very likely a place of worship. This implies that the character of the scene does not inhere in any single amenity. We always have to look to collections, mixes and sets to get a read on what makes each scene distinctive. Other sociologists and economists of culture have analysed the qualitative characteristics of localities by measuring only one type of amenity, or a few, such as restaurants, museums or bookstores. We build on this work, and use amenities as key indicators for measuring scenes. We and our collaborators go further, however, by downloading and aggregating hundreds of different types of amenities for every zip code in the USA and postal code in Canada, as well as all French communes, Spanish census tracts, and more. This gives a far more holistic picture, one that allows us to see how the same amenity (e.g. a tattoo parlour) can take on different meanings when joined by others (e.g. an art gallery or hunting lodge).

1.1.2. Multi-dimensionality. Not only does no single amenity make any particular scene, but each amenity may contribute to the overall scene in many different ways. Imported Italian cappuccino may evoke a sense of local authenticity but it might also suggest the legitimacy of tradition, doing things in the way they have been done in the past. The Japanese–French fusion restaurant may celebrate the importance of ethnic culture but simultaneously affirm the value in expressing some unique, personal twist on old techniques. The nightclub red carpet VIP area may evince glamour just as much as it demands attention to formality, adhering to codified standards of appearance like dress codes. *Both-and*, not either-or, has to be the watchword for any theory of scenes.

1.1.3. Combinatorial thinking. Further difficulties arise when we move more deeply from amenities and activities and people into what they mean. In so doing, we necessarily move to a higher level of abstraction. This is because the same qualities can be found in many different scenes, expressed by many different amenities. Because the same dimensions of meaning can be present across scenes, qualities can (and must) be abstracted from any specific scene. Each quality – local authenticity, transgression, tradition, glamour, formality – has its own character that can be articulated separately. This also implies that no single abstract quality defines any particular scene. If both ethnic neighbourhoods and neo-bohemian scenes have a dimension of local authenticity, this does not make them the same. The difference lies in how this one quality combines with others in each particular configuration – one with neighbourliness and tradition, the other with self-expression and transgression. However these combinations emerged, the resulting scene is a specific combination of multiple traits. This combinatorial logic extends the line of analysis from Richard Wagner's Leitmotifs, to Claude Levi-Strauss's myths, to scenes.

1.2. Authenticity, theatricality, legitimacy: a pragmatic approach to scenes analysis

If we try to delimit ahead of time what cultural themes can inhere in a scene, we will never be able to stop. For any quality we list, others can think of five more. At the same time, we cannot 'just look' at the world of scenes and expect some fixed set of qualities to pop out. We have to know what to look for; as William James noted in a section on 'The Realities of the Unseen' in *The Varieties of Religious Experience*, it is in the light of abstract qualities like beauty, justice, goodness or strength that things and facts appear to us at all in the first place.[2]

The most prudent course is a pragmatist middle road between systematic theory and empiricism. On this middle road, the goal is to draw conceptualizations from a range of sources that have attempted to describe urban life, including aesthetic forms like poetry, novels, religion, and film and also non-fiction, like journalism, ethnographies, surveys, case studies, social and cultural theory, and philosophy. Such sources illustrate crucial themes that have occurred to participants in and observers of scenes. From these, we can build a workable set of dimensions with which to describe a given scene.

To start, let us return to the three scenes briefly evoked above – the ethnic neighbourhood, neo-bohemia and downtown scenes. While each 'says' much, the kinds of things they say bear some sort of resemblance to one another. The images of ethnic restaurants, indie record labels and corporate logos are all saying something about who you really are, about *authenticity*. *How* they say this differs – by being from a particular place and being part of its local customs, by coming from a particular ethnic heritage, by possessing a certain brand name (Gucci, not knockoffs). These meanings resemble one another in that all point to something considered *genuine* rather than *phony*, *real* not *fake*.[3]

But scenes say more than just how to be real. There is also something in the scene about how to present yourself, in your clothes, speech, manners, posture, bearing, appearance. The checked tablecloths and family-style service of a pizza joint suggest presenting yourself in a warm, intimate, neighbourly way; the dress codes of a country club or opera house cue formality and the ripped jeans and anarchist graffiti of the worker-owned, fair-trade café invite transgression. These modes of self-presentation can be considered styles of *theatricality*.[4]

TABLE 1 Analytical dimensions of scenes I: theatricality, authenticity and legitimacy.

Theatricality	Authenticity	Legitimacy
Mutual self-display	Discovering the real thing	Acting on moral bases
Seeing and being seen	Touching ground	Listening to duty
Appropriate vs. inappropriate	Genuine vs. phony	Right vs. wrong
Appearance	Identity	Intentions to act
Performing	Rooting	Evaluating

Authenticity is about who you really are; theatricality is about how you appear. Just as important is what one believes makes one's actions right or wrong, the authorities that are taken to normatively govern one's behaviour, and scenes say something about this as well. If the Catholic mass says listen to tradition, the poetry slam MC is saying listen to yourself; if the human rights watch poster on the wall says listen to the universal voice of humanity equally, the portraits of Che Guevara, Steve Jobs and Ronald Reagan are saying listen to what great leaders say. Think of these ways of determining what is right or wrong as types of *legitimacy*, a classic topic in sociology from Max Weber to Robert Bellah.

Thus, we have three general categories of meaning at stake in a scene: authenticity, theatricality and legitimacy. Table 1 summarizes these three general analytical components of scenes. To be sure, some lines between these categories are fuzzy. Still, the differences are real, and we can recognize them relatively easily – especially when they clash. For instance, 'being real' and 'being right' can point in different directions. The charmingly authentic Italian cappuccino shop may use coffee beans harvested under exploitative conditions. The intellectually sincere person, in staying true to his real self, may violate the moral expectations of his community. Theatricality can clash with authenticity and legitimacy just as well. As a form of theatricality, flashy clothes may provide the allure of glamour; as a form of authenticity, they may reek of the poseur. Formal gowns can make an event into an occasion just as much as they can indicate a moral failure to think for oneself. While authenticity, theatricality and legitimacy need not clash – a real scene can be a good scene can be a beautiful scene – they do point at different types of criteria for evaluating the nature of the scene.

1.3. Towards a cultural logic of scene dimensions

These broad categories – authenticity, theatricality and legitimacy – help us organize the types of meaning that a scene can support or resist. However, we also need to be able to say what types of authenticity, theatricality and legitimacy a scene values (or devalues). More specific dimensions – like *local* authenticity, *glamorous* theatricality or *traditional* legitimacy – have emerged already, but it is crucial to give them more substantive content. Whatever its specific dimensions, however, a theory of scenes needs to provide some guidance about how to order those dimensions as members of a larger family. To do so, we arrange them into a pattern like the periodic table's groups of elements that, generally, become less metallic as you move from left to right. Even in the case of chemistry, though, 'exceptions to this general rule abound' (Scerri 2006, p. 11): some metals are soft and dull (like potassium and sodium), while others are hard and shiny (like gold and platinum). The same goes for the thematic elements of scenes. Rather than treat such exceptions as thorns in our side, think of them instead as spurs to further thought, new elements and new patterns.

Let us begin with the dimensions of authenticity, which convey the sources of one's being, where the 'true you' comes from. The *scope* of that 'you' organizes dimensions of authenticity. Starting at the top of table 2, the dimensions expand from *my turf* to the *world*. As we move down, the narrow and particularistic authenticity of the local contra the foreign expands outward. A 'real' rooted in state citizenship connects authenticity to a trans-local community, while diasporic and corporate sources of authenticity extend wider still; an ethnicity or a brand name can make a claim to authenticity in any country. And there is in principle no limit to the scope of reason, which can provide the true nature of not only any human but more broadly of any rational agent, Martians, angels, gods, whatever.

Theatricality is about performance, and the logic of performance (cf. Alexander 2010) runs, not from specificity to generality, but rather from external to internal and between convention and deviance. There is, first, the

TABLE 2 Analytical dimensions of scenes II: 15 dimensions of theatricality, authenticity and legitimacy.

Theatricality	
Exhibitionistic	Reserved
Glamorous	Ordinary
Neighbourly	Distant
Transgressive	Conformist
Formal	Informal
Legitimacy	
Traditional	Novel
Charismatic	Routine
Utilitarian	Unproductive
Egalitarian	Particular
Self-expressive	Scripted
Authenticity	
Local	Global
State	Anti-state
Ethnic	Non-ethnic
Corporate	Independent
Rational	Non-rational

conspicuous display of self as an object to be viewed for the sake of being viewed: the *exhibitionism* of 'look at me!' But what to look at, specifically? Table 2 shows various possibilities. You can perform according to conventional forms, *formally*, or by deviating from such forms, *transgressively*. And you can display yourself in such a way that you direct your audience towards your inner, intimate warmth, like a good *neighbour*, or towards your outer, surface sheen, *glamorously*.

Legitimacy concerns the basis of moral judgements, the *authority* on which a verdict of right or wrong is grounded. Time and space are key ways of discriminating among possible authorities. Starting from the top of the legitimacy group in table 2, *tradition* temporally orients one towards the authority of the past – as in classicism, which urges you to heed the wisdom of classic masters. The power of the present inheres in the *charisma* of great leader, who says listen to me now, past and future be damned. To orient yourself towards the authority of the future is to live not for present pleasure but rather to plan for what is to come, to treat the past not as a rule but as a source of information; this is the *utilitarian* attitude – calculating, forward-looking, weighing alternative courses. There are also spatial dimensions of legitimacy, such as the *global* ideals of egalitarianism that say what is good is what all can benefit from equally, or the legitimacy of the *individual person*, where the ultimate authority resides in you and you alone, in a unique personality revealing itself as it responds in its own way to particular situations.

2. Self-expressive legitimacy: a key dimension of scenes

A full accounting of a scene attends to multiple dimensions of legitimacy, theatricality and authenticity. To provide substantive content to such an accounting, each dimension needs to be articulated in more detail. Elsewhere, we do so for those listed in table 2 (*Scenes*, Chap. 2). Given space restrictions, we feature just one dimension of legitimacy, self-expression, since it is central to our analysis of NSMs, below.[5]

Self-expression grounds the legitimacy of a scene in its capacity to actualize an individual personality. The good person brings his own unique take, her own personal style, her own way of seeing, to each and every one of her actions. This is self-expression as an ethical task, a demand to improvisationally respond to situations in unscripted and surprising ways. Themes of self-expression run through Herder, Emerson, Thoreau and the American Pragmatists. Here is Emerson: 'Insist on yourself; never imitate. Your own gift you can present every moment with the cumulative force of a whole life's cultivation; but of the adopted talent of another you have only an extemporaneous half possession' (Emerson 2009, p. 145).

The legitimacy of self-expression continues to be affirmed in improv comedy theatres, rap cyphers and karaoke bars, in the stress on interior and product design, and in the expectation that each person curate a unique playlist for their iPod. Daniel Bell (2008) suggested that this outlook dominates the contemporary art world, from conductors to poets, and extends out from there to the general populace. Robert Bellah *et al.*'s (2008) famous case study of expressive individualism shows its religious potential ('Sheilaism'). Political scientist Ronald Inglehart (1990) has found evidence of an international shift in values, away from 'materialism' and towards personal self-development. Even so, hostility to self-expression can define a scene just as well, in evincing the pleasures of fitting into scripts and filling roles – following in a marching band, playing in lockstep with an orchestra, reciting a memorized prayer at Mass.

3. Locating scenes

Digitized data now provide ways to access and compare the scenes evoked by the materially embodied life of local communities in a far more precise and extensive fashion than ever before. These allow us to 'visit' thousands of scenes from afar. Rather than strolling from neighbourhood to neighbourhood, writing down what we see and making comparisons, we can download online information into spreadsheets that tell us how many cafés, art galleries, Baptist churches, tattoo parlours, night clubs, community centres, etc. are in each locality. By downloading information about hundreds of different types of amenities, we reduce the chances of error by not relying on a handful – or even dozens – of indicators. This richness moves quantitative analysis closer to the ethnographer's ideals of thick description and local knowledge.

This is, of course, not the only way to analyse scenes empirically. Chad Anderson (2010), for instance, used scenes concepts to create videos and photos of Seoul neighbourhoods to capture the foundations of major conflicts over the city's redevelopment strategies. Working in France, Stephen Sawyer (2011) used yellow pages data to distill Parisian scenes, and one of his students made a film about the Parisian Underground. Dozens of student papers have investigated scenes ethnographically, especially around Chicago, such as Vincent Arrigo and John Thompson's (2007) study of Bridgeport. We ourselves have employed multiple methods – including ethnography, oral history, observant participation, interviews and documentary research – in our studies of political elites' top-down style of transforming Chicago's scenes (Clark and Silver 2012, Clark forthcoming) and of local activists in Toronto organizing politically to shape the character of their neighbourhood scenes (Silver 2012b, Silver and Clark 2013).

Nonetheless, large-scale data sets are helpful for locating and comparing scenes in national and cross-national analyses. We have typically used two main sources: (1) national business censuses, which contain surprisingly rich information about restaurants, arts amenities, churches, civic and social information, and much more; and (2) online yellow pages directories, which contain more consumer-driven categorizations, like specialized shops and boutiques and multiple types of restaurants and churches. Like any data source, from ethnographic field notes to the census, each has its own error structures and assumptions (discussed in *Scenes*, Chap. 8; see also Silver *et al.* 2010). Together, however, they (along with other sources) provide a useful way to 'read' the material differences across local communities.

We often use a metric called 'the performance score' to measure scenes. It extends a certain form of Durkheimian reasoning, seeing particular amenities as indices of collective meanings (our 'dimensions'). That is, we can use tattoo parlours to indicate transgressive theatricality, Catholic churches for traditional legitimacy, nightclubs for glamorous theatricality and so on. We assigned weights for each amenity in our database on a 5-point scale, ranging from low (1) for amenities that support practices which reject a given scene dimension, like modernist art rejecting traditional legitimacy, to neutral (3) for amenities that support practices indifferent to a given dimension, to high (5) for amenities that support practices which affirm a given dimension. Table 3 illustrates the sorts of amenities we use as indicators of self-expressive scenes, as well as those we use for traditionalist, rationalist and transgressive scenes, to give a feel for the scope of our database and indicators.

Each dimension's performance score is the average weight assigned on that dimension for all amenities in a given locality (e.g. postal code or zip code). That is, a traditional legitimacy performance score of 3.2 for a particular zip code means that the average amenity in that zip code (somewhat) positively affirms the legitimacy of tradition. Each locality's scene can thus be decomposed into a symbolic profile of multiple dimensions. Performance scores are not intended as rankings but as tools for discerning what types of experiences a given locale affords, the symbolic meanings which a greater or lesser share of its amenities perform.[6] This approach has been used by our collaborator Clemente Navarro with results clearly mapped for individual Spanish cities (http://www. upo.es/cspl/scenes/). Chapter 8 of *Scenes* provides more detail about coding methods, performance scores, sensitivity checks and the like.

4. Scenes and NSMs

To illustrate the analytical value of these techniques, we now examine the sorts of locations most likely to support NSM organizations. These new (in the 1970s) civic groups were oriented to programmes – ecology, feminism, peace, gay rights, etc. – that older political parties ignored. Over time, other, more humanistic and aesthetic concerns also arose, such as suburban sprawl, sports stadiums, flowers, museums and walkability. In Europe, the state and parties were the hierarchical 'establishment' opposed by NSMs. For instance, in the 1970s in Italy, even Communists and Socialist parties rejected the new issues. In the USA, local business and political elites were more often the target

TABLE 3 Illustrative sample of amenities weighted high and low on traditionalism, self-expression, transgression and rationalism, from the Canadian amenities database.

	Traditionalist	Self-expressive	Transgressive	Rationalist
Higher weights	Bibles, synagogues, clergy, archives, religious goods, religious organizations, etiquette, ethics & protocol lessons, antique dealers, cemeteries, monuments, heritage buildings consultants, bookbinders-specialty & restoration, campgrounds, crests, mausoleums, historical places, museums, fishing & hunting, automobile antique & classic cars, Opera companies, church furnishings & supplies, churches & other places of worship, mosques, synagogues	Artists-fine arts, night clubs, fashion stylists & consultants, haute couture, graphic designers, fashion stylists & consultants, clowns tattooing, piercing & body art, schools-dramatic art & speech, art galleries, dealers & consultants, estheticians, dancing instruction, interior designers, sound recording studios, musical groups and artists, theatre (except musical) companies, hobby, toy and game stores, dance companies, live theatres and other performing arts presenters with facilities, yoga instruction, independent artists, writers and performers	Sex shops, adult entertainment, tattooing, piercing & body art, motorcycles, escort services, hemp products, casinos, nudist parks, snowboards, smokers' articles, gambling industries, esotericism – products and services, surf shops, night clubs, haute couture, art schools, escort services	Microscopes, telescopes, encyclopaedias, business consultants, accountants, lawyers, banks, bookkeeping services, insurance agents & brokers, tax return specialists, management consultants, laboratories, economic consultants, retirement and planning consultants, engineers, patent agents, expertise and technical analysis, productivity consultants, marketing consultants, industrial consultants, robotics, research and development, forensic services, statistical services, astronomy, geophysical surveying and mapping services, technical and trade schools, research and development
Lower weights	Business centres, laboratories, marketing consultants, robotics, administrative management and general management consulting services, engineers, industrial consultants, machine shops,	Uniform rental services, military goods, etiquette, ethics & protocol lessons, Bibles, business centres, business consultants, engineers, technical and trade schools, accountants, lawyers, management	Military goods, etiquette, ethics & protocol lessons, formal wear, uniform rental service, clergy, Bibles, business & trade associations, Chamber of Commerce, accounting services, lawyers, banks, tuxedos,	Esotericism – products and services, clergy, Bibles, mosques, funeral homes, religious organizations, synagogues, cemeteries, churches & other places of worship, astrologers, psychic consultants, massages,

TABLE 3 (*Continued*)

Traditionalist	Self-expressive	Transgressive	Rationalist
multimedia, hydroponics equipment & supplies, Internet-cafes, wireless communications, computer supplies & accessories, market research & analysis, research and development, sex shops, escort service, esotericism-products & services, inventors	consultants, corporate image development services, insurance agents and brokers, stock and bond brokers, tax consultants, mosques, synagogues, religious organizations, law courts	insurance, homes-elderly people, investment banking, portfolio management, mosques, uniforms, religious organizations, synagogues, religious goods, antique dealers, senior citizens services & centres, child care services, image consultants, elected government representatives, courts of law, professional organizations	homoeopathy, aromatherapy, naturopaths, chiropractors, amusement places, pilates, health resorts, nature parks, nature centres, rock climbing, skating rinks, boxing instruction, psychotherapy, hypnotherapy, sports teams and clubs, acupuncturists, herbal products, bars and pubs, psychoanalysis, musical groups and artists, dance companies, beauty salons, campgrounds, funeral homes

(see Ramirez *et al.* 2008). In either case, these citizen activists saw the traditional political process as closed, and this encouraged the more informal organization of the NSMs and their often confrontational tactics. But, as some political parties and governments embraced the new social issues, the political opportunity space in which they were operating drastically shifted. Movement leaders then broke from 'urban guerrilla warfare' and began participating in elections, lobbying and advising governments. As their issues were incorporated into the political system, their demands moderated. Yet their campaigns added a heightened sensitivity to the emotional and theatrical aspects of political life (McDonald 2006).

The influence of NSMs has been so strong that it is no exaggeration to say that the field of social research devoted to 'social movements' has been an extended attempt to explain how and why the movements of the 1960s and 1970s succeeded as much as they did. Much research on NSMs focuses on the 'successful' cases, where groups organize effectively and sometimes stage dramatic victories. This approach uncovers new tactics, rhetoric and organizational forms at work in the public sphere. Its cost, however, is that one has difficulties determining how these few successful cases differ from the many others that do not generate strong social movement organizations or tangible outcomes. The NSM rhetoric is often universalistic, concerned with issues like environmental degradation, human rights, personal expression and social justice. These apply to all human beings, wherever they happen to live and whatever their background. However, these universalistic themes do not resonate universally, and they result in significantly different styles of organization and political efficacy. Some analysts began to stress environmental characteristics, like the local political 'opportunity structure' that conditions NSMs' chances of success (McAdam *et al.* 1996). 'Framing' and 'organization' were also featured as key variables affecting the likelihood a social movement would flourish. But is it possible that more tangible local characteristics might play a role in NSM formation and success?

4.1. The specificity of the universal

Linking scenes and social movements explicitly, Darcy Leach and Sebastian Haunss (2007) have shown the importance of clusters of bars, clubs, films, concerts and parties in energizing and sustaining Germany's 'autonomous' movement. In the American context, the key scenes of NSM activism were dense, high-crime, multi-ethnic urban centres. Here, young college graduates, artists and intellectuals moved in racially diverse inner-city neighbourhoods. In many cities, these areas showed the greatest underinvestment and degradation, and 'white flight' to the suburbs was often most rapid. But a vision of an alternative future emerged among (some of) those 'left behind', one more humane, more sensitive to the ecological consequences of human actions, and able to see beauty not only in symmetry and regularity but also in discord and disorder.

Richard Sennett's (2012) *Uses of Disorder* conveys some of this general attitude. But density alone does not capture what was distinctive about these NSM incubators.

We have, for instance, already noted the presence of artists in these neighbourhoods. Artists have often been politically aligned with NSM causes, but their significance goes deeper. The artist him- or herself could be a catalyst for urban change, helping to envision urban space as a source of beauty rather than a scene of depravity, despair and dirt. The artist, in other words, renders the inner city into a resource for cultivating the self. Aesthetic experience could be a human right. Insofar as this aspiration goes against the types of culture and the vision of society favoured by the organs of the state and the corporation, it would naturally tend to take on a more transgressive, counter-cultural flavour. A different world was in the making in avant-garde paintings and poetry, and it would of course be hard for the people benefiting from the current system to accept and enjoy what was to come. It was in the wake of these experiences, well before the current vogue of treating artists as urban development agents, that some of the first and most visionary urban cultural documents were formulated.

But not just any neighbourhood in any city is experienced this way. In her *Death and Life of Great American Cities*, Jane Jacobs (1961) argued that ill-advised urban renewal projects like those of Robert Moses in New York City and Fred Gardiner in Toronto, which proposed to build huge freeways through existing inner-city neighbourhoods, would destroy the features that made them work. Particularly important to these neighbourhoods was walkability: people out on the streets, she argued, are more likely to bump into one another, encounter others different from themselves, avoid getting stuck into stultifying routines, and keep their eyes out for criminal activity. Car culture threatened the very basis of urban community, and with it the spirit of cosmopolitan diversity crucial to the progressive NSMs.

We can translate these general observations into testable claims. NSMs should thrive in dense, diverse, places where high crime co-exists with college graduates and the arts. They should be in scenes that encourage self-expression, and they should be strong where more people spend more time walking. To take on these issues empirically, we made an NSM index, which sums the number of human rights groups, environmental groups and social advocacy groups in every US zip code. It is elaborated and described further in Knudsen and Clark (2013).

Table 4 lists the 30 US zip codes with the most NSM organizations. The list naturally includes many state capitals, and Washington DC neighbourhoods are at the top of the charts. But it also suggests that NSM activity is driven by more than access and proximity to political leaders. The San Francisco Bay Area, for example, has five of the top 30, with the highest totals in the zip codes containing the Mission and Tenderloin districts. Portland's historic Goosehollow neighbourhood, whose

TABLE 4 Top 30 NSM zip codes, nationally.

Zip code	NSMs	Zip code	NSMs
20036 DC, Washington	109	60604 IL, Chicago	24
20005 DC, Washington	82	10022 NY, New York	23
20006 DC, Washington	53	22314 VA, Alexandria	23
20009 DC, Washington	49	98101 WA, Seattle	22
94103 CA, San Francisco	47	02108 MA, Boston	22
20002 DC, Washington	44	19107 PA, Philadelphia	20
95814 CA, Sacramento	37	03301 NH, Concord	20
53703 WI, Madison	32	97205 OR, Portland	20
10017 NY, New York	31	94105 CA, San Francisco	20
20001 DC, Washington	29	32301 FL, Tallahassee	19
94612 CA, Oakland	28	02116 MA, Boston	19
10001 NY, New York	27	94129 CA, San Francisco	19
10016 NY, New York	26	94102 CA, San Francisco	18
55104 MN, Saint Paul	25	10021 NY, New York	18
43215 OH, Columbus	25	48933 MI, Lansing	18

Note: This table shows the zip codes with the most NSM organizations, nationally. The NSM index sums human rights groups, environmental groups and social advocacy groups.

neighbourhood association explicitly makes walkability, parks and cultural opportunities its main goals,[7] and Seattle's dense, hip Belltown have the most in Oregon and Washington.

These 30 localities are of course a tiny fraction of the whole country. To examine characteristics of the places in which NSM's thrive in general, we performed multivariate regression analyses for all US zip codes (*Scenes*, Chap. 6).[8] We found that NSMs are found mostly in Democratic counties with high rent and high crime. *Neighbourhoods* where NSMs cluster are usually dense, have lower rent, and include strong arts concentrations along with high non-white and college graduate shares of the population. Moreover, walking is a crucially important element of an NSM-friendly scene: the US zip codes in which the most people walk to work are associated on average with a 61 percent increase in NSMs over those with average levels of walkability. But cultivating an openness to personal expression is important as well: our self-expression performance score variable is strongly linked with NSM presence. Self-expressive, walkable, dense, artistic, diverse, low rent, neighbourhoods: these are indeed places that very much resemble the scenes in Jane Jacobs's Greenwich Village and Annex neighbourhoods. But Jacobs's haunts are not unique; they embody a type of urban experience that is apparently conducive to NSM activity in general, at least in the US context.

4.2. Self-expression and the political salience of walkability

The above discussion, however, treats walkability and the cultural features of the neighbourhood (like self-expression) independently, asking how much an increase of one is associated with an increase of NSMs net of changes in the other. But of course they do not operate independently, and one of the main propositions of urban reform movements from Jacobs on was that they should not. The urban experience itself should become an uplifting opportunity, and that means taking the time to wander through it and listen to what it says. Where there is a conjunction of walking and self-expression, we are, in turn, likely to find organizations dedicated to preserving and expanding the vision of life it suggests – cosmopolitan, ready to learn from chance encounters and diverse others, out to make the world more beautiful and sustainable than it currently is.

Figure 1 shows how important this interplay between walking and self-expression is in fostering NSM political activity. The left graph indicates that, *ceteris paribus*, places with more walking are, in general, more likely to have any NSMs than neighbourhoods where there is less walking. But it also shows that this difference is greater in more self-expressive scenes: in the country's least self-expressive zip codes, the most walkable places have about 8 percent higher predicted probability of having some NSMs than the least walkable places do. But in the country's most self-expressive scenes, the most walkable zip codes exhibit a roughly 13 percent higher predicted probability of having at least one NSM than do the least walkable zips.

In the right graphic, we can see that the 'walking premium' for not only any but for many NSMs is much greater in more self-expressive scenes. The difference between walkable/less walkable increases rather dramatically, however, in highly self-expressive scenes. In less self-expressive scenes, a highly walkable zip code tends to have on average four more NSMs per 1,000 amenities than does a less walkable zip. But in the country's most self-expressive zip codes, a more walkable zip code has on average around 19 more NSMs per 1,000 amenities than does a low walkability zip.

That is, when walking and self-expression come together, the resulting scene is quite likely to contain organizations advocating for human rights, social justice and the environment. The one supports the other, as Jacobs held. A neighbourhood with people walking about is one with an audience, one that holds opportunities to see and be seen. A scene that prizes self-expression is one that legitimizes efforts to put one's ideas, insights and imagination forward before others, as an opportunity for experience and interaction. These sorts of places where public sociability and personal self-expression push one another to higher levels seem to cultivate the environments in which the NSMs have found energy, inspiration, members and supporters most in tune with their aims and ambitions.

Our results show just how much NSM organizations depend on the specific character of the situations in which they work. However universal and cosmopolitan the content of NSM goals, they appear to get much of their energy and support from the qualities of their concrete local contexts. Such

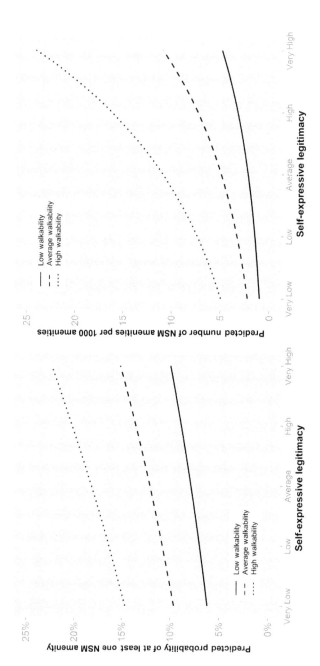

FIGURE 1 Walking and self-expression interact to predict greater numbers of NSMs. The figure is read left to right, where the y axis indicates the predicted probability of having any NSMs and the predicted number of NSMs (given that any exist) for an average US zip code (defined using the following covariates: county population, democratic vote share (1992), crime rate, and rent, zip code population density, percentage of college graduates, percentage of non-whites, percentage of arts industry concentration, rent, and change in rent). The x axis indicates an increase in the average self-expressive scene within each zip code from very low to very high.

qualities sustain a distinct style of life, one not found everywhere or even in many places – dense, walkable, self-expressive, urbane, diverse, intellectual. While each of these characteristics is important separately, when they come together, they provide powerful catalysts for NSM activism to grow. But where they are weak or absent, NSM styles and goals may seem alien and unwelcome, and they may face difficulties in taking root. Jacobs-esque settings, that is, provide a critical foundation of meanings and emotional energies for the more abstract environmental characteristics enshrined in the NSM literature's trinity of opportunity structure, framing and organization.

5. Conclusion

This analysis illustrates how powerful scenes analysis can be, but this is by no means its limit. We have found, for instance, scenes that feature self-expression and glamour strongly predict economic growth – increasing incomes, jobs, population, rent and the like (Silver *et al.* 2011). Indeed, these scenic dimensions show economic growth impacts comparable to classical variables in the urban development literature, such as education or rent. We have similarly found strong links between various scenes and population shifts and political dynamics: there are more young people in transgressive scenes, for instance, and Canadians in more transgressive and self-expressive scenes vote less conservative while those in more corporate and local scenes vote more conservative (Silver and Miller 2013). These associations again hold independently from more traditional explanatory variables, and often rival them in explanatory power. The scenes of life evinced by local amenities have real and demonstrable social consequences.

At the same time, the subtleties of scenes sensitize us to the importance of context in enhancing or shifting the impacts of other variables. That is, instead of only asking whether A leads to B, we also ask whether the relationship between A and B changes depending on context C. For example, we find that (in the USA) when technology firms are located in self-expressive scenes, they are strongly linked with local economic growth; outside of such scenes, growth is weak to non-existent (Silver 2012a). Similarly, we find that in Canada the 'artistic dividend' – that is, the boost in general economic growth associated with artist clusters (Markusen and King 2003) – is greater when artist concentrations are located in supportive scenes, but weak to absent elsewhere (Silver and Miller 2012).

Similar work is underway internationally. For instance, Navarro (2012) uses amenities to map and compare Spanish cities, in terms of how 'conventional and unconventional' their scenes are, showing that about half the cultural differences among individuals relate to individual socio-economic characteristics and half to contextual and scene characteristics. Navarro *et al.* (2012) extend this work to show that significant economic development trajectories of Spanish cities attach to scene variations. In France, Sawyer (2011) used amenities to map the scenes of Paris. They show that Parisian scenes are organized polycentrically rather than in terms of the classical 'centre–periphery' divide, and draw out the political implications of this fact for the City's ambitious *Grand Paris* project. Jang *et al*. (2011) map Seoul, Tokyo and Chicago's scenes in terms of how glamorous, bohemian, traditional and ethnic they are, finding significant differences across cities and neighbourhoods, and analysing not only demographic characteristics but also the values and identities of the people who live in distinctive scenes. This body of research clearly indicates that cultural, meaning-laden aspects of place matter in quantifiable and often surprising ways.

These are just illustrations of the kind of analyses our theory of scenes allows us to model. The findings generated by the model can be combined with other perspectives and research methods to advance our understanding of urban life. We ourselves have pointed towards one possible direction, developing a theory of the 'buzz' generated by scenes as an 'urban resource' that can enhance economic production, political power and community solidarity, in the process-making scenes potentials objects of contestation and sparks to institutional innovation (Silver and Clark 2013). Silver (2012b) applied this perspective to two neighbourhood case studies in Toronto, drawing on interviews with local arts activists, community leaders, city officials, policy and legal documents, city staff reports, and media coverage to show how political controversies over local scenes differ when the value of the scene is perceived to be rooted in stimulating economic growth or community togetherness. Related contributions explore the specific dynamics of cultural policy in case studies of different cities from the USA, Canada, France, Spain and Korea (Grodach and Silver 2012).

'Scene' is a useful concept because it is generative, opening up rather than stymieing lines of inquiry. Hence, our theory of scenes aims to hold open a fluid space for understanding – in the most capacious sense of the term – the many dimensions of meaning that resonate through the material practices of everyday life. Beyond specific concepts, methods and data, the prospect of a genuinely humanistic social science is perhaps the driving animus of scenes analysis. Such analysis is *humanistic* in virtue of granting fundamental weight to the aesthetic and ethical qualities of human experience. It is *social* in virtue of locating such qualities in various constellations of practices and settings that inspire or disgust, excite or terrify, attract or repulse. And it is *science* in virtue of making the humanistic aspects of social life part of testable explanations of human behaviour, gathering data to test such propositions and testing them. Why do certain groups of people move to some neighbourhoods rather than others? Why do some businesses thrive in some locations but not others? And why do some political movements find support in some contexts but not elsewhere? Scenes analysis can help us answer these questions.

Acknowledgements

We thank our Scenes Project colleagues for conversations, examples and support and are especially grateful to Benjamin Woo for his helpful comments on earlier drafts of this article.

Funding

This research has been supported by the Social Sciences and Humanities Research Council, The Cultural Policy Center at the University of Chicago, Urban Innovation Analysis, and the Neubauer Collegium for Culture and Society.

Notes

1   See http://www.tnc-newsletter.blogspot.com and scenes.uchicago.edu.
2   'As time, space, and the ether soak through all things, so (we feel) do abstract and essential goodness, beauty, strength, significance, justice, soak though all things good, strong, significant, and just. Such ideas, and others equally abstract, form the background for all our facts, the fountain-head of all the possibilities we conceive of' (James 1902, p. 52).
3   Specific dimensions of authenticity are drawn primarily from classical authors, though we also explored themes from recent urban scholarship and journalism. Thus, Rousseau, Herder, Wagner and the Brothers Grimm, as well as the American transcendentalists, provided our inspiration for natural, local and ethnic authenticity, which was bolstered by recent studies by Zukin (2009), Grazian (2003), among others. Rousseau and Durkheim stressed the nation-state as a fundamental source of identity and authentic reality, able to shape consciousness, local customs and more. Charles Taylor's (2007) discussions about the power of logos like Nike or Coca Cola as sources of authenticity or inauthenticity provided initial impetus for corporateness, as well as Ritzer's (2008) idea of McDonaldization. Kant and Hegel provide inspiration for including the rational intellect as a potential source of authenticity, a category stressed more recently in Daniel Bell's knowledge workers or Joel Kotkin's (2001) Nerdistan.
4   Four of our theatricality dimensions are drawn directly from recent and classic literature (e.g. Goffman 1959, Blum 2003, Lloyd 2006, Currid 2007): glamour, transgression, exhibitionism and formality. Because these are mostly urbane styles of performance, we added a fifth, neighbourliness, which builds on Jürgen Habermas and Daniel Bell's observations that the small-town Puritan ethic was more than a moral doctrine but also a mode of self-presentation stressing neighbourly intimacy and warmth.

5 Empirically, self-expressive legitimacy is often correlated with local authenticity and glamorous theatricality.

6 We analyse our data at the zip code level primarily, since this is the lowest level at which census of business information is available. Scenes, however, are clearly not identical with zip codes, or even neighbourhoods, as they can spill across such boundaries. Discerning the 'catchment' area of a scene empirically is a challenging task. We are pursuing statistical techniques for doing so. In the meantime, we join this data with ethnographic accounts that explore where some folks go to church, and clubs others go to for Saturday night. The total number of various types of amenities may also be analytically important, and we have developed other measures designed to tap into this aspect of scenes, which we explore elsewhere.

7 http://goosehollow.org/images/ghvision20110317.pdf

8 More specifically, we are summarizing results from a Hurdle Model. These models are used in situations where an outcome is relatively rare but can take on multiple values (e.g. major sports teams in US counties). Our model accounts for county population, percentage of Democratic vote share (1992) crime rate and rent, as well as zip code population density, percentage of college graduates, and percentage of non-whites, rent and change in rent (from 1990 to 2000). We also include arts industry concentration, which measures how clustered employment in an index of cultural industry organizations is, relative to all other zip codes (this is a location quotient, described in the appendix to *Scenes*, Chap. 8).

Notes on Contributors

Daniel Silver is an Assistant Professor of Sociology at the University of Toronto. He holds MA and Ph.D. degrees from the Committee on Social Thought at the University of Chicago, and BAs in philosophy and rhetoric from UC Berkeley. His research interests include social theory, cultural policy, urban sociology and cultural sociology.

Terry Nichols Clark is a Professor of Sociology at the University of Chicago. He holds MA and Ph.D. degrees from Columbia University, and has taught at Columbia, Harvard, Yale, the Sorbonne, University of Florence, and UCLA. He has published some 30 books. He has worked on how cities use culture to transform themselves, especially in books on *The City as an Entertainment Machine* and *Building Post-Industrial Chicago*.

References

Alexander, J. (2010) *The Performance of Politics*, Oxford, Oxford University Press.

Anderson, C. (2010) 'Urban scenes and urban development in Seoul: three cases viewed from a scene perspective', Unpublished thesis, University of Incheon.

Arrigo, V. & Thompson, J. (2007) 'Blue-collar bobos: scenes in Bridgeport', Unpublished student paper, Chicago, University of Chicago. Available at: https://sites.google.com/site/tncresearch/blue-collarbobos:scenesinbridgeport,chic (accessed 1 May 2014).

Bell, D. (2008) *The Cultural Contradictions of Capitalism*, New York, Basic Books.

Bellah, R., *et al.* (2008) *Habits of the Heart: Individuals and Commitment in American Life*, Berkeley, CA, University of California Press.

Bennett, A. & Peterson, R., eds. (2004) *Scenes: Local, Translocal, and Virtual*, Nashville, TN, Vanderbilt University Press.

Blum, A. (2003) *The Imaginative Structure of the City*, Montreal & Kingston, McGill-Queen's University.

Clark, T. N. (forthcoming) *Trees and Real Violins: Building Post-industrial Chicago*.

Clark, T. N. & Silver, D. (2012) 'Chicago from the political machine to the entertainment machine', in: *The Politics of Urban Cultural Policy*, eds. C. Grodach and D. Silver, New York, Routledge, pp. 28–41.

Currid, E. (2007) *The Warhol Economy: How Fashion, Art and Music Drive New York City*, Princeton, NJ, Princeton University Press.

Emerson, R. W. (2009) *Essays and Lectures*, New York, Digireads Publishing.

Goffman, E. (1959) *The Presentation of Self in Everyday Life*, Garden City, NY, Doubleday.

Grazian, D. (2003) *Blue Chicago: The Search for Authenticity in Urban Blues Clubs*, Chicago, IL, University of Chicago Press.

Grodach, C. & Silver, D., eds. (2012) *The Politics of Urban Cultural Policy: Global Perspectives*, New York, Routledge.

Hitzler, R., Bucher, T., & Niederbacher, A. (2005) *Leben in Szenen. Formen jugendlicher Vergemeinschaftung heute* [Life in Scenes: Forms of Contemporary Youth Communities], Wiesbaden, Opladen Zweite, aktualisierte Auflage.

Inglehart, R. (1990) *Culture Shift in Advanced Industrial Society*, Princeton, NJ, Princeton University Press.

Irwin, J. (1977) *Scenes*, Beverly Hills, Sage Publications.

Jacobs, J. (1961) *The Death and Life of Great American Cities*, New York, Vintage Edition.

James, W. (1902) *The Varieties of Religious Experience*, New York, Random House.

Jang, W., Clark, T., & Byun, M. (2011) *Scenes Dynamics in Global Cities: Seoul, Tokyo, and Chicago*, Seoul, Seoul Development Institute.

Knudsen, B. B. & Clark, T. N. (2013) 'Walk and be moved: how walking builds social movements', *Urban Affairs Review*, vol. 49, no. 5, pp. 627–651.

Kotkin, J. (2001) *The New Geography: How the Digital Revolution is Reshaping the American Landscape*, New York, Random House.

Leach, D. & Haunss, S. (2007) 'Social movement scenes: infrastructures of opposition in civil society', in *Civil Societies and Social Movements: Potentials and Problems*, ed. D. Purdue, London, Routledge, pp. 71–87.

Lena, J. & Peterson, R. (2008) 'Classification as culture: types and trajectories of music genres', *American Sociological Review*, vol. 73, no. 5, pp. 697–718.

Lloyd, R. (2006) *Neo-bohemia: Art and Commerce in the Postindustrial City*, New York, Routledge.

Markusen, A. & King, D. (2003) *The Artistic Dividend: The Arts' Hidden Contributions to Regional Development*, Minneapolis, MN, Project on Regional and Industrial Economics, Humphrey Institute of Public Affairs, University of Minnesota.

McAdam, D., McCarthy, J. D., & Zald, M. N. (1996) *Comparative Perspectives on Social Movements: Political Opportunities, Mobilizing Structures, and Cultural Framings*, New York, Cambridge University Press.

McDonald, K. (2006) *Global Movements: Action and Culture*, Malden, MA, Oxford University Press.

Navarro, C. (2012) *Las dimensiones culturales de la ciudad: creatividad, entretenimiento y política de difusión cultural en las ciudades españolas* [The Cultural Dimensions of the City: Creativity, Entertainment, and the Politics of Cultural Diffusion in Spanish Cities], Madrid, Catarata.

Navarro, C. J., Mateos, C., & Rodriguez, M. J. (2012) 'Cultural scenes, the creative class and development in Spanish municipalities', *European Urban and Regional Studies*, first published online, 5 September 2012.

Ramirez, A. M., Navarro, C. J., & Clark, T. N. (2008) 'Mayors and local governing coalitions in democratic countries: a cross-national comparison', *Local Government Studies*, vol. 34, no. 2, pp. 147–178.

Ritzer, G. (2008) *The McDonaldization of Society*, London, Pine Forge Press.

Sawyer, S., ed. (2011) *Une cartographie culturelle de Paris-Métropole* [A Cultural Cartography of Paris], Paris, Rapport à la Mairie de Paris.

Scerri, E. (2006) *The Periodic Table: Its Story and Its Significance*, New York, Oxford University Press.

Sennett, R. (2012) *The Uses of Disorder*, New York, Random House.

Silver, D. (2012a) 'The American scenescape: amenities, scenes and the qualities of local life', *Cambridge Journal of Regions, Economy and Society*, vol. 5, no. 1, pp. 97–114.

Silver, D. (2012b) 'Local politics in the creative city', in *The Politics of Urban Cultural Policy*, eds. C. Grobach and D. Silver, New York, Routledge, pp. 249–264.

Silver, D. & Clark, T. N. (2013) 'Buzz as an urban resource', *The Canadian Journal of Sociology*, vol. 38, no. 1, pp. 1–31.

Silver, D., Clark, T. N., & Navarro, C. (2010) 'Scenes: social context in an age of contingency', *Social Forces*, vol. 88, no. 5, pp. 2293–2324.

Silver, D., Clark, T. N., & Graziul, C. (2011) 'Scenes, innovation and urban development', in *Handbook of Creative Cities*, eds. C. Melander and D. Andersson, Cheltanham, Edward Elgar, pp. 229–258.

Silver, D. & Miller, D. (2012) 'Contextualizing the artistic dividend', *The Journal of Urban Affairs*, vol. 35, no. 5, pp. 591–606.

Silver, D. & Miller, D. (2013) 'Neo-regionalism: local scenes and party voting in Canada', presented at the American Sociological Association annual meeting, August 2013, New York.

Straw, W. (2001) 'Scenes and sensibilities', *Public*, no. 22/23, pp. 245–247.

Taylor, C. (2007) *A Secular Age*, Cambridge, MA, Belknap Press of Harvard University Press.

Zukin, S. (2009) *Naked City: The Death and Life of Authentic Urban Places*, New York, Oxford University Press.

Ayaka Yoshimizu

BODIES THAT REMEMBER

Gleaning scenic fragments of a brothel district in Yokohama

In January 2005, a large-scale raid organized by Kanagawa Prefectural Police and the municipal government eradicated sex trade businesses in Koganecho, a marginalized district in the port city of Yokohama. The array of small brothels in the district was completely uprooted, and transnational migrant women who were working there disappeared. Although the migrant sex workers are no longer present in the district and the city landscape is shifting rapidly, their ghostly 'traces' persist in the city in the forms of rumors, people's memories and affective experiences, various cultural texts and the architectural remains of former brothels, which continue to constitute the materiality of Koganecho today. While Koganecho has traditionally been regarded simply as a place to engage in illicit and 'abnormal' activities – namely, prostitution – the ghostly traces of Koganecho suggest that it was a cultural space where migrant sex workers participated in the production of everyday culture, shared experiences, affects and identities. In this article, I present an alternative way of remembering Koganecho's brothel district by using the notion of 'scene'. Based on my ethnographic research in Yokohama, I reconstruct a scene of Koganecho brothel district through these ghostly traces, primarily by presenting emotional moments of the scene remembered by local people and photographic images of the district that I produced during my fieldwork. The things people remembered were not the 'primary' activities of the scene (i.e. prostitution), but activities that took place outside the regular work hours when sex workers engaged in mundane social activities, including eating, singing karaoke, shopping and hanging out with friends. In these moments, the Koganecho scene transformed into a diasporic space where migrant women remembered and maintained relationships with family back home while building new relationships with the local Japanese.

The reality of past practice haunts the present space of the city, haunts the social relations and everyday practices. The reality of the present will now haunt memories of the past and the possibility of future practices. (Kuftinec 1998, p. 94)

Koganecho: an/other memoryscape of Yokohama

In January 2005, a large-scale raid organized by Kanagawa Prefectural Police and the municipal government eradicated sex trade businesses in Koganecho, a marginalized district in the port city of Yokohama. The array of small brothels in the district was completely uprooted, and transnational migrant women who were working there disappeared. The city and the police explicitly promoted eradication of prostitution from Koganecho with banners, creating a discourse that 'equated ... women's vanishing from public space with urban development and (post)industrial progress' (Wright 2004, p. 370). Most of the buildings that were constructed specifically for the purpose of running brothels were later rented by the city and turned into art studios and arty stores under its creative city project. Although nobody seems to know exactly what happened to the transnational migrant sex workers who used to work in Koganecho, it is likely that some were arrested during the raid or other crackdowns in the neighbourhood and deported back to their countries of origin. Rumors suggest that some left Yokohama and moved to other parts of Japan or elsewhere, such as Australia, to continue working as sex workers. Others married Japanese citizens, obtained permanent resident status and still live in Yokohama.

In this article, I view Koganecho as a cultural space by using the notion of 'scene'.[1] Traditionally, the district has publicly been regarded as a place to engage in illicit and 'abnormal' activities: to have sexual interactions with exotic others or to become sex slaves in an alienating environment. However, like in other cultural scenes, it was more fundamentally about participating in the production of 'shared experiences, affects, and identities' and 'engag[ing] with the processes of meaning-making that [took] root around cultural practices, extend[ing] over time, and creat[ing] coherence amidst city life' (Woo *et al.* 2012). In other words, I am more interested in the mundane, everyday practices, as opposed to the extraordinary, the sensational or the abnormal in Koganecho, a scene that produced its culture and identity as not only distinct from but also connected to other places. This is not to depoliticize social issues involved in the economy of sex-trade businesses or sex industries in Japan and its patriarchal and imperial nature. On the contrary, I intend precisely to politicize and disturb 'how our societies distinguish between activities considered normally 'social' and activities denounced as morally wrong' (Agustin 2005, p. 619). I hope thereby to open up imaginative possibilities to work towards building more ethical relations to places and people that are regarded as 'unworthy' of being remembered.

Koganecho, or 'Gold Town', came to be a brothel district after the end of Second World War. Unlicensed little brothels called *chon-no-ma* (a literal translation would be 'a little moment or space') developed underneath the Keikyu train railway overpass along the Ooka River. They offered services for low-income Japanese men who could not afford 'higher-end' sex workers called *yo pan* ('westerners-only'), who were across the river and offered exclusive services for American GIs stationed in Japan during the Allied Occupation. Sex workers in *chon-no-ma* were also distinguished from traditional *yujyō* ('pleasure women') in Maganecho Yukaku, a more privileged and licenced red-light district of Yokohama that was active until prostitution became criminalized under the Anti-Prostitution Act in 1956. Unlicensed but tolerated, Koganecho survived long after 1956. Indeed, as Japan's economy grew, it started to absorb transnational migrant women, many of whom were trafficked from developing countries in East Asia, Southeast Asia, South America and the former Soviet Republics. These women would eventually constitute the majority of *chon-no-ma* sex workers.[2] Many of them worked in Koganecho to support their families back home. Indeed, it was common among female Thai migrants who entered Japan through the trafficking system to work as sex workers for the first three months to pay the 'debt' imposed on them by *chon-no-ma* owners and the crime organizations that facilitated their entrance into the country. Following this initial phase, they would start sending a large portion of their earnings home to their family to build a house or to send their children to school. At its peak, there were roughly 250 *chon-no-ma* underneath and along the Keikyu railway and over 1,000 women working in the sex trade in the area. Each *chon-no-ma* was shared by two to four women, depending on the number of rooms in the building, and they usually took turns by splitting the time into day and night shifts. Koganecho was 'open' twenty-four hours a day, seven days a week.

A number of small crackdowns happened during the 60-year history of the area, but it never occurred to locals that the *chon-no-ma* district of Koganecho would be completely demolished. Koganecho and *chon-no-ma* were one and the same, and the district seemed to stay unchanged. In fact, small changes in the landscape did happen gradually. For example, willows, a symbol of traditional Japanese pleasure districts, used to line the Ooka River, but they were replaced with cherry trees in the 1970s when the municipal government attempted to improve the district's gloomy image. Then in the late 1990s, *chon-no-ma* and other small bars had to move out from under the railway overpass when it was renovated to make the overpass earthquake-resistant. This resulted in the outer expansion of the *chon-no-ma* district around the railway. Even while the demography of the sex workers changed, however – from Japanese to Taiwanese, to Filipino in the 1980s, and then to mostly Thai in the 1990s, later mixed with Chinese, South Americans, Russians and others in recent years – people believed that *chon-no-ma* would somehow survive.

Known as a scene of crime, drugs, prostitution and disease, Koganecho was learned deeply in the skin of those who grew up in the neighbourhood. It was understood to be a place embodying all sorts of dangers, immorality and shame, populated by 'bad' men (*yakuza*) and 'bad' women (prostitutes). It was the kind of place kids were supposed to avoid, and children did not have to be told this by adults because you would feel the tension immediately after crossing the boundary of Koganecho; you simply did not want to go over there. The *chon-no-ma* was also inscribed in the popular imaginations by films and novels, where the area was often portrayed as the lowest end of society, a breeding ground for *yakuza* battles, murders and the drug trade (e.g. *Tengoku to jigoku* 1963, Miri 1998, Matsumoto 2003).

Members of the local community gave different explanations for why the *chon-no-ma* in Koganecho had to be uprooted. The official justification offered by the municipal government of the City of Yokohama and its young and energetic mayor, Hiroshi Nakata, was that the demise of the *chon-no-ma* would improve the image of the city by ridding it of the 'unfavourable', which was necessary to prepare for the 2009 Expo and the celebration of the 150th anniversary of the Port of Yokohama. Some speculated that Koganecho had become too popular and public on the Internet; as a consequence, the police could no longer unofficially tolerate the businesses. Another story says that a seal called Tama-chan appeared in the Ooka River in September 2002 and attracted families with small children, which consequently exposed Koganecho too visibly to the public, leading the government to shut down the district (Tamura, personal communication, 31 January, 2012). Less politicized views include beliefs that old-fashioned, district-based prostitution is obsolete with the rise of new communication technologies that allow consumers to have sex workers come to them anywhere in the city with a quick phone call or text message, that men could no longer afford sexual services due to the economic recession and that Koganecho had in fact become less vibrant than it was before the 2000s. According to these views, in other words, *chon-no-ma* were in decline in the underground economy of Yokohama, and the police did not see as much incentive as in the old days to tolerate such businesses. I would add that there were other contexts that facilitated the city's decision to demolish the district, including the fear of AIDS that emerged among locals in Koganecho during the 1990s,[3] international pressure on the Japanese Government to prevent human trafficking, which became pronounced in the 2000s,[4] and newly implemented security measures that, beginning in 2003, aimed to remove undocumented migrant sex workers.

After the demolition of the *chon-no-ma* district, two dominant practices remained to shape how the Koganecho district's past was remembered. First, popular representations of *chon-no-ma* emerged in popular culture.

These non-fiction books and blogs written by male authors highlight sexual and sensational aspects of life in Koganecho and, as a result, objectify migrant women as passive sexual objects (Yagisawa 2006, *Kogane-cho no tenshi* 2008, Danbara 2009, *Ah, Yokohama Koganecho* 2010–12). Second, the government and some local residents attempted to erase and forget Koganecho's post-war history entirely through a 'clean-up' project that uprooted *chon-no-ma* businesses and replaced them with an entirely new landscape under the city's creative city project.

When I launched my project on the memoryscapes of Koganecho in 2012, I wanted to problematize the uprooting of the district, but I was also dissatisfied with overly romanticized pictures of *chon-no-ma*. Koganecho has always been charged with moral discourses that judge the primary activity in the area – i.e. prostitution – as either liberating or enslaving, empowering or dehumanizing.[5] From the outset of my research, I was motivated to move beyond these dichotomies and see Koganecho as a diasporic cultural space where women, whatever the circumstance that brought them there, lived and made their lives meaningful by producing shared understandings of the place as they negotiated their relationships with other migrant workers, their *chon-no-ma* owners, clients and local residents. Thus, my criticism of the crackdown is not that it shut down a space for intimate and liberated forms of in-person sexual activities and expression but that it eradicated a space where the lifeworlds of migrant sex workers were grounded. I also see such actions as an active effort of forgetting that negates the contributions the *chon-no-ma* scene made in creating the physicality, materiality and imagination of the city (Riano-Alcala 2006, pp. 101–130, Burk 2010, p.112).

In the remainder of this paper, I discuss how Koganecho's scene is and can be remembered – as a way that lets us *feel* Yokohama's history and cultural landscape – by the traces that are left behind. By using the notion of 'scene', I attempt to illuminate Koganecho as a space of everyday cultural practices instead of an exotic place for illicit sexual and sensational activities or an instrumentalized zone for institutionally driven 'revitalization' projects. While fragmented, traces of a Koganecho scene will show us that migrant sex workers actively made the place into a site of lived experience – meaningful, affective and culturally, socially and economically vibrant. These are precisely the aspects of Koganecho that the municipal government has failed to acknowledge. My discussion is based on two phases of fieldwork I conducted in Koganecho and its neighbourhood from January 2012 to April 2012 and from November 2012 to March 2013.

Gleaning scenic fragments in a former brothel distric

I take another photograph of the glass entrance of an empty *chon-no-ma*. They look like abandoned houses. Very bleak, almost dead. I photograph myself reflected on their glasses. What I see in the reflection is the total absence of women who used to take in men through these doors. The doors, which functioned as the opening to their body-worlds, are closed completely now. The reflection shows the impossibility of knowing them and their bodies. I simultaneously collect traces of my presence in front of these entrances, my own reflections that will disappear as soon as I walk away. (Fieldnotes, 6 January, 2012; figure 1)

FIGURE 1   Photographs by author, 5 April 2012.

Writing about the past scene of Koganecho is a burdensome duty for me. Having conducted nine months of fieldwork in Koganecho and its neighbourhood, fully immersing myself there and hearing stories about its past from local people, I am still not comfortable speaking about how things used to be there. My academic impulse to 'capture' the scene in a way that is as comprehensive as possible always ended up being denied when I encountered the complexities of the history of the place. It flows out of my grasp every time I convince myself that I am finally approaching it, and my view of the scene is always limited, blurred or both.

When I launched my fieldwork in 2012, I was a complete outsider to the local community. I had only made one short, preliminary visit in the winter of 2010, and I had no personal relationship with the residents. Not a single *chon-no-ma* business remained by then, and, with very limited experience or knowledge of sex trade businesses and culture in Japan, it was difficult to imagine what things were like in the old days. In fact, even if I had known about Koganecho and happened to be in Yokohama before 2005, I would not have been able to visit and walk in the area easily, as women who are not 'professional' were not welcomed in the area. Indeed, a culture of looking, or '*flanerie*, the voyeuristic art of strolling in a city' is still 'a male practice' (Guano 2003, p. 359) in brothel districts.

Getting any reliable information about Koganecho is daunting and in fact almost impossible due to its illicit nature. While prostitution was criminalized under the Anti-Prostitution Act of 1956 in Japan, *chon-no-ma* businesses in Koganecho were tolerated by the police – most likely in exchange for bribes – until they were finally demolished in the 2005 raids. *Chon-no-ma* were not directly owned and managed by *yakuza*, but the district was part of their 'territory', and the businesses were under their 'protection' in the sense that *chon-no-ma* owners paid *yakuza* members 'street fees'. Koganecho was like an underground extraterritorial space ruled by a different set of laws, and there was an unspoken consensus not to publicly mention it, just like other places where a blind eye is turned to criminal activity. Things that happened there were not publicly spoken or recorded, and the *yakuza* who policed the district did not permit activities that might disturb the businesses, including taking photographs of *chon-no-ma*. By doing so, they also provided a measure of protection to Koganecho's undocumented sex workers, keeping their identities from being exposed to the wider public.

Once the district was demolished in 2005, its past was silenced under an invisible pressure from authorities to 'improve' the image of the neighbour-hood. In fact, according to owners of small businesses that currently occupy former *chon-no-ma* buildings, they were under surveillance by the police at first for fear that they were intending to offer sexual services. It was not uncommon for officers to come into their stores to investigate their businesses without any advance notice. At the same time, there were invisible pressures that aimed at silencing people who remember Koganecho from the old days and do not necessarily agree with how the *chon-no-ma* district is perceived by the government authority: 'The atmosphere of this neighbourhood didn't allow us to talk anything related to sex in general', said several business owners in Koganecho (Fieldnotes, 6 March, 2012).

Despite the authorities' effort to erase the history of prostitution in the district, I also felt that elements of cultural life produced before the uprooting have not been completely erased from the district. Rather, they linger there like ghosts. In *Ghostly Matters*, Avery F. Gordon (2008) suggests that 'haunting is one way in which abusive systems of power make themselves known and their impacts felt in everyday life, especially when they are supposedly over and done with … or when their oppressive nature is denied' (p. xvi). It is in this sense I think that Koganecho is haunted by traces of migrant sex workers – their practices, relationships and affective experiences – that have been removed and concealed by the authorities but are very much still alive and present as persistent 'imprints' left in the scene (Burman 2006). In fact, the more I spent time in Koganecho and its neighbourhood, hearing stories of the district in the old days, the more I noticed the presence of a 'scenic coherence' (Straw 2001, p. 255) that continues to define the local culture despite the district's complete transformation over the past decade. This coherence can be found in the ways people remember Koganecho and continue to live in the place. Such practices and local habits enabled me to see something like what Toni Morrison (2004) calls 'rememories', ghostly 'picture[s] floating around out there outside [the] head', that stay unchanged (p. 43). I was interested in exploring how one might become accountable to these ghosts by following their 'bare trace[s] [which can be] visible to those who bother to look' (Gordon 2008, p. 22).

Here I define 'traces' not as 'facts' about the history of Koganecho in a realist sense but rather as sites for a 'culturally mediated material practice' of memory where memories of Koganecho are produced out of the phenomeno-logical experiences of differently positioned subjects (Riano-Alcala 2006, p. 11). These memories are 'spatialized in the city' (Edensor 2005) by being associated with particular objects and places. Ghostly traces are sometimes visible and sometimes not. They are 'processual and transient' and appear 'only briefly at moments' when they evoke memories of Koganecho (Yoneyama 1999, p. 114). Throughout my fieldwork, I engaged in 'memory work', which Annette Kuhn (1995) defines as a 'method and a practice of unearthing and making public untold stories' (p. 8) and involves critical and creative work similar to Benjamin's historical materialism: 'working backwards – searching for clues, deciphering signs and traces, making deductions, patching together reconstruc-tions out of fragments of evidence' (pp. 3–4). I tried to identify and record what is left behind, what stays the same and also what is emerging out of the place today, primarily by collecting stories and photographs.

Photography tends to be imagined as the 'pure index' (Metz 1985), a 'trace' (Sontag 1973, p. 154) of people and things from the disappearing record of the past. At the same time, photographs also reveal what is *absent* in the space that is captured, allowing the viewer to recognize invisible presence; things that are 'invisible' but not 'not-there' (Gordon 2008, p. 17). As McAllister (2006) points out, the 'photograph does not just 'preserve', trapping whatever it captures in a static temporal order. It has the capacity to envision a time and place beyond the past/present captured' in the image (p. 149). In my research, I took photographs as an act of visualizing traces or absent bodies of migrant sex workers, *both* to remember the present/past *and* to envision the future. In other words, by making the invisibile visible, photographic images of Koganecho generate ghostly moments where a forgotten or repressed past can be brought back in ways that suggest how these spaces could be used and lived in the future. It is in this sense that I engage with photographic images as 'both representation *and* presentation, still *and* animate, dead *and* alive like the ghost' (Roberts 2013, p. 387).

In the initial stage of my fieldwork, I repeatedly visited Koganecho and collected things left behind from the time prior to 2005 by taking photographs of *chon-no-ma* buildings. However, it felt like I was not capturing anything in these photographs – not even the absence of bodies – because I simply did not have the knowledge and imaginative resources to understand what that absence and loss really mean. These images did not evoke any sense of history, emotions or feelings but total emptiness. To come to sense ghostly traces, I had to keep visiting and walking in the neighbourhood over extended periods of time, to develop relationships with locals at bars and coffee shops, to see the new businesses now central to the scene in Koganecho and to know the restaurants, karaoke bars and pubs owned and run by members of the Thai community, many of whom are former sex workers who used to work in Koganecho. Only then did I start to see some of the traces that appear in people's stories. Indeed, over time, these traces became like affective marks imprinted on the bodies of those I met. Later, I was able to witness traces of the past in people's everyday practices (e.g. how local people socialize and develop relationships), in architectural remains (e.g. former *chon-no-ma* buildings), among objects left behind in former *chon-no-ma* buildings, and on things that (semi-)permanently stay in the area (e.g. the Keikyu Line train overpass, the Ooka River, bridges, cherry trees along the river). The emptiness that pervaded my photographs of *chon-no-ma* started to gain meaning after I spent enough time in the neighbourhood and made Koganecho a part of my everyday life. At the same time, I immersed myself in the 'afterlife' of Koganecho to the extent that I became part of the fabric of the everyday scene. I even felt an urge to leave my own trace there so that it would remember me after I left. In a sense, the ghosts of Koganecho haunted me.

In what follows, I present tiny fragments of the Koganecho scene remembered by local people who were involved in migrant sex workers' everyday life. Due to the intimate relationships they had – and continue to have – with the sex workers and the place, the scene evokes strong emotional responses. I did not collect stories directly from migrant women themselves, and I do not argue that the scene I present here accurately represents how it was felt and experienced by the sex workers. I am also hesitant to claim that the empathetic stories I heard from my informants are the most ethical versions of memories of Koganecho. As I have discussed elsewhere (Yoshimizu 2010) and as has been discussed by other scholars (Ahmed 2004, Shuman 2006, Pratt 2009), empathetic and emotional responses to others' living situations can be problematic because they often serve to empower the empathizer more than the empathized by creating an illusion that experiential differences can be overcome by emotional affiliation. Most of my informants were Japanese citizens and men whose social positions are, obviously, significantly more privileged than those of migrant sex workers. However, I still believe that their memories of the scene are much more sensitive to the everyday reality of the women working in Koganecho away from their homeland than more publicized (official and popular) discourses of Koganecho that render them as criminals or sexual objects. My intention is not to present an 'accurate' and 'authentic' version of what Koganecho used to be but to offer another way of remembering the place, one that may be more ethical than others.

Bodies that remember

There is one picture of Koganecho that visualizes how I imagine its cultural scene, as a site of lived experience, might have been before 2005 (figure 2). This is a photograph, which I took during my fieldwork in 2012, of a block of

FIGURE 2   Photograph by author, 29 March 2012.

former *chon-no-ma* buildings. These buildings were renovated and are now occupied by locals running small businesses, such as coffee shops and bars. I took the photograph of stores I had become very familiar with from across the Ooka River. What fascinates me about this image is not the *chon-no-ma* buildings themselves, but the reflections of lights on the dark surface of the river, which I captured accidentally. These are store lights and pink paper lanterns that decorated both sides of the river for the up-coming Cherry Blossom Festival. Glossily but softly, lights in blue, red, yellow, green and orange diffuse on the river and interweave with each other, creating a magical, dream-like space on the water. As the photograph was taken in the spring time under cherry blossom trees in bloom, these colourful lights also evoke images of liveliness and hope, together with images of nighttime desires and excitement. In fact, the image captured my desire and longing for Koganecho, a place I was soon to leave.

Some of my informants recalled Koganecho from the past exactly as a 'dream-like' place (Fieldnotes, March 27, 2012) or a 'festival-like' place (Fieldnotes, 22 March 2012). Especially during the weekends, the streets of Koganecho were full of men – young and old, working-class and middle-class, locals and outsiders, *yakuza* and police – parading along the array of *chon-no-ma* buildings. Food vendors were open along the river, catering to both sex workers and their clients wanting to have a quick meal and drinks. All *chon-no-ma* used pink lights, illuminating the entire district in pink. In the 1990s and 2000s, women working in *chon-no-ma* shared a diversity of racial, cultural and national backgrounds. Women from East Asia, Southeast Asia, South America and the former Soviet regions put themselves in a wide variety of costumes – 'ranging from skintight outfits to high-school uniforms, China dresses, bikinis, *kogyaru* (highschool gal)-styles, and hostess-styles' (Danbara 2009, p. 272) – and solicited men in front of their stores. While Koganecho is often described as a place of outlaws and illicit activities, it was also a place that embraced diversity and difference. For instance, one of my informants said:

This part of the city attracted various people from all over the place, people who didn't have status or places of belonging. Koganecho used to have a capacity to accept them all, although this capacity is linked to its illegality … For example, you would know that the person sitting next to you is an undocumented migrant, but you wouldn't mention it. People's status isn't important. (Tamura, personal communication, 31 January, 2012).

Koganecho offered a different, non-official, subversive and diverse space, a space of the 'carnival' to borrow Mikhail Bakhtin's term (1984).

Such images of Koganecho, however, only reveal one part of the district's cultural scene. I argue that a cultural scene is not homogeneous; it is differentiated or experienced differently depending on one's relationship to the scene. Koganecho could have been experienced as an extraordinary, festival-like or dream-like place, particularly by male clients and onlookers, but it could also have been experienced as an ordinary, everyday, or mundane place by other participants of the scene, including sex workers themselves and those who were involved in related businesses or who had close relationships with the sex workers. I argue that in order to understand the ordinariness of Koganecho, we need to pay attention to practices that happened around or beyond the sex trade businesses; we have to push the boundary of the 'scene'.

Straw (2004) notes that a scene 'designates particular clusters of social and cultural activity without specifying the nature of the boundaries which circumscribe them' (p. 412). One would not be able to delineate the boundaries of Koganecho as a cultural scene with a physical map, even if the place called Koganecho exists as an officially designated district and as a train station. Rather, it was made up of both actual place(s) and imaginary space(s) in which cultural, social and economic activities took place centred around the sex trade and related activities. For instance, in the 1990s when Thai women made up the majority of sex workers in Koganecho, businesses catering to Thai sex workers also flourished in Wakabacho, a district right across the Ooka River. Within a small district of Wakabacho, a number of Thai restaurants, karaoke bars, food delivery businesses, dance clubs, grocery stores, video stores and gambling venues developed, creating a Little Bangkok where Thai women hung out with their friends, boyfriends and regulars. Many also lived in the area. Although prostitution itself may not have taken place in Wakabacho and onlookers would only see the *chon-no-ma* storefronts as the Koganecho scene, those who had closer relationships to Thai sex workers talk about activities taking place across the river as part of the Koganecho scene. Because regulars and boyfriends often gain access to sex workers' lifeworld outside *chon-no-ma* by financing dinner, paying rent for apartments and sometimes part of their 'debts', the scene of Koganecho expanded through the movement of sex workers from one side of the river to the other, where the boundary of work and private life becomes much more blurred. While Thai restaurants were often used by sex workers to meet their clients, mostly regulars, to spend extra time outside *chon-no-ma*, one recalled that Thai restaurants were also used like Thai migrants' living rooms. Intergenerational groups would have their supper and workers would watch recorded Thai TV dramas or lie on the sofa during slow hours. Thus, like other cultural scenes, the scene of Koganecho 'realign[ed] the cartographies of city life' (Straw 2001, p. 252) beyond their primary activities, which were intended to only occupy the *chon-no-ma* district.

Those who have a more nuanced view of the Koganecho scene also often recall moments in which Thai sex workers' everyday experiences of being part of a diaspora were highlighted. Scenes where they call their family back home by payphone, sing Thai songs at karaoke bars or show pictures of their children and share their family stories with locals further expand and multiply the Koganecho scene, transforming the margin of the city into a dynamic 'diasporic space' (Burman 2001) with 'different everyday chronotopes' (Burman 2010, p. 107) where everyday lives here and now are connected to lives lived 'over there', across the Pacific, in the past, but also in the present and likely the future. When these moments are recalled, Koganecho gains affective tones, painted with the empathetic feelings for sex workers who longed for their homeland. These moments infused Koganecho with a sense of 'yearning', in Burman's (2010) term, a combination of intense desire for loved ones left behind back home (past), a strong motivation to continue their current life in order to financially support them (present) and aspirations to reunite the family and have a better life once they complete their work (future).

Below, I present everyday moments from the scene, fragments of mundane activities that constituted migrant sex workers' everyday practices in the city. These mundane activities took root around or outside of the primary scene of Koganecho (the scene of 'prostitution') both spatially and temporarily during the quiet time, between work, after work or in the scenic space across the river in Wakabacho. These activities constituted an expanded scene in Koganecho and produced an 'affective surplus' (Straw 2001, p. 252) that transformed the primary scene of Koganecho into a diasporic space that made up a significant part of transnational migrants' lives in Yokohama.

Descriptions of these moments were collected from people who had different relationships to the scene: some of them have visited Koganecho with varied frequency as clients; one owned a business in Koganecho that catered to sex workers and male visitors; some owned businesses that catered to Thai sex workers; some informants were husbands of Thai women who are part of the larger Thai migrant community of former sex workers; most of my informants have lived and/or worked in the neighbourhood for a number of years, if not their entire lives. Among these participants' stories and rememories, the affective surplus produced in Koganecho through migrant women's everyday practices clearly haunts the place today, persistently inscribing its past onto the bodies of those who remember and recollect what it used to be. Each scenic moment also includes a photograph of the place and a short additional description of how the place used to be and/or how it has been transformed in the last decade (figures 3–7).

Moment 1: Chon-no-ma

> The streets of Koganecho in the daytime were much quieter. I used to like to see the daytime scene of Koganecho where girls were having their mundane lives. When not many passersby are around they would come out from their stores and have chitchats on the street. One time I came out early on Sunday morning assuming most stores would be closed but they were already open. I saw Thai girls leaning on the counter and taking a nap in the store. At five o'clock in the evening girls in the daytime shift get off work, change their high-school uniforms to jeans and T-shirts, get on their bikes, talking cheerfully and leave, crossing the bridge. (Shikiyama, amateur photographer and community historian, personal communication, 4 March, 2012)

FIGURE 3 Streets of Koganecho today are quiet at both daytime and night-time. Most of red awnings have been removed by police and some local residents because they symbolize and remind people of prostitution businesses of old days. There used to be pubs and *chon-no-ma* located underneath the railway, but they had to move out for its renovation in the late 1990s. The construction is still ongoing at some parts of the underpass today. Photograph by author, 9 January 2013.

Moment 2: public phone booth

> You know those days cell phones were not available like today. Girls used to call their loved ones back home using public paid-phones. There are some phone booths along the river. I often saw them in those booths, speaking into the phone receiver and crying ... (Tamura, bar owner and a tour guide in Koganecho, personal communication, 4 March, 2012)

FIGURE 4 Public phone booths along the Ooka River are still there, except for 'pink billstickers' or sex flyers that used to fill up the space in the old days. International phone cards used to be one of the most popular items sold at Thai grocery stores in Wakabacho, and they allowed migrant women to call their family with reduced rates when the international call was still expensive and the Internet was not available. During my research, I rarely saw a person in those booths. Photograph by author, 6 March 2012.

Moment 3: food cart

> I used to own a little food cart along the river. I had some chairs and a bamboo screen to give customers some privacy. There were two more carts beside mine owned by non-Japanese people. It was a simple business

that only required me to have a little apron. I usually opened at 6 PM until the following morning, if there were any customers. On weekends lots of people would parade on the street just like on festival days. It was fun. I enjoyed the atmosphere. I had close relationships with my customers too. Girls would come by individually early in the evening before work or late at night after work. I sympathized with them like my own daughters. They used to say, 'I will save money and go home. I miss my kids'. They are still so young, like 22 or 23. Some girls had pictures of their kids and showed them to me. I felt bad, you know. (Katayama, former-vendor in Koganecho, personal communication, 22 March, 2012)

FIGURE 5 There used to be food carts in the space where a police box is standing today (on the right side of the photograph). Behind the police box is the railway with a newly installed structure underneath. This is part of the 'art' project funded by the City of Yokohama and the overpass underspace is currently used as an artist-run-coffee shop/live house/community library. This structure was designed with the objective of making the space more 'transparent', which is apparent in the large windows that make the activities happening inside visible to the outside. Photograph by author, 6 January 2012.

Moment 4: grocery store

My store was open 24 hours. We had Thai groceries, including dried food, fresh fruits and vegetables, spices, videos, magazines, phone cards, and so on. Girls used to come as a group of four or five after work, either after their daytime shift or nighttime shift. They would get tons of food and alcohol and leave. Some girls talked to me that they'd work hard to save money for their kids' university education. Occasionally, one of them came by and asked, 'Can I have some drinks here?' I'd say, 'All right, let's drink', and share some bottles. She would talk about her kids and burst into tears, saying she has to work some more years. Girls working this area were young and had two or three-year-old kids back home. (Numata, former-grocer in Wakabacho, personal communication, 9 March, 2012)

FIGURE 6 Numata closed his business a few years before the interview was conducted. The number of Thai migrants dramatically decreased after the uprooting of Koganecho, and he lost the majority of his customers. Most Thai businesses around the area, including karaoke bars, food delivery businesses, dance clubs, grocery stores, video stores and gambling venues, are gone now as well. Photograph by author, 31 January 2012.

Moment 5: karaoke bar

When Thai women were working as prostitutes in Koganecho, lots of Thai men worked as manual labourers at factories. Just like girls, those men used to go to Thai karaoke bars in Wakabacho after work to sing traditional Thai songs. This is music from the Northeastern region of Thailand and it

FIGURE 7 A few Thai karaoke bars/restaurants remain in Wakabacho today. They are open from the evening to the following morning, catering primarily to Thai women who work at night and want to spend their after work hours socializing with their friends or do extra-work by meeting their regulars. In addition to being everyday socializing places, these venues also used to hold live shows by professional singers travelling from Thailand. When these events took place the restaurants were packed. Other special occasions that attracted their customers include their birthdays and Christmas/New Year holidays. Photograph by author, 26 December 2012.

sounds like *enka* [traditional Japanese ballads]. They take turns, sing one after another and cry, missing their family back home. On the TV screen you see migrant fathers working away from home, just like those at the bar. It felt that they were singing for their kids. I often saw their tears flowing non-stop. (Chikada, Representative Director of Terra People Act Kanagawa, personal communication, 27 November, 2012)

These snippets of stories offer fragments of the expanded scene of Koganecho. They capture the lived experiences of transnational migrants, who not only worked *in* Koganecho but also worked *on* it, actively participating in the creation of the affective culture of the scene. Most of the descriptions given by my informants evoke a persistent sense of the desire, longing and yearning that would have surged, circulated, floated and been exchanged in the everyday scene of Koganecho. They also tell us that Koganecho was a diasporic space where transnational migrant sex workers developed intimate relationships with other workers at *chon-no-ma* (Moment 1), while getting to know and making friends with local Japanese residents through routine activities like eating, shopping (Moments 3 and 4) and sharing stories about family back home (Moment 2). The expanded scene of Koganecho, including Thai karaoke bars, restaurants and gambling venues, was gathering places for both female and male Thai workers. Due to its diasporic nature, Koganecho attracted transnational migrants who were not sex workers themselves but who participate in its scene and play significant roles in coproducing its affective culture (Moment 5). I mean by this that, to borrow Burman's (2010) terms, Koganecho was a scene of diasporic 'emplacement'; it created a form of community through migrants' 'coming into relation with other city residents and their multiple affiliations' (p. 103) in circumstances that otherwise would have been alienating.

At another level, these fragments of the Koganecho scene reveal that a place can be viewed, felt and experienced differently depending on one's relationship to the scene and other participants. The Koganecho scene can be expressed in a variety of ways even among 'idle onlookers' (Blum 2002) who do not necessarily participate as regulars. Tourist-like passersby may, for example, only think of the Koganecho scene as the *chon-no-ma* storefronts with pink illuminations and sex workers in seductive outfits, while locals who have some degree of understanding of transnational migrants' lives tend to include migrant women's everyday activities as part of the scene. Likewise, the scene of Koganecho may have been felt and experienced differently among regulars, depending on the level of commitment devoted to their relationships with sex workers. Some may have more interests in a sensational aspect of activities that took place in *chon-no-ma*, while others have more nuanced emotional investments into the scene due to their involvement in the migrants' community through their personal relationships with sex workers.

The stories I heard from those who had close or intimate relationships with Thai sex workers also suggest that the boundaries of the Koganecho scene was always tested and 'practiced' (De Certeau 1984) through tactical uses of space by the sex workers and other members of the community who were extremely vulnerable due to their 'illegality' and 'deportability' (De Genova 2002) as undocumented migrants engaged in criminalized activities like prostitution and gambling.[6] The following recollection of a gambling venue offers a fragment of the esoteric face of the scene produced by undocumented Thai migrants. This was part of Thai sex workers' everyday activities that took place in Wakabacho.

Moment 6: baccarat room

> If you were Japanese and wanted to go to a Thai baccarat place you must have been accompanied by a Thai person. Their security was very strict. Once you were in you could stay there overnight, however long you wished. Food was free, cigarettes were free, everything was free. They were open 24 hours. At a busy time there were almost 30 people in a little apartment. The most popular game was baccarat. Everything went super fast. The dealer, who always had to be female, distributed cards, two cards per person. One game lasted only for a minute. Then they counted bills quickly. There would have been five or six Thai mafia guys checking from behind to see if anyone was cheating. Those who won pay 10% of their earning to the banker. There used to be five or six gambling venues in some apartment buildings. They constantly changed the venues to avoid crackdowns. (Takizawa, Thai restaurant owner, personal communication, 16 March, 2012)

Boundaries of the Koganecho scene, therefore, were indeed 'elastic' and 'flexible' (Straw 2001, p. 248). Migrants tactically reshaped the boundaries of the scene, according to their immediate needs; they left and abandoned the spaces they occupied and created new venues for their activities through their 'spatial practices' (De Certeau 1984) in order to avoid crackdowns. At the same time, the boundaries were fixed and fixing, extremely difficult to transgress, precarious and always under threat due to the strategies deployed by authorities to control immigration flow, crimes and sex trade businesses. For example, the scenes of crackdown were often recollected by locals as part of the larger Koganecho scene.

Moment 7 and 8: crackdown

> I was looking down on the street from my apartment. There were lots of Columbian street prostitutes fighting against a hundred police officers. That was a large-scale crackdown, lots of officers were brought from elsewhere. I saw about ten girls arrested. (Takizawa, Thai restaurant owner, personal communication, 27 November, 2012)
> I sometimes had to protect my customers from police. Those days when policing (of undocumented migrants) was strict, officers would ask my customers to show their passports right in front of my store. I had to drive police away claiming that they were interfering with my business. I still saw some girls arrested because they didn't have their passports with them. (Numata, former-grocer in Wakabacho, personal communication, 9 March, 2012)

Crackdowns became a regular activity of police and immigration officers when the municipal government started to move forward with its project to 'clean-up' the *chon-no-ma* district and turn it into a 'crime-free' zone in the early 2000s. A final massive raid in January 2005 completely uprooted *chon-no-ma* businesses in Koganecho, terminating nearly 60 years of low-end prostitution in the district.

Despite the government's effort to displace migrant sex workers, eradicate sex trade businesses and erase the post-war history of Koganecho altogether, the cultural scene of Koganecho has not completely disappeared. Edensor's words well capture the working of the ghostly presence of Koganecho culture from the old days:

> because of imperatives to bury the past too swiftly in search of the new, [the modern city] is haunted in a particularly urgent fashion by that which has been consigned to irrelevance but which demands recognition of its historical impact. (2005, p. 829)

Koganecho, its 'social relations and everyday practices' in the present, is haunted by the 'reality of past practice' (Kuftinec 1998, p. 94), which has left persistent imprints in the city.

In April 2012, over seven years after the uprooting, a young Russian woman was murdered in an apartment located in the former *chon-no-ma* district. At first, news reports did not reveal her personal background except for her age and her status as 'unemployed' (Naka-ku no roshia-jin jyosei satsugai jiken 2012), but there was an unspoken and automatic consensus among locals that she was a sex worker, as many sex workers were murdered when the district was still active before 2005.[7] As one Koganecho business owner put it, 'No matter how hard the police try to "clean up" this place that doesn't work. Koganecho never changes' (Fieldnotes, 25 April, 2012). Rumors about the incident circulated in Koganecho for some days, as if to reactivate memories of the past scene. Being repositories of fragments of the Koganecho scene, people who remember it from the old days continue to constitute the materiality of the city through their conscious or unconscious act of remembering the past scene and identifying what has not changed.

Conclusion

In this article, I have presented memories and stories of the Koganecho scene from the time when it was vibrant as a brothel district populated and lived by transnational migrant sex workers. I have paid attention to moments that emotionally stand out in the memories of people who were part of Koganecho's scene and of migrant sex workers' everyday lives. Because of their particular relationships to the place and to the migrants, many of these moments were remembered in empathetic ways, which do not objectify the migrant women as exotic and sexualized bodies, as in popular, sensational representations of Koganecho. The things people remembered were not the 'primary' activities of the *chon-no-ma* district but activities that took place outside regular work hours, when sex workers took part in mundane social activities like eating, singing karaoke, shopping and hanging out with friends. In these moments, the Koganecho scene transformed into a diasporic space, where migrant women remembered and maintained relationships with family back home while building new relationships with the local Japanese. These moments remind us that what the municipal government eradicated from Koganecho was not 'criminal', 'immoral' or 'dangerous' activities and people but a space in which people had their everyday lives, creating local and transnational linkages that made the area vibrant.

In fact, what is officially declared to have disappeared in the inner-city of Yokohama with the uprooting of the *chon-no-ma* district of Koganecho – namely, prostitution of undocumented transnational migrant women – continues to exist in other parts of Yokohama and elsewhere.[8] During my research, informants told me that some women left Yokohama after the uprooting and moved to the Japanese countryside or abroad – to Australia, for instance, where they are able to continue working as sex workers. In addition, young migrants keep coming into Japan to engage in prostitution in a neighbouring city, participating in the reproduction of the Koganecho scene today. I heard a recent story about young Thai women who work as sex workers outside Yokohama but who still used the Thai restaurants in Wakabacho to meet clients outside their regular work and to hang out with friends. I also saw migrant women standing at corners of Wakabacho streets at night, trying to solicit passersby. Thus, the prostitution of migrant women goes on in the area – and in ways that are further underground and perhaps less organized, more individualized and more deterritorialized.

Meanwhile, some of the everyday activities that were part of the Koganecho scene can still be witnessed in the diasporic space that was produced before the uprooting and continued afterwards. Some Thai businesses such as restaurants and karaoke bars are still surviving in Wakabacho. Although the number has decreased significantly, in the neighbourhood I saw a new Thai karaoke bar starting up and one Thai restaurant renovating itself from a diner to a karaoke bar designed to be part of the nightlife scene of Yokohama's Thai migrant community. Migrants' night-time culture did not completely disappear, in other words. In fact, it is coming back in subtle ways. New scenes are emerging in the afterlife of Koganecho, for example, many Thai women who stayed in Yokohama after the uprooting now work in massage parlours (apparently, their services are not explicitly sexual as the government regulation has been much stricter in the neighbourhood). Scenes where a group of Thai women sing Thai songs at karaoke bars, socialize at restaurants and hang out at their workplaces just like being in their living room are still active in the present Thai community. While what used to be the 'primary' activity of Koganecho does not exist anymore, other activities that were part of Koganecho culture remain in its everyday scenes in less visible ways.

Acknowledgements

I would like to thank Stuart Poyntz and Benjamin Woo for their editorial suggestions. I also acknowledge Japanese Government Support for Long-Term Study-Abroad, Pacific Century Graduate Scholarship, CanWest Global Graduate Fellowship in Communications, William & Ada Isabelle Steel Memorial Graduate Scholarship, COGECO Graduate Scholarship in Communication and Michael Stevenson Graduate Scholarship, which have made my present research possible.

Notes

1   For other works that offer cultural analyses of commercial sex, see Agustin (2005, 2007).
2   Feminist scholars such as Ehrenreich and Hochschild (2002) may view this as Japan's neoimperialist 'extraction' of women and their emotional/affective labour from the developing countries. While migrant women's entrance to Japan was largely organized by crime organizations Japanese Government silently accepted 'import' of women into sex industries. In fact, until recently so-called 'entertainers' visas' issued by the Japanese Government allowed entrance of a number of women, most not only from the Philippines but also from Korea, Taiwan and Thailand (Komai 2000), who actually ended up being drawn into sex industries. Requirement to obtain the visa became stricter in 2005 after the USA identified this problem in its *Trafficking in Person Report* 2004 and placed Japan in the Watch List for its lack of comprehensive law against trafficking (Department of State, United States of America 2004, p. 96).
3   Yokohama hosted the 10th International AIDS Conference in 1994 as the first venue in Asia.
4   The Second World Congresses on Commercial Sexual Exploitation of Children (CSEC) took place in Yokohama in December 2001 and Japan signed the UN protocol to Prevent, Suppress and Punish Trafficking in persons, especially Women and Children in December 2002 (International Labour Organization 2005, p. 50). In 2004, Japan was categorized as a destination country for trafficked persons by Department of State of the USA (see Note 1).
5   Whether transnational migrant women were 'forced' to engage in prostitution in Japan (and thus they are 'trafficked victims' and 'sex slaves'; Morita 2004, Otsu 2004, Saito 2009, Ono 2010) or they made their own 'choice' to work in the capacity and migrate to Japan (and thus they are 'migrant sex workers'; Ito 1992, Kajita 1994/2001) remain a controversial issue. Meanwhile, in her

study of Thai migrant sex workers in Japan, Aoyama (2009) pays attention to the grey zone between 'forced' and 'voluntary' prostitution and discusses the process in which women *become* sex workers out of necessities and/or aspirations. Likewise, to what degree they were aware of the nature of their work prior to their arrivals in Japan has been a debated issue. See Watanabe (1998) for some cases of Thai women working as sex workers in Japan, including in Yokohama, who had varied quantity and quality of information on the nature of the work before they made a decision to come to Japan.

6   For other examples of spacial practices of sex workers, see Bailey *et al.* (2011) and Hubbard and Sanders (2003).

7   On 8 May 2012, the Kanagawa Prefectural Police arrested a Peruvian man, the victim's partner, for murdering the woman (Sengetsu, Koganecho no manshon de… 2012). No additional information about herself or her occupation was revealed by news media.

8   In his study of the transition from regulated prostitution to abolition in Salt Lake City, Nichols (2002) suggests that abolition of prostitution in the city did not lessen the number of sex workers, but it made sex workers' lives more difficult and dangerous by forcing them underground or to the streets. Viewing from a global perspective, Kempadoo (2005) suggests that even deportation of migrant sex workers does not usually 'eradicate' prostitution, forced or voluntary, but simply 'displaces' it (p. xvi).

Notes on Contributor

Ayaka Yoshimizu is a doctoral student of the School of Communication at Simon Fraser University. Her current research interests include transnational migration, urban memory, diasporic identity and culture, body and affect. Her dissertation research examines the displacement of transnational migrant sex workers from port city Yokohama, Japan, and reconstructs its cultural landscape by unearthing memories of the sex workers through her ethnographic work. She has published widely in cultural studies, literary studies, anthropology and human geography.

References

Agustin, L.M. (2005) 'New research directions: the cultural study of commercial sex', *Sexualities*, vol. 8, no. 5, pp. 618–631.

Agustin, L.M. (2007) 'Introduction to the cultural study of commercial sex: guest editor', *Sexualities*, vol. 10, no. 4, pp. 403–407.

Ahmed, S. (2004). *The Cultural Politics of Emotion*, Edinburgh, Edinburgh University Press.

Ah, Yokohama Koganecho, gado-shita no sure [A Thread under the Railway], 2010–12. Available at: http://kilauea.bbspink.com/test/read.cgi/club/1288533299/ (accessed 5 March 2012).

Aoyama, K. (2009) *Thai Migrant Sex Workers: from Modernization to Globalization*, New York, Palgrave Macmillan.

Bailey, A., Hutter, I. & Huigen, P. P. P. (2011) 'The spatial-cultural configuration of sex work in Goa India', *Tijdschrift voor economische en sociale geografie*, vol. 102, no. 2, pp. 162–175.

Bakhtin, M. (1984) *Rabelais and His World*, Bloomington, Indiana University Press.

Blum, A. (2002) 'Scenes', *Public*, vol. 22/23, pp. 7–35.

Burk, A. L. (2010) *Speaking for a Long Time: Public Space and Social Memory in Vancouver*, Vancouver, University of British Columbia Press.

Burman, J. (2001) 'At the scene of the crossroads, "somewhere in this silvered city": diasporic public spheres in Toronto', *Public*, vol. 22/23, pp. 95–202.

Burman, J. (2006) 'Absence, "removal," and everyday life in the diasporic city: antidetention/antideportation activism in Montreal', *Space and Culture*, vol. 9, no. 3, pp. 279–293.

Burman, J. (2010). *Transnational Yearnings: Tourism, Migration, and the Diasporic City*, Vancouver, UBC Press.

Danbara, T. (2009) *Kieta Yokohama shofu-tachi* [Vanishing Yokohaman Prostitutes], Tokyo, Data House.

De Certeau, M. (1984). *The Practice of Everyday Life*, Berkeley, University of California Press.

De Genova, N. P. (2002). 'Migrant "illegality" and deportability in everyday life', *Annual Review of Anthropology*, vol. 31, no. 1, pp. 419–447.

Department of State, United States of America. (2004) *Trafficking in Persons Report* [online] Available at: http://www.state.gov/documents/organization/34158.pdf (accessed 14 May 2013).

Edensor, T. (2005). 'The ghosts of industrial ruins: ordering and disordering memory in excessive space', *Environment and Planning D: Society and Space*, vol. 23, no. 6, pp. 829–849.

Ehrenreich, B. & Hochschild, A. R. (2002) 'Introduction', in *Global Woman*, eds. B. Ehrenreich & A. R. Hochschild, New York, Metropolitan Books, pp. 1–14.

Gordon, A. (2008) *Ghostly Matters: Haunting and the Sociological Imagination*, Minneapolis, University of Minnesota Press.

Guano, E. (2003). 'A stroll through la Boca: the politics and poetics of spatial experience in a Buenos Aires neighborhood', *Space and Culture*, vol. 6, no. 4, pp. 356–376.

Hubbard, P. & Sanders, T. (2003). 'Making space for sex work: female street prostitution and the production of urban space', *International Journal of Urban and Regional Research*, vol. 27, no. 1, pp. 75–89.

International Labour Organization. (2005) *Human Trafficking for Sexual Exploitation in Japan* [online] Available at: http://www.ilo.org/sapfl/Informationresources/ILOPublications/lang–en/docName–WCMS_143044/index.htm (accessed 27 November 2011).

Ito, R. (1992) '"Japayuki-san" gensho saiko [Reconsidering 'Japayuki-san' phenomenon]', in *Gaikokujin rodosha ron* [Foreign Worker Studies], eds. T. Iyotani & T. Kajita, Tokyo, Kobundo, pp. 293–332.

Kajita, T. (1994/2001) *Gaikoku-jin rodosha to nihon* [Foreign workers and Japan], Tokyo, Nihon Hoso Shuppan Kyokai.

Kempadoo, K. (2005) 'From moral panic to global justice: changing perspectives on trafficking', in K. Kempadoo, ed. *Trafficking and Prostitution Reconsidered: New Perspectives On Migration, Sex Work, and Human Rights*, Boulder, Paradigm Publishers, pp. vii–xxxiv.

Kogane-cho no tenshi [Kogane-cho Angel]. (2008) Available at: http://koganean-gel.blog111.fc2.com/ (accessed 9 May 2013).

Komai, H. (2000). 'Immigrants in Japan', *Asian and Pacific Migration Journal*, vol. 9, no. 3, pp. 310–326.

Kuftinec, S. (1998) '[Walking through a] ghost town: cultural hauntologie in Mostar, Bosnia-Herzegovina or Mostar: a performance review', *Text and Performance Quarterly*, vol. 18, no. 2, pp. 81–95.

Kuhn, A. (1995) *Family Secrets: Acts of Memory and Imagination*, London, Verso.

Matsumoto, K. (2003) *Koganecho Crush*, Tokyo, Jitsugyo no nihon sha.

McAllister, K. (2006) 'Photographs of a Japanese Canadian internment camp: mourning loss and invoking a future', *Visual Studies*, vol. 21, no. 2, pp. 133–156.

Metz, C. (1985) 'Photography and fetish', *October*, vol. 34, pp. 81–90.

Miri, Y. (1998). *Gold Rush*, Tokyo, Shinchosha.

Morita, S. (2004). 'Pornography, prostitution, and women's human rights in Japan', in *Not for Sale: Feminists Resisting Prostitution and Pornography*, eds. R. Whisnant & C. Stark, North Melbourne, Spinifex, pp. 64–84.

Morrison, T. (2004) *Beloved*, New York, Vintage Books.

Naka-ku no roshia-jin jyosei satsugai jiken. (2012) *Kanaloco*, April 23. Available at: http://news.kanaloco.jp/localnews/article/1204230001/ (accessed 6 January 2014).

Nichols, J. (2002). *Prostitution, Polygamy, and Power*, Urbana, University of Illinois Press.

Ono, S. (2010) 'Ido no shiten kara mita nihon no jinshin torihiki taisaku no imi [On the anti-trafficking policy in Japan: with the special reference to migration]', *Jenda kenkyu* [Gender Studies], vol. 13, pp. 47–72.

Otsu, K. (2004). 'Jyosei no ie HELP kara mieru jyosei-eno boryoku = DV soshite jinshin baibai [Violence against women = DV seen from Women's House HELP and human trafficking]', *Nihon seishinka byoin kyokai zassi* [Journal of Japan Psychiatric Hospitals Association], vol. 23, no. 7, pp. 685–692.

Pratt, G. (2009) 'Circulating sadness: witnessing Filipina mothers' stories of family separation', *Gender, place & culture*, vol. 16, no. 1, pp. 3–22.

Riano-Alcala, P. (2006). *Dwellers of Memory: Youth and Violence in Medellin, Colombia*, New Brunswick, Transaction Publishers.

Roberts, E. (2013). 'Geography and the visual image: a hauntological approach', *Progress in Human Geography*, vol. 37, no. 3, pp. 386–402.

Saito, Y. (2009). 'Gurobarizeshon-ka no jinshin baibai to kazoku no henyo [Human trafficking and the change of families of human trafficking survivors under the globalization]', *Hikaku kazoku-shi kenkyu* [Comparative Studies of Family], vol. 24, 111–138.

Sengetsu, Koganecho no manshon de…. (2012) *Hamarepo.com*, May 18. Available at http://hamarepo.com/story.php?story_id=1081 (accessed 6 January 2014).

Shuman, A. (2006) 'Entitlement and empathy in personal narrative', *Narrative Inquiry*, vol. 16, no. 1, pp. 148–155.

Sontag, S. (1973) *On Photography*, New York, Picador.

Stoller, P. (1997) *Sensuous Scholarship*, Philadelphia, University of Pennsylvania Press.

Straw, W. (2001) 'Scenes and sensibilities', *Public*, vol. 22/23, pp. 245–257.

Straw, W. (2004) 'Cultural scenes', *Loisir et société* [Society and Leisure], vol. 27, no. 2, pp. 411–422.

Tengoku to jigoku [High and Low]. (1963). Film. Dir. Akira Kurosawa, Japan, Toho.

Watanabe, S. (1998) 'From Thailand to Japan: migrant sex workers as autonomous subjects', in *Global Sex Workers*, eds. K. Kempadoo & J. Doezema, New York, Routledge, pp. 114–123.

Woo, B., Poyntz, S. R. & Rennie, J. (2012) 'Cultural scenes: case studies in the social analysis of the media-oriented practices of youth', Paper presented at a *joint session of ARCYP and ACCUTE*, Kitchener–Waterloo, ON, May.

Wright, M. W. (2004) 'From protests to politics: sex work, women's worth, and Ciudad Juárez modernity', *Annals of the Association of American Geographers*, vol. 94, no. 2, pp. 369–386.

Yagisawa, T. (2006) *Koganecho Maria*, Tokyo, Mirion Shuppan.

Yoneyama, L. (1999) *Hiroshima Traces: Time, Space, and the Dialectics of Memory*, Berkeley, Los Angeles, University of California Press.

Yoshimizu, A. (2010) 'Nanay: drawing a new landscape of diasporic mothers', *Topia: Canadian Journal of Cultural Studies*, vol. 27, pp. 153–172.

Will Straw

SOME THINGS A SCENE MIGHT BE

Postface

I am honoured to contribute some closing remarks to this issue of *Cultural Studies* devoted to the idea of cultural scenes. I am writing this at the beginning of a six-month leave from teaching and am reminded of my very first sabbatical in 1990–1991. This was the year in which I wrote my first article on the notion of scenes and coedited, with John Shepherd, the issue of this journal in which that article appeared. My article, inspired by rich exchanges with Holly Kruse, Barry Shank and others, has had a longer shelf life than anything else I have written. It has brought me cherished friendships and collegial relationships with scholars in Brazil, France and elsewhere; it has ensured that, even when I felt I had nothing more to say on the subject of popular music, I was still offered a seat at the table with those who study it.

The work of Kruse, Shank and myself on scenes 'landed' in popular music studies at a fortuitous time, marked by an observable spatial turn in cultural analysis more generally. The spatiality implicit in the idea of scene has inoculated it from the risk that it simply become one more label (like *subculture* or *fandom*) for the groupings of people which take shape around cultural objects or activities. I sometimes think that this inoculation protected the idea of scene until it could take its place within the ascendant urban cultural studies of the last decade or so. In 2014, *scene* circulates in a variety of different theoretical and cultural spaces. In Brazil, it is one influence on rich, multilayered studies of musical cultures, like those produced by my dear colleagues Janotti and Perreira de Sá (2013). In North America, *scene* has entered into debates over the status of culture as amenity – debates which surround the contested work of Richard Florida but which recently have found their fullest academic development in the 'scenes perspective' developed by sociologists originally based at the University of Chicago. (See the article by Silver and Clark in this issue.) In French-language work in sociology and urban studies, the notion of *scene* is being set into productive tension with concepts like *field* and *network*, whose prominence in Francophone social theory over the last quarter century is well known.[1] And, clearly, in the articles assembled in this issue of *Cultural Studies*, we have rich evidence of the usefulness of the term *scene* outside of the exclusive study of popular music.

The adaptability of *scene* to these different contexts is ensured in part by two inescapable features of the term: on the one hand, its persistence within everyday and extra-academic talk about culture, notably within the ubiquitous 'creative city' discourse of recent years; on the other hand, the unsettled and oft-noted flexibility of the term, an effect of the haziness for which it is sometimes dismissed and of a fluidity often seen as the source of its generative power.

In the remarks that follow here, I want to delve into some of the things that a scene might be and some of the ways in which scenes might usefully be imagined. I will do so by drawing out some of the claims or insights I have found in the selection of articles gathered in this issue of *Cultural Studies*. The concepts organizing this postface are little more than notions grabbed from a potentially limitless list, but they are the ones I have found most useful in thinking about scenes and discussing them with others, in classrooms or other contexts of exchange.

Scenes, I suggest, might be seen as all of the following: as *collectivities* marked by some form of proximity; as *spaces of assembly* engaged in pulling together the varieties of cultural phenomena; as *workplaces* engaged (explicitly or implicitly) in the transformation of materials; as *ethical worlds* shaped by the working out and maintenance of behavioural protocols; as *spaces of traversal and preservation* through which cultural energies and practices pass at particular speeds and as *spaces of mediation* which regulate the visibility and invisibility of cultural life and the extent of its intelligibility to others.

The scene as collectivity

One genealogy of the scenes perspective follows the concept out of subcultural theory, and is principally concerned with the sort of collectivity which a scene might be. This concern was at its most explicit, perhaps, in David Hesmondhalgh's influential article (2005) on 'Subcultures, scenes or tribes', whose title offers (and ultimately rejects) a typology of forms with which to designate the copresence of people. One of the earliest questions poised to the notion of scene was whether it could be imagined outside of relationships of physical proximity. Were the affinities of people dispersed across space – a shared taste for a genre of music, for example – enough to generate a scene? Was it necessary that these people, physically separated, engage in ongoing communication and other forms of collective interaction in order to constitute a scene? If a scene was to be more than the statistical accumulation of consumers around a cultural object or practice, what levels of self-conscious collective identity and ongoing sociability were required to make it so?

The articles gathered here set scenes, for the most part, in distinctively bounded localities of variable scale: the brothel area of Yokohama, Japan (Yoshimizu), the Queen Street West neighbourhood in Toronto (Deveau), 'downtown' Manhattan (Eichhorn), Sydney, Australia (Drysdale), the Windsor/Detroit border region (Darroch) and individual zip codes across the USA (Silver and Clark). The analysis of the Bangladeshi Heavy Metal scene by Quader and Redden captures scenic activity as a national phenomenon but is based on fieldwork carried out in a single city, Dhaka.

Grimes's article on the video game *LittleBigPlanet* is the only essay here whose chosen scene bears no relationship to physical proximity. It pushes the notion of scene as collective unity in productive new directions and in doing so holds out the promise that game studies may be one of the fields in which the theorization of scene is renewed most vigorously. Video games, Grimes shows here, not only link together spatially dispersed gestures of affinity (like the simultaneous playing of a game) but also serve as the ground for other, more complex sorts of collective behaviour. Games allow for collectivities of people distributed in space to produce spectacles out of intense and focused interaction. Indeed, we may see the complex and roughly simultaneous interaction of players' bodies in multi-user games as producing new sorts of physical 'proximity' inviting further theoretical reflection. At the same time, sociability and affective surplus take shape in the collective playing of games, rather than (as is often the case in geographically dispersed music scenes) emerging in communicative activities distinct from those acts in which the key object of attachment is consumed. As Grimes suggests, the 'scene' of the video game is poised conceptually between two other kinds of spaces: on the one hand, privatized (and thus 'unscenic') spaces, like basement computer rooms, in which individual consumers play; on the other hand, the higher-level, 'highly corporately controlled space[s]' of mediated player networks which transcend the spatiality of any single instance of collective game-playing. The scene of collective game-playing Grimes studies draws creative energies from the privatized space of the player even as it works to pull back (and win territory) from the more abstract ground of corporately constructed brand-space.

The scene as a space of assembly

By suggesting that spaces are 'spaces of assembly', I mean that scenes perform the often invisible labour of pulling together cultural phenomena in ways which heighten their visibility and facilitate their circulation to other places. Scenes, in this respect are spaces of enlistment and convergence, which act in dynamic fashion upon creative labour to constantly reorder its locations and outcomes. Electronic music activity in Montreal, for example, is sometimes pulled together within a scene anchored by the Mutek recording label and festival; in turn, a 'Mutek scene' travels to other cities, like Mexico City or Barcelona, where it both brings together instances of local electronic music activity and itself becomes part of larger electronic music scenes in those cities. Scenes are caught up in the processes of nesting and fractal duplication which undermine attempts to map them as simply adjacent places on topographical surfaces.

Darroch's rich examination of cultural scenes in the border regions of Detroit, Michigan, and Windsor, Ontario, captures the multi-scalar structure of such scenes. Detroit's music, contemporary art and other scenes are often grouped within a more broadly identified Detroit 'creative' scene which has become the focus of international attention. Windsor, in turn, has its own cultural and artistic scenes, whose relationship to the cultural activity of Detroit is complex. For example, scholars and artists in Windsor may pull cultural activity transpiring across the border into their construction of an international 'cross-border' scene. That 'cross-border scene' might be the name we give to exclusively Windsor-based activity which takes the border as its object and purpose but the term may also designate histories of cross-border interaction and name a unity which encompasses all of this interaction. In some instances, Detroit functions within this cross-border scene as something like a source of the raw cultural material upon which Windsor activists and scholars work. In other instances, people and resources in both countries are seen as partners in the elaboration of a cross-border scenic identity.

Across these differences of scale, clusters of cultural phenomena with the status of scenes are pulled within larger scene-like clusters or spun off conceptually as adjacent scenes. Scenes are 'points of assembly' in that sense that, at all levels of scale, they gather together cultural phenomena and endow them with a coherence. That coherence is one precondition of their being joined to other scenes or of their pulling away from other scenes in processes of autonomization. Tourist guides these days struggle to capture the complex topographies produced when, say, foodie/restaurant or design/retail scenes form on the edges of gentrifying artistic scenes and then develop their own dynamics and trajectories of expansion. A music or visual arts scene may be surrounded by restaurants, bars and boutiques which serve as the supports for the former (in the way Howard Becker saw art worlds as requiring cafes and artistic supply shops). Alternately, all of these things may join together as roughly equal partners in a more unified scenic effervescence (Becker 1982, p. 4).

The scene as workplace and space of transformation

Scenes are workplaces in the sense that much of the activity which transpires within them involves a transformative work carried out upon materials and resources. If this work is not normally the most visible element of a scene, it is, nevertheless, useful to ask of a scene what transformation of materials goes on within it. Whatever else happens within Montreal's Mile End neighbourhood music scene, significant amounts of time and interaction are expended in discovering and repurposing objects (old clothes, furniture and vinyl records, for example) and spaces (lofts and apartments) and drawing these together within practices whose outcome is a relatively coherent collective identity. The recognition of scenes as workspaces runs through several of the articles collected here. The artistic activity that Darroch observes in Detroit involves, at least partly, the transformation of Detroit's cultural legacies (of techno music and muralist modernism) through acts of updating, recreation or homage. This work is often the locus of the experimentation which gives certain scenes their avant-garde character. Windsor, Darroch suggests, offers 'an arena for experimentation in which artists and students work with and against the urban environment'. For the heavy metal musicians studied by Quader and Redden, the underground scene in Dhaka grounds its relative autonomy in the ways in which it is an incubator of experimentalism and innovation.

Eichhorn's article on the role of copy machines in the Downtown New York scene of the 1970s and 1980s is in part about how information about a scene is disseminated through photocopied media. However, it is also about a scene-like culture of production engaged in making photostatic objects which expressed sensibilities and documented or promoted various activities of the neighbourhood. Were photocopiers part of the communicative infrastructure of a separate scene (that of Downtown art-making), or may we speak of a copying scene in which this art was one of several 'raw materials' (alongside resumes and missing animal announcements) underpinning the late-night sociability and exchange of the late-night copy shop? Scenes possess a *trompe-l'oeil* character in as much as slight shifts of attention may make seemingly subsidiary practices into their core organizational centre. Like the science laboratory studied by Latour and Woolgar (1986), whose key outputs are scientific articles (rather than 'discoveries' or the other outcomes usually associated with laboratories), scenes often invite a defamiliarizing analytic gaze which upsets the customary ordering of their primary and secondary activities.

The scene as ethical world

To say that scenes are *ethical worlds* risks obscuring the collisions of value and sensibility which gather within them. Nevertheless, the elaboration of scenic identity out of disparate cultural phenomena often follows the shaping of tastes, political identities and protocols of behaviour which set the boundaries (however fragile) of a scene and serve as the basis for its self-perpetuation. The ethical structure of scenes is built upon low-level, implicit rules like those which govern greeting rituals or the buying of drinks. The most interesting dynamics take shape in a back-and-forth between those values which preside over specifically cultural activities and those directed at broader phenomena like capitalism or gentrification. To return to the Mile End neighbourhood of

Montreal in which I live, the commitment to preserving certain features of local life (pre-gentrification markers of ethnicity, like Italian coffee shops or Portuguese bakeries) is tightly interwoven with the anxieties of musicians and other musicians about hype or selling out. These two impulses interact in what we might see as ongoing displacements: the risk of preciousness which might settle around the musician's commitment to artistic purity is hidden within a broader and more generous commitment to the preservation of community; at the same time, any appearance of self-interested exclusivism in the resistance to further gentrification may be expressed in a more noble form as a commitment to protecting the cultural space fought for by authentic cultural producers.

Deveau's article on the alternative stand-up comedy scene in Toronto's Queen Street West neighbourhood captures some of these dynamics in sharply observed fashion. The anti-establishment ethos which surrounded the Rivoli Theatre, site of the ascendancy of comedy troupe *The Kids in the Hall* to network television success, is able to accommodate the troupe's success by leveraging an image of itself as an underground cultural incubator in which genuine culture is to be found. (It thus joins a long series of such places of discovery, like the Cavern Club in Liverpool or the Pasadena Playhouse Theatre in Los Angeles, whose reputations as genuine were not diminished by their capacity to launch success.) Recurrent reference by members of *Kids in the Hall* to the Rivoli as the place in which they are 'discovered' both reinforces this sense of the Rivoli as a place of underground innocence and confirms the Kids' own pedigree as products of the underground. In this case, the discovery of artists performing at the Rivoli, and their ascension to higher levels of success, is the result of visits to a Rivoli-centred scene by representatives from the outside world, not of the scene's complicity with that world.

The scene as space of traversal, acceleration and deceleration

Scenes are the spaces through which cultural forms and practices move at variable speeds. It is always possible to designate, as scenes, phenomena of sufficient longevity that different cultural practices succeed each other within them: the Downtown New York scene, the college-based poetry scene, Montreal's *musique actuelle* scene. Some will want to see each of these clusters of practice (like those which produced *No Wave* as one moment in the history of Downtown New York culture) as producing its own scene; others find it more interesting to designate, as scenes, those cultural spaces which maintain some consistency while accommodating the passage of different practices or styles through them. A useful question, then, is that of the effect of scenes upon cultural time. If scenes are spaces within the circulation of culture, do they accelerate the movement of styles and forms or slow down that movement? Do scenes act as archival spaces of preservation and memory, anchoring cultural activity in rituals of living and being together? Or by subjecting cultural activity to intense collective attention, do scenes produce rapid obsolescence and thus function as places of forgetting? In Detroit, Darroch suggests, ruins function as both of these: as the marks of a historical decline too devastating to be easily reversed (the scene as space of deceleration) and as spaces of opportunity open to relatively easy transformation through artists' projects and urban activism (the scene as accelerative space).

We may point to something of a reversal in the function or ascribed meaning of scenes in recent years. A quarter century or more ago, it was easy to imagine scenes as territories of effervescent, fragile cultural activity whose commitment to invention and change stood in contrast to the unchanging permanence of a city's architecture and social relations. Increasingly, it seems, scenes are cherished for their decelerative properties, for their role as repositories of practices, meanings and feelings threatened by the processes of gentrification and commodification. The articles by Drysdale, Deveau and Yoshimizu are all concerned with the ways in which histories of use inscribe themselves upon places and confront the destabilizing effects of gentrification and property development.

The Wheel Club is an event held every Monday night in a tavern in Montreal's west end. It has existed for many years as a time/space in which a stable core of older country musicians plays with successive generations of younger players, for an audience which is genuinely intergenerational. Anyone can get up and play, but there is a prohibition on the performance of songs composed after 1966 (the year in which, the event's key organizers believe, good country music ceased to be written). At one level, the Wheel Club scene might be seen as simply decelerative and museum-like, ensuring the ongoing availability of particular historic forms of country music. However, the event's openness to musicians new on the scene has meant that its canonical corpus of pre-1967 country music is regularly reinterpreted by the bearers of identities distinct from those which first popularized this music: by transgender cow-punks, rockabilly purists, hipster ironists, people of colour and others. In this respect, the Wheel Club is a socially accelerative scene, its stable musical repertory serving as the point of continuity against which shifting configurations of cultural identity become visible.

In Drysdale's analysis of the Sydney, Australia, drag king scene, the withering of the places and events constitutive of that scene was accompanied by a strengthening of the collective memories which gave coherence to the scene and invested these changing spaces with meaning. '[A]necdotes', Drysdale writes, 'capture the simultaneous ephemerality of social moments and their retrospective consolidation into collective forms of recognition'. Put differ-ently, the accumulation of traces and memories in Sydney's Newtown district acts as a decelerative force, slowing an otherwise rapid transformation of the area's meanings and values which might come with gentrification. Roughly similar processes unfold in the remnants of the Koganecho district examined by Yoshimizu. The distinctiveness of this case, however, comes from the ways in which the uprooting of the Koganecho scene led to the dispersal of many of its key people and practices elsewhere. The memory traces of Koganecho's history as a site of sexual commerce mark 'particular objects and places', and new, fragmentary forms of its past sex trade are now to be found in the district, but key components of its past have been broken apart and dispersed.

The scene as space of mediation

The question of a scene's mediation is less one of its presence within media than of its status as a space of transit between visibility and invisibility. Among the many uncertainties which hover over the notion of scene, that of its decipherability and observability is key. For Silver and Clark (in this issue), as for Alan Blum (2003, pp. 165–167) and others, scenes are defined in a large measure by their theatricality and by their status as publicly observable clusters of urban sociability. Conversely, in the article by Deveau, and in many studies which delineate the logics of hipsterdom or undergrounds, scenes are marked by an obscurity whose result is that their purpose and constitutive logics escape comprehension. The knowability of scenes may require a labour of memorialization; for Drysdale, scenes not only look outwards but also 'face backwards, anticipating their retrospective narration as socially intelligible moments'. In Eichhorn's study of the Downtown New York copy scene, it is, rather, a question of mediation: documents produced in moments of hidden labour circulate, often without attribution, as the tokens of scenic activity.

Scenes make cultural activity visible and decipherable by rendering it public, taking it from acts of private production and consumption into public contexts of sociability, conviviality and interaction. In these public contexts, cultural activity is subject to the look which seeks to understand Just as clearly, though, scenes make cultural activity invisible and indecipherable by 'hiding' cultural productivity behind seemingly meaningless (or indistinguishable) forms of social life.

Five years ago, when both national and international media sent reporters to cover Montreal's high-profile Mile End cultural scene, these countervailing logics of a scene played themselves out in ways that were both revealing and amusing. Journalists hovered around either of the two Italian coffee shops, the conventional ports of entry to this scene, uncertain as to where to begin. They were unsure whether the easily observed bubbling social effervescence in these places was the scene itself or a set of distractions which camouflaged a real, more secret scene to which they would never find access.

Afterthoughts

If *scene* has a future, this may have much to do with the multiple directions in which it may be pulled by prominent recent tendencies within cultural analysis. One of these tendencies feeds an interest in materialities – in infrastructures, objects, assemblages and surfaces. The status of *scene* in relation to the materialities of culture warrants further reflection, which work like that of Grimes in this issue begins to address. Scenes may hover above the materialities of cultural life as their expressive surplus, designate the social glue which makes these material elements cohere, or organize the mobility of material forms and their attachment to place. Another tendency in cultural analysis will pull the concept of scene towards an interest in affect. As Drysdale's article here shows, scenes might be considered spaces for containing and stabilizing affectual relationships to cultural practices or forms, or for embedding such relationships in behavioural routines or ways of being together. At the same time, the language of affect theory may usefully specify the supplementary levels of effervescence, theatricality, solidarity or tension which make a scene different from a simple network, cluster or locality. Indeed, as cultural analysis more broadly moves between poles which have been designated, variously, as those of structure and agency, infrastructure and affect, or circulatory matrix and creative act, *scene* may continue to name the conceptual space in which the distance between these poles is crossed.

Note

1   See, for example, the description of the international colloquium, 'Champs, mondes, scènes au prisme des réseaux. Quelles implications en sociologie de l'art et de la culture?', to be held in Montreal in October, 2014: http://w3. aislf.univ-tlse2.fr/spip/spip.php?article2368.

Notes on Contributor

Will Straw is the director of the McGill Institute for the Study of Canada and professor within the Department of Art History and Communications Studies at McGill University in Montreal. He is the author of *Cyanide and Sin: Visualizing Crime in 50s America* and over 100 articles on cinema, music and popular culture. He is currently the director of an interdisciplinary research project on 'Media and Urban Life in Montreal' and a multi-university research project on 'The Urban Night as Interdisciplinary Object' (theurbannight.com).

References

Becker, H. S. (1982) *Art Worlds*, Berkeley and Los Angeles, University of California Press.

Blum, A. (2003) *The Imaginative Structure of the City*, Montreal, McGill-Queen's University Press.

Hesmondhalgh, D. (2005) 'Subcultures, scenes or tribes? none of the above', *Journal of Youth Studies*, vol. 8, no. 1, pp. 21–40.

Janotti, J., Jr. & Pereira de Sá, S. eds. (2013) *Cenas musicais* [Musical Scenes], São Paulo, Brazil, Editora Anadarco.

Latour, B. & Woolgar, S. (1986) *Laboratory Life: the Construction of Scientific Facts*, Princeton, NJ, Princeton University Press.

Index